ATTACHMENT IN INTELLECTUAL AND DEVELOPMENTAL DISABILITY

Wiley Series in

CLINICAL PSYCHOLOGY

Adrian Wells *School of Psychological Sciences, University*
(Series Adviser) *of Manchester, UK*

For other titles in this series please visit www.wiley.com/go/cs

ATTACHMENT IN INTELLECTUAL AND DEVELOPMENTAL DISABILITY

A Clinician's Guide to Practice and Research

Edited by Helen K. Fletcher, Andrea Flood and Dougal Julian Hare

This edition first published 2016
© 2016 John Wiley & Sons, Ltd

Registered Office
John Wiley & Sons, Ltd, The Atrium, Southern Gate, Chichester, West Sussex, PO19 8SQ, UK

Editorial Offices
350 Main Street, Malden, MA 02148-5020, USA
9600 Garsington Road, Oxford, OX4 2DQ, UK
The Atrium, Southern Gate, Chichester, West Sussex, PO19 8SQ, UK

For details of our global editorial offices, for customer services, and for information about how to apply for permission to reuse the copyright material in this book please see our website at www.wiley.com/wiley-blackwell.

The right of Helen K. Fletcher, Andrea Flood and Dougal Julian Hare to be identified as the authors of the editorial material in this work has been asserted in accordance with the UK Copyright, Designs and Patents Act 1988.

All rights reserved. No part of this publication may be reproduced, stored in a retrieval system, or transmitted, in any form or by any means, electronic, mechanical, photocopying, recording or otherwise, except as permitted by the UK Copyright, Designs and Patents Act 1988, without the prior permission of the publisher.

Wiley also publishes its books in a variety of electronic formats. Some content that appears in print may not be available in electronic books.

Designations used by companies to distinguish their products are often claimed as trademarks. All brand names and product names used in this book are trade names, service marks, trademarks or registered trademarks of their respective owners. The publisher is not associated with any product or vendor mentioned in this book.

Limit of Liability/Disclaimer of Warranty: While the publisher and authors have used their best efforts in preparing this book, they make no representations or warranties with respect to the accuracy or completeness of the contents of this book and specifically disclaim any implied warranties of merchantability or fitness for a particular purpose. It is sold on the understanding that the publisher is not engaged in rendering professional services and neither the publisher nor the author shall be liable for damages arising herefrom. If professional advice or other expert assistance is required, the services of a competent professional should be sought.

Library of Congress Cataloging-in-Publication data applied for

Hardback ISBN: 9781118938034
Paperback ISBN: 9781118938041

A catalogue record for this book is available from the British Library.

Cover image: Getty/BrSav.

Set in 10.5/13pt Palatino by SPi Global, Pondicherry, India

1 2016

CONTENTS

About the Contributors vii

Foreword xiv

Acknowledgements xvi

Chapter 1 Introduction 1
Dougal Julian Hare, Helen K. Fletcher and Andrea Flood

Chapter 2 An Overview of Attachment Theory: Bowlby and Beyond 8
Helen K. Fletcher and Deanna J. Gallichan

Chapter 3 Attachment Relationships Between Parents and Their Children: The Impact of 'The Loss of the Healthy Child' 33
Helen K. Fletcher

Chapter 4 Assessing Attachment Relationships in People with Intellectual Disabilities 59
Samantha Walker, Victoria Penketh, Hazel Lewis and Dougal Julian Hare

Chapter 5 Autism Spectrum Disorder and Attachment: A Clinician's Perspective 79
Ewan Perry and Andrea Flood

Chapter 6 Maintaining the Bond: Working with People who are Described as Showing Challenging Behaviour Using a Framework Based on Attachment Theory 104
Allan Skelly

Chapter 7 Psychotherapy and Attachment Dynamics in People with Intellectual Disabilities: A Personal View 130
Pat Frankish

Chapter 8	Adult Attachment and Care Staff Functioning.......................151 *Carlo Schuengel, Jennifer Clegg, J. Clasien de Schipper and Sabina Kef*	
Chapter 9	Have a Heart: Helping Services to Provide Emotionally Aware Support............172 *Amanda Shackleton*	
Chapter 10	Attachment Trauma and Pathological Mourning in Adults with Intellectual Disabilities......................197 *Deanna J. Gallichan and Carol George*	
Chapter 11	Attachment, Personality Disorder and Offending: Clinical Implications..........223 *Lesley Steptoe, William R. Lindsay, Caroline Finlay and Sandra Miller*	
Chapter 12	Getting Intimate: Using Attachment Theory to Understand Intimate Relationships in our Work with People with Intellectual Disabilities............244 *Nancy Sheppard and Myooran Canagaratnam*	

Index.................................266

ABOUT THE CONTRIBUTORS

Myooran Canagaratnam has worked as a Consultant Child and Adolescent Psychiatrist in the Lifespan ASD and Learning Disability Service at The Tavistock Clinic, London, UK since 2011. He is the Child and Adolescent Psychiatry Academic Programme Director and Lead for Undergraduate Medical Education at the Tavistock. He is particularly interested in the contribution of biological, psychological and social factors to the presentation of developmental conditions across the lifespan, the role of attachment in social and emotional development and the broad range of psychotherapeutic interventions which can help support individuals with these conditions and their families.

Jennifer Clegg is Honorary Associate Professor at the University of Nottingham, UK. Prior to retiring in 2015, she was a Consultant Clinical Psychologist and qualified family therapist working for Nottinghamshire Healthcare NHS Trust. She has espoused a relational approach to research and practice in ID throughout her career, publishing both empirical and case-study articles on attachment. A recently concluded longitudinal research project with a cohort of school leavers critically examined concepts framing ID policy and practice such as Inclusion and Adulthood. She also writes on the history and ethics of clinical practice. Jennifer provided clinical support to an acute Assessment and Treatment Service for adults with ID and mental health problems or challenging behaviour and their families, alongside nursing and other colleagues. For eight years, this service used Jacques Heijkoop's Discovery Awareness, a Dutch relationship-building method grounded in developmental psychology, with considerable success.

J. Clasien de Schipper is Assistant Professor for Clinical Child and Family Studies at VU University, Amsterdam and is a member of the Academic Workplace on Child Abuse and Neglect. Her research focus is on attachment, attachment disturbances, challenging behaviour, child abuse and trauma, mechanisms of change in intervention and specific and non-specific treatment factors. She was trained in observing attachment behaviour by Dr Robert Marvin, Dr Elisabeth Carlson, Dr Alan Sroufe, Dr Sarah Mangelsdorf, Dr Jolien Zevalkink, Dr Neil Boris and Dr Jim Elicker. She has carried out research on attachment behaviour in daycare centres, group care for young people with intellectual disabilities, foster families and children exposed to inter-parental violence or sexual abuse.

Caroline Finlay graduated from the University of Dundee, Scotland, UK in 2013. Following this she completed a masters degree studying Psychology Therapies in Primary Care. During this time she became interested in learning disabilities and currently works in a learning disability and challenging behaviour service.

Helen K. Fletcher is a Chartered Clinical Psychologist specializing in working with people with intellectual disabilities. She has over twelve years of experience working with children and adults with ID within the NHS in Community, Inpatient and Tier 4 Specialist Teams including The Tavistock Centre, London, UK. Helen completed her training at University College London, undertaking research on attachment and ID which was supervised by Professor Howard Steele. Her particular interest is the relationship between attachment and parents' reactions to their child's diagnosis of ID. She has presented on this topic at National Psychology Conferences. Helen is a Visiting Tutor for the Oxford Institute of Clinical Psychology Training and joint module organizer for the teaching on intellectual disabilities and older people. She has extensive experience of reviewing and marking academic submissions through her role as Examiner for the Oxford Doctoral Course in Clinical Psychology.

Andrea Flood is a Chartered Clinical Psychologist with extensive experience of working with children and adults with intellectual disabilities and their families in both NHS and social care settings. She currently works as a Clinical Teacher on the Doctorate in Clinical Psychology Programme at Liverpool University, UK. Her clinical experience includes both diagnostic assessment and post-diagnostic support for children and young people with ASD. This fostered an interest in the clinical implications of attachment theory in this field. She is also involved in developing supported living services for individuals with ID who have been living in out-of-area placements. Andrea is a co-author of the Manchester Attachment Scale – Third party observational measure (MAST).

Pat Frankish has many years of experience working therapeutically with people with disabilities. Her interest stems from an early life in close contact with long-stay hospital patients. She was aware of their attachment difficulties as a child and has worked hard to redress the balance of their emotional lives and needs. Her doctoral research established a measurement tool for levels of emotional development and consequent attachment needs. She has worked in all levels of security, including high, has been President of the British Psychological Society and now has her own independent business after retiring from the NHS. She provides training for all levels of staff from how to provide a therapeutic environment on a day-to-day basis, through to how to be a Disability Psychotherapist.

Deanna J. Gallichan (née Mason) is a Consultant Clinical Psychologist with the Community Learning Disabilities Team in Plymouth, UK. She has worked with people with intellectual disabilities since qualifying in 2006 from the University of Exeter. Prior to clinical training she completed a PhD at the University of Birmingham. She has additional training in family therapy and systemic practice. Deanna has a particular interest in attachment theory, using it to inform her clinical formulations and interventions with individuals and families, and in consultation with staff teams. She is trained in the use of the Adult Attachment Projective (AAP), and is a certified reliable AAP judge. She has published research with Carol George exploring the use of the AAP to measure attachment state of mind in adults with intellectual disabilities.

Carol George is Professor of Psychology at Mills College, California, USA. She received her doctorate in developmental psychology at the University of California, Berkeley. She is considered an international expert in attachment across the lifespan. She has authored numerous research articles, book chapters and books on adult and child attachment and caregiving, including *Attachment Disorganization* (1999), *Disorganized Attachment and Caregiving* (2011) and The Adult Attachment Projective Picture System. Carol has been at the forefront of developing attachment assessments for children and adults, including the Attachment Doll Play Projective Assessment, the Caregiving Interview, the Adult Attachment Interview and the Adult Attachment Projective Picture System. She teaches courses in development, infancy and attachment, co-directs a master's degree programme in infant mental health, trains and consults on the application of attachment assessment in research and clinical settings and is on the Editorial Board of *Attachment and Human Development*.

Dougal Julian Hare is a Chartered Clinical Psychologist with a quarter of a century of experience in working with people with intellectual and developmental disabilities, particularly those on the autistic spectrum. Following studies at Durham and London, UK, he undertook his clinical training at the University of Leeds and has worked as a Consultant Clinical Psychologist in the NHS and in the charitable and private sectors. He is currently Reader in Clinical Psychology at Cardiff University where he is the research director for the South Wales Clinical Psychology training programme. Dougal has published extensively in the field of intellectual disabilities, with a particular focus on behavioural phenotypes, movement and sleep disorders and attachment. He has also been an editor for *Autism* and the *Journal of Applied Research in Intellectual Disabilities*.

Sabina Kef is an Assistant Professor in the Department of Educational and Family Studies at the VU University in Amsterdam, The Netherlands. As a senior researcher she is supervising several national and longitudinal projects on social relations, social support, psychosocial development, job satisfaction, social participation and parenting of families of persons with intellectual or visual disabilities. Furthermore, she is involved as a coach in a masterclass called 'Scientific research for professionals working in the field of support for persons with disabilities'. She is a board member of different national committees for research, journals/newsletters, societal projects and policy initiatives for parents of persons with disabilities.

Hazel Lewis is a Trainee Clinical Psychologist at the University of Liverpool, UK. Prior to training, she worked with adults with severe and enduring mental health problems at Guild Lodge Secure Services as an Assistant Psychologist. She later trained as a Psychological Wellbeing Practitioner within Wigan IAPT Primary Care service. Influenced by her experiences of working with service users with interpersonal difficulties who often struggle to form relationships, she has an interest in attachment and challenging behaviour.

William R. Lindsay is Professor of Learning Disabilities at the University of Abertay, Dundee, Scotland, UK and Honorary Professor at Deakin University, Melbourne, Australia. He has published over 350 research articles and book chapters, published five books and given many presentations and workshops on cognitive therapy and the assessment and treatment of offenders with intellectual disability. He has always been a working clinician and his current research and clinical interests are in dynamic risk assessment, sex offenders, personality disorder, alcohol-related violence and CBT, all in relation to intellectual and developmental disability.

Sandra Miller is a speciality doctor in Learning Disability. She originally qualified from Dundee University, Scotland, UK, in 1985 and thereafter trained and worked in General Practice. She has worked both in psychiatry and in hospital medicine throughout her career. Her interests include systemic working, attachment and resilience.

Victoria Penketh is a Chartered Clinical Psychologist specializing in working with people with mental health, attachment and forensic needs. Victoria completed her Clinical Psychology training at the University of Manchester, UK. She undertook research on attachment leading to the development of the Manchester Attachment Scale – Third party observational measure (MAST). Other research interests include mother–infant interactions that promote a secure attachment for mothers living with psychosis. She has over eleven years' experience of working with children, adolescents and adults with complex needs and intellectual disabilities. She is currently working within an inpatient service to increase access to psychological therapies and promote the assessment, formulation and treatment of attachment needs.

Ewan Perry qualified as a Clinical Psychologist from the University of Manchester, UK, in 2009. He works with adults with intellectual disabilities in Manchester as part of a multi-disciplinary community team. Ewan has developed an interest in working with people on the autism spectrum and he currently leads on the development of the Autism Spectrum Disorder care pathway for the service. In his clinical work, he integrates interpersonal and psychodynamic ideas, systemic approaches and positive behaviour support in an attempt to address the emotional and behavioural needs of his clients. He has been involved in the selection and teaching of Trainee Clinical Psychologists and provides regular clinical placements to trainees in the hope that he can inspire them to consider working within the varied, challenging and rewarding field of intellectual disability.

Carlo Schuengel is Full Professor and Leader of the Section of Clinical Child and Family Studies and Associate Dean for research at the Faculty of Behavioural and Movement Sciences of VU University, The Netherlands. He is also a member of the executive committee of

EAMHID and Associate Editor of *Child Development*, a leading scientific journal. From 1999 he has directed the research programme on Challenges in Childrearing Relationships. During this period, he has engaged with multiple large organizations that provide care and support for people with intellectual disabilities to forge long-term partnerships for practice-based research. He has been an advisor for 20 dissertations, many of which are in the field of intellectual disabilities. His research, published in over 100 journal articles and book chapters and well-cited, spans topics from attachment, parenting, maltreatment and intervention, to social development and mental health. His theoretical and methodological approach to research and practice has been shaped, to a large extent, by attachment theoretical research.

Amanda Shackleton is a Clinical Psychologist with many years of experience working with people with intellectual disabilities in the NHS, UK. She has always worked primarily with people showing distressed or challenging behaviours. Her interest in psychotherapy and attachment ideas began after seeking to address the limits of behavioural approaches. Completing four years of training in Disability Psychotherapy has profoundly changed her clinical practice. She currently works in independent practice utilizing psychotherapy and attachment ideas within a service which supports people with intellectual disabilities and forensic issues. Amanda regularly delivers training around Disability Psychotherapy to a range of audiences.

Nancy Sheppard trained at the University of East London, UK, in 1996 and has been working in the field of intellectual disabilities since. She worked as a Consultant Clinical Psychologist within the original Learning Disabilities service at The Tavistock Clinic, London, offering psychodynamic and attachment-based work to children and adults and their families. During this time, Nancy took up a significant training role, offering teaching and support to staff at all levels. Nancy has been keen to make psychodynamic thinking and models of attachment accessible to staff working with people with intellectual disabilities, contributing to Sally Hodges' book *Psychodynamic Counselling for People with Learning Disabilities* (2003) and chapters in Simpson and Miller's *Unexpected Gains* (2004). Previously Head of CAMHS Psychology at The Tavistock Clinic, she currently manages the CAMHS team in the Camden integrated service for children with disabilities and is a Trustee and Training Committee member of The Institute of Psychotherapy and Disability.

Allan Skelly is Consultant Clinical Psychologist within the National Health Service in Tyneside, UK. He has published research into the effectiveness of psychological and multi-disciplinary interventions in community and inpatient settings; the effectiveness of group and individual psychodynamic therapy in people with intellectual disabilities; the process of change in psychodynamic phenomena within therapy; and the role of attachment narrative style in therapy. More recently, he has advocated for the incorporation of attachment theory into the practice of Positive Behaviour Support in the UK, both as a risk factor and a construct of outcome. Allan is currently Honorary Secretary of the Faculty for People with Intellectual Disabilities within the British Psychological Society.

Lesley Steptoe currently works in the Forensic Service for offenders with intellectual disability in NHS Tayside, UK. She gained her PhD at the University of Abertay, Dundee, investigating attachment issues in offenders with intellectual disability. Similar to her research interests, on which she has published extensively, her clinical interests include risk assessment, sexual offending, personality disorder and quality of life.

Samantha Walker is a Senior Clinical Psychologist, who has experience of working with children and adults with intellectual disabilities and their families in both NHS and social care settings. She currently works independently for Socrates Clinical Psychology in Huddersfield, UK. Her clinical experience includes the assessment of autism and differential diagnosis around attachment, and post-diagnostic support to children and adults. She also works within the expert witness arena for family and criminal courts. Her interest in attachment theory began whilst completing her doctoral thesis in the area of attachment assessment with people who have an intellectual disability. Her research provided the foundation for the development of the Manchester Attachment Scale – Third party observational measure (MAST), of which she is a co-author.

FOREWORD

When John Bowlby died in 1990 at the age of 83, he had already seen the proofs of his last book *Charles Darwin: A New Life*, which was published after his death. It is not often we have the chance to experience a genius writing about a genius and Bowlby accesses the emotional losses and joys of Darwin in a way that sheds insight without demeaning any of Darwin's brilliance. Indeed, looking at attachment, loss and somatizing in Darwin through the prism of Bowlby's own clinical and theoretical contributions adds to our knowledge of both men.

As well as all the other connections between these two men, who both created paradigm shifts, there is one that is particularly apposite for this seminal book. Both men had the experience of intellectual disability in their families (Darwin's son and Bowlby's grandson) and both men loved the family member with a disability. Indeed, in the early days of The Tavistock Clinic Mental Handicap Workshop (the correct terminology at that time), both John Bowlby and his daughter told me with great pride that he had diagnosed the disability before other doctors had and that because of all the love and family support, the child had exceeded all expectations.

Intellectual disability can create such loss and exclusion that it feels warming that the father of attachment theory was not part of such processes. Attachment theory has allowed us to find a way of evaluating social and emotional richesse, hope, risks, forensic concerns, safeguarding issues and generational transmission. It has engendered internationally accepted research tools that have meaning for the emotional health of each country. It is a lifesaving body of theory and practice.

This book, the first to formally, academically, clinically and theoretically extend the applications of attachment theory to the population of those with intellectual disability who are excluded from so much mainstream research, is a fitting quarter-century tribute (post Bowlby's death) to the continuing and deepening legacy of his work.

Children and adults with intellectual disability face a different world to many of their peers. Cognitive and emotional capacities can be significantly impacted on by disability, which then requires rethinking of provision and research tools. Dependency needs, extra losses and lack of emotional and sexual fulfilment impinge on and affect the nature of attachment processes and relationships. These issues have not been explored adequately. The impact on care staff of different attachment patterns in this field also requires further attention to avoid the damaging dissociative defence of looking at behaviour only to avoid the pain of emotional meaning.

Whilst disability psychotherapists in the UK mention attachment and remain connected under the umbrella of the Institute for Psychotherapy and Disability (e.g. Blackman, Corbett, Frankish, Hollins, Kahr, Sheppard and Sinason), attachment has not been the core of the work. There has been a growing need for a book that finally privileges the subject and its applications across different clinical populations within the Intellectual Disability field. Attachment patterns, assessment, children, families, services, forensic populations, autism and challenging behaviour all come under helpful and knowledgeable scrutiny.

Helen Fletcher, Andrea Flood and Dougal Julian Hare are to be congratulated for righting this omission in such a positive, rigorous and informative way. Together with their fine selection of senior contributors they have extended the attachment map, and this book is a crucial addition to the field.

John Bowlby was a profoundly honourable man who followed his clinical and academic understanding even when it led to unpopular fields. He was ahead of his time in realizing the importance of secure, consistent relationships and the impact of loss on children. As a psychoanalytic historian and clinician speaking at the Bowlby Centre's 25th Anniversary Conference in honour of John Bowlby, Professor Brett Kahr spoke of the towering impact of the man and his legacy whilst pointing out a final evaluation of his work was not yet complete. Indeed, it is still too early to appreciate properly the internationally accumulating legacy left by Bowlby. However, an important book like this raises a warm glow of attachment in the disability field and spreads a major legacy in a deeply successful way.

Valerie Sinason PhD MACP M. Inst. Psychoanal., FIPD is President
of the Institute of Psychotherapy and Disability

REFERENCE

Bowlby, J. (1990) *Charles Darwin: A New Life*. New York: Norton & Company Inc.

ACKNOWLEDGEMENTS

We would like to thank all the authors who have contributed to this book and worked so hard on their chapters, in addition to their full work lives and other commitments. Book editing and writing chapters is a time-consuming business and we would like to thank our families for their support, patience and encouragement over the two years of working on the book.

Helen would like to give thanks to Rob, Sue and Keith for helping look after the girls to free up essential blocks of time for book writing. Special thanks to Rob for his support and encouragement and for being so patient during the long nights of work as the book deadline approached. To Sophie and Chloe, who have taught Helen most about attachment theory in real life, this book is dedicated to them with special love. Thank you also to Andrea and Dougal for sharing the journey of book editing, which has been so stimulating and challenging.

Dougal would like to thank Liza Dysch for her help with copy-editing and proof-reading various chapters, Adrian Wells for his support of this book from its inception, his co-editors for their patience and hard work in seeing this project to completion and, of course, Jayne Bromhall. He would like to dedicate this book to his dad, Kenneth Geoffrey Hare, who was one of the pioneer clinical psychologists in the UK before a distinguished career as an educational psychologist in West Cumbria.

Andrea would like to thank Bret for all his support, encouragement and continued dedication to sharing equally the important task of nurturing their amazing daughters. She would also like to thank Ruby and Alexa, for the joy they bring every day, and bringing meaning to much of what is written about in this book. This book is dedicated to them all with love and appreciation. Thanks go to Helen and Dougal for their perseverance and wisdom, with particular gratitude to Helen for the time she committed when the rest of the country was asleep. Finally, a special thank you goes to Elaine Thomson, who provided inspiration, knowledge and mentorship at the very beginning of Andrea's journey, and whose influence has been profound and long-lasting.

Many people have supported us by reading drafts of the chapters, giving incredible feedback which helped to shape and improve the chapters. Helen would like to thank the following people for their time and assistance in reading and commenting on her chapters: Louise Acker, Amy Critoph, Kate Ferrara, Sue, Keith and Claire Fletcher, Rob Fletcher-Dallas, Barbara Hurtado, Lynne Jones, Marielle Lord, Sophie Mills, Catherine Naysmith, Laura Sanchez-Horneros, Nancy Sheppard and George Young. A special thanks to Deanna Gallichan for her time and assistance in reading, commenting on and shaping up the chapters.

Various professionals from Wiley have supported us throughout the writing and editing of the book. Thank you to Darren Reed for supporting us with the development of the book proposal and for overseeing the book. Also thanks to Roshna Mohan, Karen Shield, Amy Minshull and Aneetta Antony for answering our questions and guiding us in the process when needed. We would like to acknowledge Helen Heyes for her copy editing work and Dr Laurence Errington for his Indexing skills.

Finally and most importantly, we would like to thank the people with intellectual and developmental disabilities and their support networks who have inspired us to work in an attachment-informed way and allowed us to share part of their lives with them.

Chapter 1

INTRODUCTION

Dougal Julian Hare[1], Helen K. Fletcher[2] and Andrea Flood[3]

[1]*South Wales D. Clin. Psy. Programme, Cardiff University, UK*
[2]*Bucks Community Learning Disabilities Team, Southern Health NHS Foundation Trust, High Wycombe, Buckinghamshire, UK*
[3]*University of Liverpool, Liverpool, UK*

> There is nothing more practical than a good theory.
>
> Kurt Lewin (1952)

AIMS OF THE BOOK

This book has been written by clinicians and researchers to tell the story of their experiences of applying attachment theory to their work with children and adults with Intellectual and Developmental Disabilities. Although attachment theory is well established in psychological and therapeutic work in mainstream populations, it remains a developing area of research and practice for those working with people with Intellectual Disabilities (ID). This book outlines the challenges of researching attachment in ID populations, provides a careful review of the available literature and discusses the implications for clinical work. The content draws on the extensive clinical experience of the contributors and presents a guide to offering attachment-informed clinical assessment, formulation and intervention to people with ID in various clinical settings.

Attachment theory is not aligned to any one clinical approach and can be integrated into the full range of psychological interventions: from

---

Attachment in Intellectual and Developmental Disability: A Clinician's Guide to Practice and Research, First Edition. Edited by Helen K. Fletcher, Andrea Flood and Dougal Julian Hare.
© 2016 John Wiley & Sons, Ltd. Published 2016 by John Wiley & Sons, Ltd.

Behavioural to Psychoanalytic, Systemic to Cognitive Behavioural Therapy. As a universal developmental theory it is also relevant to people from every country and culture, although, of course, different family contexts will create natural variations in the way children are raised. This book uses case studies taken from clinical practice (although adapted in order to make them anonymous) to give detailed examples of how attachment behaviours may present in clinical work, and ways to understand and reduce distress related to attachment trauma and losses. Although many of the cases are drawn from clinicians working in the National Health Service (NHS) in the United Kingdom, they have been chosen to illustrate common difficulties which confront people with ID, their families and paid carers, wherever they are living.

We are sure that many clinicians are working with people with ID using aspects of attachment theory, possibly naming it as such or using other language to describe it. We hope that this book will build upon their excellent work and confirm the theoretical rationale behind their ways of working. For people in training who are new to working with people with ID, we hope this book will give them ideas on how to work in a truly person-centred, ethical way, looking at people's enduring relationships and the challenges people with ID and their families and carers may face.

The idea for the book emerged in email correspondence following the IASSIDD and DCP Faculty for ID *Advancing Practice* event, held in 2011 in Manchester in the UK. Carlo Schuengel delivered a keynote speech on Attachment and ID and there were other stimulating presentations focusing on attachment in ID. Following this, a small group of people came together to form a collaborative network with a shared interest in research and clinical work using attachment theory in ID settings. The idea of writing a book together was welcomed instantly by the group.

As the editors of this book, we hope that you will find it an interesting and practical guide to using attachment theory to improve the lives of people with ID. We wanted to unpick and demystify some of the more technical parts of attachment theory so as to help clinicians to feel confident in talking about and using such ideas. We also wanted readers to see real examples of how attachment theory has informed work in different settings and services and to be able to take away practical ideas to use in their work without having to do any further training or go on a particular course.

Books such as this cannot, of course, be written solely on the basis of enthusiasm and goodwill. We have to engage with the ongoing issue within clinical psychology of what constitutes 'evidence'. This presents particular difficulties in the field of ID, where there are many challenges to using the well-established research methods that are used to explore models of distress and approaches to intervention in mainstream populations. Randomized controlled trials are rarely used in ID research, perhaps due to difficulties in gathering a suitably large and homogenous group of research participants. However, the apparent lack of 'evidence' in ID populations more generally may reflect not only the challenges in research design, but also a more widespread disinterest and dismissal of important issues for people with ID. This could be related to issues of stigma and disempowerment of people with ID, particularly for those whose communication difficulties mean their 'voices' may not be heard without others advocating for them. Within this book, the contributors have drawn upon a wide range of evidence including clinical trials and outcome studies, single-case studies, experimental research, innovative approaches such as Q methodology and practice-based evidence. The latter is vital in supporting the all-important 'how to' element that is emphasized throughout this book.

CURRENT CONTEXT OF ID SERVICES IN THE UK

There has been much talk of the need for compassionate care in the light of the abuse perpetrated upon people with ID at the Winterbourne View care home in Gloucestershire, UK, which was brought to light in 2011. The shocking images filmed by the BBC *Panorama* TV programme during an undercover investigation were a stark reminder that many people with intellectual disabilities still lack safe and nurturing places to live. It was evident right from the beginning of this chain of events that there was a culture of callous indifference and cruelty alongside a fear of speaking out or 'whistleblowing' in order to protect those vulnerable people who were being abused. Following investigation of these horrific crimes, senior figures in the UK have turned their attention to fundamental failures in the commissioning and delivery of services, particularly when individuals with ID are experiencing a period of acute distress or crisis. There is a commitment to enable individuals supported in out-of-area services to return 'home', the development of pooled budgets at a local level and an increasing emphasis on the importance of people with ID being legitimate partners in the change process.

Unfortunately, progress has been slow. Important work has been done to change inspection and regulatory systems and attempts made to improve skills and boost empathy in direct care staff, however many barriers remain. Notably, there has been little attention given to the very complex issue of the nature and quality of the relationships between people requiring support and those who provide this. It is precisely here that attachment theory has so much to offer in terms of both understanding and improving such relationships to the benefit of all parties in ID services. Therefore, whilst attachment theory cannot overcome the systemic barriers to the wholesale change in culture that is required, we think that the current book, with its over-riding emphasis on practice, is both timely and imperative with relevance across a range of settings and services.

> I've learned that people will forget what you said, people will forget what you did, but people will never forget how you made them feel.
> Maya Angelou

CONTENT OF THE BOOK

In Chapter 2, Helen Fletcher and Deanna Gallichan summarize the theoretical basis for attachment theory, describing the milestones that have occurred in understanding parent–child relationships and their role in long-term psychological functioning. This chapter is intended to set the scene for the remaining chapters in the book, so that readers without any prior knowledge of attachment theory can become familiar with basic elements and key concepts of the model. This is followed by a further chapter by Helen Fletcher in which the impact of having a child with a disability is explored from the perspective of the parents, with particular reference to both early attachment relationships and later presentations in a clinical setting. Chapter 4 by Sam Walker, Victoria Penketh, Hazel Lewis and Dougal Hare reviews the assessment of attachment in people with ID in clinical practice, with an emphasis on the validity and feasibility of available techniques, and presents a clinical 'toolkit' to this end. In the fifth chapter, Ewan Perry and Andrea Flood examine the oft-problematic issue of attachment and autism spectrum disorder (ASD), with an emphasis on the importance of primary attachment relationships for the psychological well-being of individuals with ASD and useful recommendations for applying attachment theory in adults with ASD. Chapter 6 by Allan

Skelly examines the value and utility of using attachment theory when working with people whose behaviour challenges services. He highlights the risk of services minimizing the importance of a person's life history and personhood through focusing primarily on challenging behaviours. The chapter presents a detailed 'worked-through' case example, which illustrates how clinical outcomes can be improved by ensuring attachment theory is at the heart of interventions such as positive behavioural support. In the seventh chapter, Pat Frankish presents a distillation of her extensive psychotherapeutic work with people with intellectual disabilities. She describes the necessary focus on attachment dynamics and the onus placed on the therapist to provide a 'secure base' within a validating and often long-term therapeutic relationship.

In Chapter 8, Carlo Schuengel, Jennifer Clegg, J. Clasien de Schipper and Sabina Kef write about the vitally important topic of attachment relationships between care staff and people with intellectual disabilities. Their chapter presents the results of recent research on professional caregivers and the impact of their mental representations of attachment on the quality of interaction with their clients. They provide a practical overview of the human resources necessary for offering good quality care, including issues of carer selection, training and supervision. In the ninth chapter, Amanda Shackleton draws upon and develops Pat Frankish's work to understand how the attachment experiences of people with intellectual disabilities can affect their emotional development and how such issues can be worked with in clinical practice via assessment and appropriate intervention tailored to their emotional stage of development. Central to this work is engineering secure attachments and emotional safety by working via staff teams and through individual therapy. Deanna Gallichan and Carol George then discuss their work using the Adult Attachment Projective with adults with ID, through the lens of attachment trauma. They focus on experiences of abuse including the common experience of bullying, and discuss the ways in which these threats can be compounded by helplessness and lack of adequate protection by caregivers. In Chapter 11, Lesley Steptoe, Bill Lindsay, Caroline Finlay and Sandra Miller examine the relationship between attachment experiences, emotional regulation and the subsequent development and presentation of personality disorder in offenders with ID. This chapter draws on their extensive experience of working with this population in secure clinical settings. In the final chapter, Nancy Sheppard and Myooran Canagaratnam examine how attachment influences close and intimate relationships for people with ID undergoing therapy at The Tavistock Clinic, London. They explore a variety of such relationships including attachment relationships between parents and adult children, sibling relationships, friendships, romantic relationships and relationships between parents with ID and their children.

LANGUAGE AND TERMINOLOGY

We decided to use the term Intellectual Disabilities (ID) throughout the book as this language is being used increasingly internationally to refer to individuals who are described as having 'Learning Disabilities', 'Global Developmental Delay' and, historically, 'Mental Retardation'. Of course, language and terminology is forever changing and the people we work with (who are given such labels and diagnoses) are rarely empowered to choose the terminology used by clinicians and researchers. Each author has used different language to describe their attachment-informed work and therefore there are slight differences in the terminology used throughout, reflecting the contributors' individual perspectives and writing styles.

HOW TO USE THIS BOOK

We have edited the book in order to provide the necessary theoretical and practical resources for using attachment theory in everyday clinical practice with people with ID. To this end, each chapter has been written as a stand-alone chapter with the necessary cross-referencing to enable the reader to read as much or as little of the book as desired without too much overlap among chapters. The various chapters use clinical case examples both to illustrate theoretical issues and to provide practical ideas for using attachment theory in clinical work. When appropriate and possible, these examples are supplemented by a clinical toolkit of assessments and procedures.

It is important that the ideas and practices described in this book are utilized within a broader framework of good practice in clinical psychology and psychotherapy. This, of course, includes our normal practice of working under the Human Rights Act (1998), the Mental Capacity Act (2005) and the Mental Health Act (2007) in the UK. In addition to this, it is necessary to work collaboratively and sensitively with both the person with ID and those who support them, in order to develop a meaningful formulation that integrates historical information, current contingencies and systemic influences. In particular, when working with behaviours described as 'challenging' that place people at risk of harm, it is necessary to ensure both an effective risk management strategy and robust mechanisms to provide emotional support for families and staff before addressing the possible role of historical factors. With these in place, an assessment of psychological functioning and presenting needs, taking into account relational histories and attachment dynamics, can be undertaken. In particular, when working with staff teams and families, it is important to be mindful that they may be feeling 'stuck' with a problem that they feel they cannot influence and may have experienced previous professional input as chaotic, unhelpful or disempowering. Such situations often suggest, or even demand, the use of attachment theory, but it is vital that ideas and approaches are introduced and presented in a comprehensible and practical manner.

To conclude this introduction, we would ask that you read this book with the stance that, as clinicians, our theoretical interest must never be merely academic, for the aim of our work is primarily to relieve distress and promote the wellbeing of other people. Moreover, to do this effectively, we must recognize that none of us, whether described as having an intellectual disability or as neurotypical, are wholly autonomous individuals, and that people need people.

> Piglet sidled up to Pooh from behind. 'Pooh?' he whispered.
> 'Yes, Piglet?'
> 'Nothing,' said Piglet, taking Pooh's hand. 'I just wanted to be sure of you.'
> A.A. Milne

Chapter 2

AN OVERVIEW OF ATTACHMENT THEORY: BOWLBY AND BEYOND

Helen K. Fletcher[1] and Deanna J. Gallichan[2]

[1] Bucks Community Learning Disabilities Team, Southern Health NHS Foundation Trust, High Wycombe, Buckinghamshire, UK
[2] Community Learning Disabilities Team, Plymouth Community Healthcare CIC, Plymouth, UK

Attachment theory describes one of the most simple and basic requirements of all animals: that of protection and survival of their young. Although it was originally thought to be a physical mechanism, Bowlby (1969) argued the importance of both emotional and physical aspects of attachment relationships. Attachment theory has been comprehensively written about and researched over the past 40 years and continues to be regarded as a central concept in psychology and psychotherapy. This is because it offers a structure through which to study and understand the development of people's enduring emotional connections with their primary carers and a template with which to consider their later interactions and relationships with others. In addition to this, there is now a convincing amount of research connecting psychological distress in adulthood with difficulties and traumas in early attachment relationships (Dozier, Stovall-McClough and Albus, 2008; Mikulincer and Shaver, 2012). This has stimulated the development of a variety of therapeutic interventions which aim to promote better quality attachment relationships between children and their carers or to help older children and adults to understand the impact their early relationships have had on their emotional functioning, personality and behaviours.

Attachment in Intellectual and Developmental Disability: A Clinician's Guide to Practice and Research, First Edition. Edited by Helen K. Fletcher, Andrea Flood and Dougal Julian Hare.
© 2016 John Wiley & Sons, Ltd. Published 2016 by John Wiley & Sons, Ltd.

Although Bowlby's work did not focus on families with intellectual disabilities (ID), clinicians have long applied attachment theory to help understand the needs of individuals with ID and the difficulties resulting from problems in their early attachment relationships. The psychological difficulties that have been observed in people with a history of insecure attachment (Main, Kaplan and Cassidy, 1985) or mistreatment from parents (Main and Hesse, 1990) are of central importance to people with ID. This is because people with ID are at increased risk of having difficulties in their attachment relationships as well as being more likely to have experienced physical and emotional abuse from others (Van IJzendoorn et al., 1992; Wright, 2013).

The aim of this chapter is to provide an introduction to attachment theory and its clinical applications to set the scene for the rest of the book. It will include:

- An overview of attachment theory as described by Bowlby;
- A description of the work carried out by Mary Ainsworth, Mary Main and Pat Crittenden in developing classifications of attachment and expanding upon Bowlby's attachment theory;
- A discussion of contemporary neuroscience related to attachment theory;
- An overview of therapeutic work regarding attachment theory in non-ID populations.

Throughout the chapter there will be discussion of the application of attachment theory and mainstream interventions to individuals with ID. A case example will also be used to help explain and illustrate the application of attachment theory within ID populations.

DEVELOPMENT OF ATTACHMENT THEORY

John Bowlby's interest in attachment relationships developed whilst he was working in a home for 'maladjusted boys' shortly after graduating from university. During this time he worked with two boys with very different responses to being separated from their mothers. One behaved in a remote, affectionless way with a tendency to isolate himself, whilst the other boy followed Bowlby around constantly. Bowlby noted that similar patterns of behaviour were observed in adults with emotional difficulties, who presented as either clinging and demanding or as having difficulty forming emotional connections with others. This led him to hypothesize that early relationships and separations had a significant impact on later development of personality and psychological problems.

Bowlby became strongly influenced by the observations of his colleague James Robertson, who was studying the reactions of children who were separated from their mothers during periods of hospitalization. Bowlby reported that children responded to their mother's absence with a 'powerful sense of loss and anger' (Bowlby, 1969, p. xiii) and when reunited, reacted either by clinging intensely to their mother or rejecting her and appearing detached. This typical pattern of protest, despair and detachment (see Table 2.1) seen in children older than six months of age led Bowlby to develop his theory of attachment, stating that 'the young child's hunger for his mother's love and presence is as great as his hunger for food' (Bowlby, 1969, p. xiii). This marked a move away from the views of contemporary

Table 2.1 Phases of protest, despair and detachment, see Kobak and Madsen (2008)

Protest	Began as parent prepared to leave. Characterized by intense distress (e.g. crying, screaming, anger, pounding the door, shaking the cot). Lasted from a few hours up to a week. Child appeared to retain hope that their mother would return. Attempts by other adults to soothe the child unsuccessful; some children actively rejecting other caregivers. Crying may subside but return at bedtime or during the night. Dominant emotions: fear, anger, distress.
Despair	Physical movements diminished, child withdrew or disengaged. Behaviour indicated hopelessness that parent would return. Likened to deep mourning, as though the child interpreted the separation as loss (Bowlby, 1973). Withdrawal often misinterpreted as recovery. Hostile behaviour could increase over time. Dominant emotion: sadness.
Detachment	Child actively turned attention to environment. No longer rejecting alternative caregivers; sociable with peers. Apathetic when mother returned, some treating her like a stranger. Detachment alternated with clinging and fear that she would leave again. Following reunion, children would exhibit fear if nursery workers visited their home. Dominant emotions: appearing emotionally numb alternating with fear.

psychoanalysts and social learning theorists, which held that children's bonds with their mothers were developed primarily through the mother feeding them (Cassidy, 2008). Bowlby drew upon ethological studies by Lorenz (1935) and Harlow (1958) which demonstrated that both geese and rhesus monkeys developed attachments to 'mothers' that did not feed them but which gave comfort. Bowlby formulated a principle that in order for a person to have good mental health, the child needs to experience a 'warm, intimate and continuous relationship with his mother (or permanent mother substitute) in which both find satisfaction and enjoyment' (Bowlby, 1973, p. 11).

Bowlby's work on separation significantly shaped policies and led to important changes in the way children are looked after within hospitals, child care and systems of fostering and adoption in the UK (Rutter, 2008). Children's services are now aware of the importance of maintaining as much contact as possible between children and their primary caregivers. Where children are removed from their birth families, they are placed within family home environments wherever possible and supported to develop attachment relationships with new carers. This is a significant shift from the historic model of placing children in orphanages and children's homes with a small number of staff looking after large numbers of children. Although these changes have taken place in non-ID groups and in the care of children, we still see that in ID services children and adults are often in placements with high turnover of staff, where there is poor continuity of care and limited opportunities for developing secure relationships (see Chapters 7 and 9 for further discussion).

Behavioural Systems

Bowlby's (1969) development of attachment theory was based upon evolutionary theory and ethology. He proposed that attachment behaviours are organized within a 'behavioural system' which promotes proximity between children and their mothers in response to real or perceived threats, in order to help them to survive. When activated, the child's attachment behavioural system acts to achieve the goal of proximity to the attachment figure in the most effective way it knows how. Babies may cry or hold their arms out, whilst older children may crawl, run or call out to their parent. As soon as the goal of proximity to the attachment figure is achieved, the child feels safe and their attachment behavioural system is deactivated.

Crucial to Bowlby's theory was the idea that the attachment behavioural system works in concert with several other behavioural systems to ensure survival of the species. These include the fear, exploratory, sociable/affiliative and caregiving behavioural systems. Thus, a child who feels fearful when approached by a stranger will use attachment behaviour to get closer to their attachment figure (e.g. holding out their arms to be picked up). Should the attachment figure be unavailable, the child faces not only the fear of the unfamiliar situation, but also the anxiety of not being able to access their source of protection and comfort (see Kobak and Madsen, 2008). As the attachment behavioural system is not thought to be contingent on pleasure, children will develop attachments to their parents even if they are not meeting their physiological needs or are behaving in abusive ways (Bowlby, 1956).

The parent's caregiving system evokes a biological, pre-programmed urge to care for and protect their child. When the caregiving system is activated, the parent is maintaining proximity and closeness to their child, providing a safe haven or secure base for them; for example, seeing their toddler climbing on a chair, a parent will move closer, allowing them to explore but remaining ready to catch them should they slip. This means that the child's attachment system can be deactivated as long as they do not perceive any threats, freeing them to explore. A child will only explore their surroundings comfortably, or seek friendships with peers, if they feel confident in the availability of their attachment figure, should they need them (see Cassidy, 2008 for further discussion on behavioural systems). However, if a parent's caregiving system is deactivated, then the attachment system may need to become activated, for example if a parent suddenly leaves the room. It is thought that this is why being left can be disturbing to a child and can lead to attachment behaviours such as protest and despair.

Bowlby (1969) hypothesized that the development of a secure attachment relationship is dependent on a smooth interaction between the parents' caregiving behaviours and the child's attachment behaviours. In favourable conditions, it is assumed that children form secure relationships with their mothers and other important figures which serve a protective function.

Internal Working Models

Bowlby's approach to the unconscious, termed 'internal working models' (IWM), departed from his background in psychoanalysis, and was influenced by information processing, cognitive psychology and neurophysiology (Bowlby, 1980). He proposed that as children grow older, and less in need of direct physical proximity and protection from their caregivers, attachment relationships are increasingly governed by IWMs of attachment. These begin developing towards the end of the first year of life and develop rapidly during the second and third years, alongside the development of language and motor skills. The child's day-to-day experiences with their caregiver were thought to give the child a working model of *'who his attachment figures are, where they may be found and how they may be expected to respond'* (Bowlby, 1973, p. 203).

Bowlby (1973) wrote that a key concern for an individual with regards to their internal working model of their 'self' is whether they are acceptable to their attachment figures or not. An internal working model of self as being valued, accepted and competent will be developed in the context of an internal working model of 'other' being emotionally available and protective when needed and supportive of the individual's exploration. Parents who are unresponsive and unavailable or rejecting in their patterns of responses will be connected to internal working models of self as unacceptable, devalued and incompetent.

In any attachment relationship, two internal working models are at play: that of the child and the caregiver. Secure attachment requires that both are continually evaluated and revised in response to developmental changes and life events. In early childhood, attachment security relies on the consistent support of a responsive, trustworthy caregiver. As children grow, they are able to draw on their internal working model of their attachment figure even when they are not physically present. They also start to become aware that their parents sometimes have needs and motivations that are different to their own, and that negotiation is sometimes necessary to work through relationship conflicts and adjust goals (see Bretherton and Mulholland, 2008 for further discussion). Internal working models, therefore, aid the ability of attachment relationships to become 'goal-corrected' partnerships which develop some time after the third year of life when children's verbal skills and ability to think about another person's perspective are developing. Developing understanding about a parent's state of mind is helpful for children in managing times where their parent is unavailable due to illness, stress or travel. This means they are less likely to feel intentionally rejected by their parent and better able to deal with such periods of adversity. Achieving a goal-corrected partnership is likely to be more difficult for children with ID due to communication difficulties and insufficient understanding of theory of mind. It might be hypothesized that individuals with ID are likely to remain more dependent on physical proximity to feel safe and secure.

Bowlby (1969) suggested that insecure attachment relationships developed when internal working models were not updated and revised, leaving them inadequate and inaccurate. Therefore, if caregivers/family members do not update their internal working models in line with developments in their child's cognitive, social and physical development, this will increase the risk of subsequent difficulties in their attachment relationships. This is important to consider when working with families who have children with ID, as parents' distress and grief may negatively affect their ability to attune to the reality of their children's actual abilities and may also lead to a child viewing themselves as being unacceptable due to their disability (see Chapter 3).

Ainsworth's Development of Attachment Classifications

Whilst Bowlby was working at The Tavistock Clinic in London, he met Mary Ainsworth, who joined his research team to explore the effect of 'early separation from mother' on people's personalities. Ainsworth used detailed observations of Ugandan mother–child pairs and white middle-class American families to determine the types of responses which led to different classifications of attachment behaviours. She then studied the reactions of the American children (aged 12–20 months) to experiences of separation from their mother in a controlled laboratory experiment called the 'strange situation' (Ainsworth *et al.*, 1978). This experiment involves the child being separated from and then reunited with their mother. The child's reactions are videotaped and then coded according to their responses. Ainsworth found clear links between sensitive and responsive parenting and secure attachment behaviour in children (Ainsworth *et al.*, 1978). Ainsworth and colleagues developed a detailed coding system for the strange situation from which they identified three main classifications of attachment behaviours. A fourth classification of disorganized attachment was later added by Ainsworth's graduate student Mary Main along with Judith Solomon (Main and Solomon, 1986; 1990) and Mary Main's husband Erik Hesse (Main and Hesse, 1990). See Box 2.1 for a summary of the classifications.

Box 2.1 Strange Situation Classifications

Secure autonomous (B): A secure attachment allows children to explore away from their parents in safe, non-threatening situations, returning to the safety of their parents in threatening circumstances for comfort and protection. Children who have secure attachments appear to have an internal model of their caregiver in which they expect their mother to be available and responsive to them. They are confident and at ease that their attachment needs will be met. In the strange situation, these children used their mother as a safe base from which to explore, showed signs of missing her during separation, greeted her after separation, indicated distress if upset, were comforted by her and then returned to play and explore quite quickly.

Anxious-avoidant insecure (A): Children with insecure attachment appear to have an internal working model of their caregiver that expects they will not be available and responsive. Those with avoidant attachments try to manage rejecting behaviours from their caregiver by minimizing their display of attachment behaviours. During the strange situation, these children explored readily with little secure-base behaviour, showed little distress when left, ignored or turned away from their mother when she returned and focused more on the toys.

Anxious-ambivalent/resistant insecure (C): Children with ambivalent attachments appear to maximize their attachment behaviours by remaining close to their mothers but getting little comfort from them (Ainsworth *et al.*, 1978). In the strange situation, these children showed distress on entering the room and did not want to explore, protested loudly during separations and wanted to be picked up on reunion. However, they did not get comfort from being held and some appeared overtly angry with their mother. They struggled to return to play.

Disorganized (D): Children who may have been frightened by their caregivers experience a dilemma. Although they may behave in ways which indicate organized secure or insecure attachment patterns, they also behave in unusual ways such as freezing, exhibiting signs of fear and disorientation. Such patterns of behaviour are frequently observed in children who have been maltreated (Main and Solomon, 1986). In the strange situation, their behaviour did not seem to have a clear goal. Children sometimes showed fear/apprehension when approaching their parent or appeared confused and disorientated. Children may be classified as D in addition to A, B or C.

It is important to note that the three organized attachment strategies of secure, insecure avoidant and insecure ambivalent are thought to be adaptive and reflect a strategy by which the child can maximize their proximity to their primary carer dependent on their carer's characteristics. The fourth attachment classification of disorganized is related to parents who behave in ways which unpredictably frighten their children through showing their own fear or through maltreatment of their children. This has been found to be clinically important and predictive of negative outcomes for the child regarding their experience of stress, emotional distress and behavioural disturbances including aggressive behaviours and dissociative behaviours (see Van IJzendoorn, Schuengel and Bakermans-Kranenburg, 1999 for a detailed review).

The development of the strange situation stimulated a considerable body of further research examining attachment behaviours in infants and internal working models of attachment in older children and adults. Attachment in adults has been assessed using a variety of techniques including interviews, Q-sorts and Projective assessments. The Adult Attachment Interview (AAI; George, Kaplan and Main, 1984/1985/1996) and Mary Main's AAI coding system (Main and Goldwyn, 1984; 1998) are used widely in research due to their excellent validity and reliability. The AAI is a structured interview which explores the participant's early attachment experiences and the impact these have had on the individual as an adult. The interview comprises 20 questions which have standardized follow-up probes/questions and normally lasts for approximately one hour (see Chapter 4 for further information about the interview and classifications of attachment).

It has been reported that children classified as being secure are more resistant to stress and better able to recover from adverse life experiences (Pianta, Egeland and Sroufe, 1990). Insecurely attached children (avoidant, ambivalent or disorganized) have been found to be more at risk of psychological and interpersonal problems (Main, Kaplan and Cassidy, 1985). A substantial body of research has shown a relationship between AAI classifications and mental health status, with insecure attachment being overrepresented in clinical populations. In particular, 'unresolved' individuals emerge as being especially at risk of psychopathology, including depression, anxiety disorders, PTSD, dissociative disorders, eating disorders and borderline personality disorder (see Dozier, Stovall-McClough and Albus, 2008 for more details).

The Dynamic Maturational Model of Attachment and Adaptation

Patricia Crittenden's Dynamic Maturational Model (DMM) of attachment proposes that an individual develops self-protective strategies as they mature, which interact with their context. Crittenden (2008) stresses that an individual's attachment strategies are adaptive and developed in response to the available resources from the primary caregivers. Later psychopathology is viewed as being due to earlier misperceptions, misattributions and misdirected behaviours which were carried forward. Crittenden proposes that adaptation is more important than security, as the ability to select an appropriate strategy to maintain safety in different contexts is possible to achieve, but controlling the safety of one's environment is not. She suggests that in adulthood, children with secure strategies have to 'earn' their balanced strategy by learning to understand danger, and children with anxious strategies achieve a balanced strategy by learning about comfort and safety. In terms of treatment, the goal is for individuals to be able to generate and use self-protecting strategies in the right context at the right time.

Crittenden also stresses the importance of children being both protected and exposed to danger in order to help them to recognize danger and develop strategies for self-protection. She uses the concept of the zone of proximal development (Vygotsky, 1978) to explain the importance of parents offering the right level of support and protection to their children for their particular stage of development. When parents misjudge their children's needs by either failing to offer help when needed or offering too much help and protection, they hinder their child's development, leading to discomfort in the child–parent relationship. This is of particular relevance to families with children with ID who may struggle to understand their children's communications and needs.

Crittenden described a group of individuals who inhibit their own affect and instead focus on protecting their attachment figure by cheering them or caring for them. Crittenden suggests that this pattern of caring for others, which Bowlby (1973) termed 'compulsive caregiving', often leads to adults finding employment in jobs caring for needy or vulnerable people. Understanding carers' attachment strategies may be useful when engaging them in interventions or looking to offer them appropriate emotional support (see Chapter 8).

INTERGENERATIONAL ATTACHMENT

There is a large body of research which has found that mothers' attachment patterns, as measured by the AAI (George, Kaplan and Main, 1984/1985/1996; Main and Goldwyn, 1984, 1998) are predictive of their child's attachment patterns, as measured by the strange situation (Fonagy, Steele and Steele, 1991; Benoit and Parker, 1994; George and Solomon, 1996; Van IJzendoorn and Bakermans-Kranenburg, 1996). Fonagy *et al.* (1993) attribute the relationship between the mother's secure/autonomous AAI classification and their child's secure attachment behaviour on the strange situation to the parent's self-reflective functioning. They state that parents who have greater capacity for self-reflection are more sensitive to their child's perspective and emotions. This means that they are better able to respond sensitively to their child's attachment behaviours and meet their needs. It is possible that an individual with a past history of insecure attachment may be classified as secure on the AAI and vice versa. This is because the AAI is a measure of the individual's current state of mind, which may have been affected by environmental or interpersonal experiences in adolescence or adulthood, such as being in a romantic relationship that has developed into a secure attachment relationship (Fox, 1995). Fonagy *et al.* (1991) suggested that the ability to predict attachment classification is not related to past experiences *per se* but in the 'overall organization of mental structures underlying relationships and attachment related issues' (p. 901).

ATTACHMENT AND CULTURE

Van IJzendoorn and Sagi-Schwartz (2008) presented a review of cross-cultural patterns of attachment and reported that the three main patterns of attachment (secure, avoidant and ambivalent) have been found in every culture where attachment has been studied. They acknowledged cultural variations but concluded that, in general, cross-cultural studies provide support for attachment theory.

Both Bowlby (1969) and Ainsworth (1967) stated that most infants develop multiple attachment relationships but proposed that there is an attachment hierarchy with preferred attachment figures. Cassidy (2008) explains that attachment figures are often fathers, grandparents, aunts, uncles and older siblings and that day care providers and even other children have been reported to serve as attachment figures. Bowlby explained that the tendency of a child to prefer a particular attachment figure could be seen in institutional care where they would choose a particular carer as 'belonging' to them. Similarly, people with ID are often reported to seek a preferred member of staff and to develop a stronger connection to them than other staff, which can be experienced as problematic for the carers (Clegg and Sheard, 2002).

CRITICISMS OF ATTACHMENT

Fox (1995) presented a detailed critique of the AAI stating that there was insufficient evidence to suggest that attachment is stable over time and that the AAI may well be 'just another interesting personality measure' (p. 409). Fox considered that retrospective reports of attachment and coherency of speech are significantly affected by the individual's current psychological state and environmental factors, and hence argued that there is no evidence that retrospective reports on the AAI are related to earlier security of attachment in the individual. In a reply to Fox, Van IJzendoorn (1995) argued that the AAI is not meant to represent the adult's childhood attachment strategy, but aims to access the adult's current state of mind and representations with regard to attachment. He also stated that there is convincing evidence that adult attachment representations and infants' attachments are strongly related (see the research cited within the section on intergenerational attachment).

The AAI has also been criticized for being overly 'deterministic' and reducing attachment to a dichotomous classification (Dunn, 1993). In fact, the AAI contains 12 subclassifications (Hesse, 2008), but these are rarely reported in empirical studies, probably due to issues with statistical power. Moreover, beyond the academic study of attachment, the AAI and similar measures provide rich qualitative data which go far beyond the overarching attachment classification and can be used in therapeutic encounters in clinical settings.

PAST AND PROXIMAL LOSSES

The loss of an attachment figure can cause severe distress and grief. Reactions include searching for the lost person, disbelief that they are gone, fears of having caused the loss and disorientation in situations where the lost person would normally have been present. Resolution of the loss indicates that the individual is able to accept the loss as permanent and stop searching for their loved one. They are also able to access memories of the lost person without becoming disorientated and no longer fear that they caused the loss. Those who are unresolved continue to experience symptoms of distress and disorientation and have conflicting internal models of their self and others.

The experience of intense fear and helplessness associated with trauma can lead to psychological and behavioural disorganization, particularly if the child is mistreated or abused by their caregiver (Main and Hesse, 1990). There is evidence to suggest that mothers who are unresolved regarding past losses and traumas are more likely to have children with a disorganized attachment strategy (Main and Hesse, 1990). The disorientation experienced by mothers who are classified as unresolved on the AAI is thought to cause them to behave in ways which unpredictably frighten their child. The child then experiences the dilemma of wanting to approach their caregiver for protection and comfort but simultaneously experiencing the caregiver as the source of fear. Some parental behaviours may be obviously traumatic (e.g. abuse or neglect) and others more subtle, such as passive helplessness or attempting to solicit care from the child (see Barnett et al., 1999).

Pianta et al. (1996) suggest that parents' caregiving systems can be disrupted by *past* losses and traumas to the attachment system, or by *proximal* losses and traumas such as giving birth to a child with a disability or chronic medical condition. Such an experience presents a threat to the parent's attachment caregiving system, as the parent is unable to protect their child from the threat to their health and development. Such a situation may disorganize the caregiving system and cause conflict and anxiety which arouse the parent's own attachment systems. The process of resolving the child's diagnosis is similar to resolution of other losses and traumas. It involves integrating new information about their child into their existing representational models without distorting information (Pianta et al., 1996). See Chapter 3 for more details.

This chapter so far has presented an overview of attachment theory and the considerable body of research work which took place following Bowlby's work to expand on his ideas. The next section will discuss the developments in neuroscience relating to attachment theory and clinical applications of attachment theory in mainstream populations. Consideration will be given as to how these can be applied usefully to people with ID and their care networks.

DEVELOPMENTS IN NEUROSCIENCE

Although the functioning of the brain remains an area of science with many questions unanswered, there have been significant developments in neurology and neuroscience which have increased knowledge of the way children's brains develop. Research has focused both on genetics and social and environmental factors. Hughes and Baylin (2012), in their book *Brain-based Parenting: The neuroscience of caregiving for healthy attachment*, describe the neurobiological processes that influence children's attachment behaviours, parents' caregiving behaviours and parent–child interactions. They identify five domains of caregiving, namely: approach, reward, child reading, meaning making and executive systems, and discuss how the processes of the brain are involved in each system. Links are made between the activation of neural systems, the release of neurotransmitters and hormones and affect-inducing experiences. Examples include the increase in cortisol during stressful situations and the release of oxytocin and dopamine during positive experiences, including parental joy and bonding.

Hughes and Baylin explain that when parents experience high levels of stress, this can place them in a 'mindless' rather than a mindful state, such that they are relying on more primitive brain processes where emotions and actions are poorly regulated. They suggest that if parents remain in this state of mind and are unable to repair these lapses of mindful parenting, they can become stuck in patterns of blocked care where they are not able to nurture their children. Children are thought to 'shut down' neurologically as a self-protective mechanism when they experience painful emotions or shame. However, this can lead to a dissociative style of emotional defences which creates problems later in intimacy and parenting. They explain the importance of parents' reflective functioning, using higher level cognitive brain processes to make sense of emotions, events and behaviours. This allows for emotional safety in the relationship between parents and children where difficulties can be thought about and worked through rather than responded to with primitive emotions and reactions.

Although there is not yet a clear understanding about the neuronal mechanisms involved in intergenerational transmission of attachment, theorists have found evidence linking 'mind-minded' comments from mothers to their infants with secure attachment (Bernier and Dozier, 2003) and children's mentalization, verbal and narrative skills in later years (Meins *et al.*, 2003). Fonagy and Target (1998) use the term 'mentalization' to describe the ability to understand and reflect on one's own and other people's mental states and understand that these are connected to behaviours.

Music (2011) explains that children who receive 'mind-minded' attention from their carers, focusing on and reflecting on the child's mental state, are more able to reflect on both their own and other people's emotions, which aids their development and social functioning in family and peer relationships. Thus, by being thought about, a child's mind actively grows and develops. Perry (2002) reports that children who have experienced extreme neglect or trauma have significantly smaller brains than other children, although, encouragingly, evidence suggests that if children are adopted early enough, their brain circumference will increase back to the same size as other children's. This provides hope that intervention can help children's development in terms of their biopsychosocial functioning. This research is important in helping professionals to identify the skills and qualities which need to be developed to help support children's development, learning and emotional wellbeing for those deemed to be at risk of poor outcomes.

ATTACHMENT-BASED INTERVENTIONS

Clinicians and researchers have worked to develop early intervention programmes to support families at risk, in order to improve attachment relationships, reduce emotional distress and reduce patterns of behaviour which may lead to negative outcomes for children later in life. They have also been interested in understanding the impact of the foster carer or adoptive parent's attachment strategy on the child who has been fostered or adopted.

A full review of the literature is not possible here, but a brief review of different attachment-based interventions is presented. Consideration will be given as to whether these approaches have been used with individuals with ID or have any scope to be.

- Video interaction guidance (VIG) involves parents being guided to review and reflect on video clips of their interactions with their child. It has been shown to enhance positive parenting skills, reduce parents' stress and help the child's development (Kennedy, Landor and Todd, 2011). VIG is recommended as an evidence-based practice which can improve maternal sensitivity and mother–child attachment for mothers with depression or infants showing behavioural

difficulties in the National Institute for Health and Care Excellence (NICE) guidance for Social and Emotional Wellbeing: Early years (2012). Video feedback is also mentioned in the NICE guidance for Autism (2013) as part of the psychosocial intervention work which should be offered to support children's relationships with others.
- The Circle of Security (Cooper *et al.*, 2005) comprises a 20-week group intervention designed to help families with children up to four years of age who are at risk of attachment trauma. It aims to increase parents' awareness of their child's attachment needs and to develop healthier attachment relationships between parents and children. It uses comprehensive assessments such as the strange situation, Parent Development Interview (Aber *et al.*, 1989) and Adult Attachment Interview to tailor the intervention to each family's strengths and needs. Group discussion, psycho-education and video feedback are then used to inform families about the importance of parents providing a secure base from which their children can explore and a safe haven to welcome them back to when they need help or comfort. The Circle of Security promotes the idea of the parent being 'bigger, stronger, wiser and kind' at all times. It explores parents' own histories and how this can lead to miscueing children because of parents' own emotional defences. The programme uses diagrams and a video animation of the 'Circle of Security'. Parents then learn and practise caregiving skills and responses. The programme is being validated at present through the 'Head Start' programme in the USA, with early findings indicating a significant shift from disordered to ordered patterns of attachment and increased security of attachment (Cooper *et al.*, 2005).
- Dyadic Developmental Psychotherapy was developed by Daniel Hughes (Hughes, 2011) and involves therapy sessions with a child and their caregiver using PACE, which stands for a 'playful, accepting, curious and empathic' approach. The therapist attunes to the child's emotional state and experiences when they are talking about distressing experiences of mistreatment and abuse. They use their body language, facial expressions and tone of voice to show that they are connected to the child's emotions and to reflect this back to the child to regulate their emotions and co-create a coherent narrative of events. The primary caregiver/parent is asked to help create a safe and containing home environment for the child. Cognitive behavioural strategies are also used within the approach.
- Infant–parent psychotherapy is an intervention for families with children under five years of age experiencing trauma and

impoverishment. The treatment involves long-term weekly psychotherapy sessions with parents and their children focusing on the parents' early attachment relationships, experiences of abusive parenting practices and current life stresses. Evidence has shown effectiveness in improving mother–child interactions and security of children's attachments to their mothers following interventions (Cicchetti, Rogosch and Toth, 2006; Doughty, 2007) and in reducing children's behavioural problems and mothers' distress (Lieberman, Van Horn and Ippen, 2005; 2006).

A meta-analysis of the effectiveness of attachment-based interventions (Bakermans-Kranenburg, Van IJzendoorn and Juffer, 2003) reported that the most effective interventions involved a 'moderate' number of sessions and had a clear-cut behavioural focus. Use of video feedback was found to improve the parental sensitivity and security of the child's attachment relationships over interventions which did not use video feedback.

The mainstream attachment-based interventions discussed above show clear evidence of positive outcomes following intervention. It is positive to note that these modes of working appear to be easily transferable to people with ID and in line with the type of interventions and support which are already being offered in services supporting children and adults with ID.

The common factors evident throughout the different approaches are summarized in Box 2.2.

> **Box 2.2 Key Components of Mainstream Attachment Interventions**
>
> - Psychoeducation about children's attachment needs, signals and behaviours.
> - Development of sensitive, attuned responses to children in the context of a mutually pleasurable relationship (e.g. using play).
> - Review of parents'/carers' responses using video feedback to facilitate development of caregiving behaviours which offer a sensitive response and safe base.
> - Reflection of parents'/carers' own attachment experiences and states of mind with respect to attachment and therapeutic support to discuss the impact of these on caregiving relationships.

As the chapter draws to a conclusion, the impact of ID on caregiving and attachment will be illustrated using a case example to draw together the different threads of attachment theory and attachment-based interventions.

Case Example: Sylvie

Background information: Sylvie, a three-year-old girl with cerebral palsy and moderate learning disabilities, was referred to the local Child Development Team for assessment and therapy. Sylvie's family was from Portugal and had come to the UK to find a better quality of life through work opportunities. Sylvie had little control over her body, she was unable to crawl or roll and used a buggy to travel. However, she was able to communicate using vocalizations and facial expressions to express her feelings. Sylvie would cry for extended periods of time and her parents, Mr and Mrs M, reported that it would be impossible to understand why, soothe her and stop the crying. Mrs M felt despairing that she could not comfort or soothe her. She reported that distraction did not work and that she would often end up placing Sylvie in her play pen in her bedroom and walking into the other room as she could not bear to hear the crying any longer. Sometimes Sylvie would stop crying by herself after a long period of time but sometimes the crying would continue until Mr M came home. Then Sylvie would greet him with a smile and stop crying. Mrs M felt jealous and angry that Sylvie appeared to prefer being with her father and responded differently to him. Mrs M explained that she no longer tried to comfort or distract Sylvie as nothing ever worked, but this led to her feeling awkward in front of other people as they were confused as to why she was not doing anything. Sylvie's parents were distressed about her disability and found it hard to accept that she had a learning disability as well as her physical disability. Despite their distress they were seen to be caring and attentive parents who attended regular appointments for Sylvie's therapy and carried out her physio and speech and language therapy exercises at home.

Formulation: Mrs M appeared to be experiencing significant distress about Sylvie's disability and this was impacting on her ability to offer sensitive caregiving and understand Sylvie's emotional communications. Their relationship had developed into restricted routines, with little mutual enjoyment or interaction between them. Sylvie was able to show pleasure in her relationship with Mr M by laughing and smiling when he came home from work and played with her. This led to feelings of relief for Mrs M when Sylvie stopped crying but also anger and resentment that she was not able to comfort Sylvie in the same way. Mrs M then withdrew emotionally from Sylvie and no longer attempted to comfort her or interact with her when she was crying. Sylvie was unable to maintain proximity to her parents physically, so it was hypothesized that she used vocal communication and facial expressions to draw or call her parents to her. However, she was unable to gain consistent comfort from them, leading to her developing ambivalent attachment behaviours where she would continually cry to call Mr and Mrs M to her but not gain comfort from their cuddles and responses. This left them in a cycle where there was a lack of smooth interaction between Mr and Mrs M's caregiving systems and Sylvie's attachment systems, leading to further frustration and distress for the family.

Intervention: Psychology sessions were offered to support Mr and Mrs M with the emotional impact Sylvie's disability was having on them and to discuss their thoughts and emotions about her diagnosis. In addition, help was offered to think about Sylvie's crying behaviours and to try and find ways of responding which would help them all. However, Mr and Mrs M found it hard to engage in psychology sessions and to discuss their feelings and Sylvie's feelings. They wanted practical ideas to try but were also struggling with hopeless and helpless feelings that things were unchangeable. Mrs M felt that Sylvie was not connected to her emotionally and that she was not distressed when Mrs M moved away from her or was out of sight. This made her reluctant to try engaging with and interacting with Sylvie, as she found the feelings of rejection unbearable on top of her grief at Sylvie's disability. Therefore, within the multi-disciplinary team it was agreed that physiotherapy and speech and language therapy tasks would be used to develop engagement, physical proximity and interactions between Sylvie and Mrs M.

Outcome: Focusing on practical and physical caregiving tasks worked well and gave Mrs M the opportunity to develop better

> sensitivity to Sylvie's emotions and communications. The psychology work stopped and intervention moved to a consultative model speaking to the multi-disciplinary team about their therapy work and the progress which Sylvie and her family were making. The crying behaviours reduced in intensity and frequency, although they still happened a few times per week. Psychology support was later offered to help Sylvie's transition to a specialist nursery. Mrs M was able to have a break whilst Sylvie was at nursery and this helped her to have some respite and she reported feeling she was coping much better. Sylvie rarely engaged in the crying behaviours at nursery and did not show any separation anxiety when left at nursery. Mrs M reported that it felt a relief to her when she dropped Sylvie off and she was very happy with the staff and felt confident that Sylvie would be well cared for.

SUMMARY

This chapter has provided a broad overview of attachment theory and attachment-based interventions, looking at their historical development and considering how these concepts are important to every human being. Recent developments in neuroscience have offered new understanding about the brain processes involved in children's development of attachment relationships and the physical impact of neglect and abuse. However, it is not yet clear how these processes are affected by ID and related conditions such as autism spectrum disorder (ASD).

Attachment theory has particular relevance in helping us understand and support those who have struggled to find emotional containment and safety in their early relationships and who are experiencing psychological and behavioural distress. For people with ID, there are many reasons why they are at increased risk of having disrupted attachment relationships and emotional distress. This raises the need for development of appropriate clinical interventions which foster understanding and support of the attachment needs of this client group. It is immensely encouraging that several attachment-based interventions are showing promising outcomes for children at risk of attachment trauma. These interventions appear to have good clinical utility in working with people with ID.

It is hoped that this chapter has provided a useful overview of attachment theory to set the scene for the remainder of the book by connecting attachment theory and mainstream interventions to the needs of people with ID. The following chapters will present up-to-date research and clinical practice detailing ways of working with people with ID in order to assess, understand and support their attachment needs.

ACKNOWLEDGEMENTS

Special thanks to Pat Frankish for her time and help in developing this chapter.

REFERENCES

Aber, J., Slade, A., Berger, B., Bresgi, I. and Kaplan, M. (1985–2003) *The Parent Development Interview: Interview Protocol*. Unpublished manuscript: Barnard College, Columbia University, New York.

Ainsworth, M. (1967) *Infancy in Uganda: Infant care and growth of love*. Baltimore: Johns Hopkins University Press.

Ainsworth, M.D., Blehar, M., Waters, E. and Wall, S. (1978) *Patterns of Attachment: A Psychological Study of the Strange Situation*. Hillsdale, NJ: Lawrence Erlbaum.

Bakermans-Kranenburg, M.J., Van IJzendoorn, M.H. and Juffer, F. (2003) Less is more: Meta-analyses of sensitivity and attachment interventions in early childhood. *Psychological Bulletin*, 129:195–215.

Barnett, D., Hill Hunt, K., Butler, C.M., McCaskill IV, J.W., Kaplan-Estrin, M. and Pipp-Siegel, S. (1999) Indices of attachment disorganzation among toddlers with neurological and non-neurological problems. In J. Solomon and C. George (eds) *Attachment Disorganization* (pp. 189–212). New York: The Guilford Press.

Benoit, D. and Parker, K.C.H. (1994) Stability and transmission of attachment across three generations. *Child Development*, 65: 1444–1456.

Bernier, A. and Dozier, M. (2003) Bridging the attachment transmission gap: The role of maternal mind-mindedness. *International Journal of Behavioral Development*; 27: 355. DOI: 10.1080/01650250244000399.

Bowlby, J. (1956) The growth of independence in the young child. *Royal Society of Health Journal*, 76: 587–591.

Bowlby, J. (1969/1997) *Attachment and Loss. Vol. 1: Attachment*. UK: Pimlico.

Bowlby, J. (1973) *Attachment and Loss. Vol. 2: Separation: Anxiety and Anger*. New York: Basic Books.

Bowlby, J. (1980) *Attachment and Loss. Vol. 3: Loss: Sadness and Depression*. New York: Basic Books.

Bretherton, I. and Mulholland, K.A. (2008) Internal Working Models in Attachment Relationships: Elaborating a Central Construct in Attachment Theory. In J. Cassidy and P. Shaver (eds) *Handbook of Attachment: Theory, Research, and Clinical Applications* (pp. 102–127). London: The Guilford Press.

Cassidy, J. (2008) The Nature of the Child's Ties. In J. Cassidy and P. Shaver (eds) *Handbook of Attachment: Theory, Research, and Clinical Applications* (pp. 3–22). London: The Guilford Press.

Cicchetti, D., Rogosch., F.A. and Toth, S.L. (2006) Fostering secure attachment in infants in maltreating families through preventive interventions. *Development and Psychopathology*, 18: 623–649.

Clegg, J. and Sheard, C. (2002) Challenging behaviour and insecure attachment. *Journal of Intellectual Disability Research*, 46(6): 503–506.

Cooper, G., Hoffman, K., Powell, B. and Marvin, R. (2005) The circle of security intervention: Differential diagnosis and differential treatment. In L.J. Berlin, Y. Ziv, L. Amaya-Jackson and M.T. Greenberg (eds) *Enhancing Early Attachments: Theory, research, intervention and policy* (pp. 127–151). New York: The Guilford Press.

Crittenden, P. (2008) *Raising Parents: Attachment, Parenting and Child Safety*. Collumptom, UK: Routledge/Willan Publishing.

Doughty, C. (2007) *Effective strategies for promoting attachment between young children and infants*. Christchurch, New Zealand: New Zealand Health Technology Assessment (NZHTA).

Dozier, M.K., Stovall-McClough, C. and Albus, K.E. (2008) Attachment and Psychopathology in Adulthood. In J. Cassidy and P. Shaver (eds) *Handbook of Attachment: Theory, Research, and Clinical Applications* (pp. 718–744). London: The Guilford Press.

Dunn, J. (1993) *Young Children's Close Relationships: Beyond Attachment*. London: Sage.

Fonagy, P., Steele, M., Moran, G., Steele, H. and Higgitt, A. (1993) Measuring the ghost in the nursery: An empirical study of the relation between parents' mental representations of childhood experiences and their infants' security of attachment. *Journal of the American Psychoanalytic Association*, 41(4): 957–989.

Fonagy, P., Steele, H. and Steele, M. (1991) Maternal representations of attachment during pregnancy predict the organisation of infant–mother attachment at one year of age. *Child Development*, 62: 891–905.

Fonagy, P. and Target, M. (1998) Mentalization and the changing aims of child psychoanalysis. *Psychoanalytic Dialogues: The International Journal of Relational Perspectives*, 8(1): 87–114.

Fox, N.A. (1995) Of the way we were: Adult memories about attachment experiences and their role in determining infant–parent relationships: A commentary on Van IJzendoorn. *Psychological Bulletin*, 117: 404–410.

George, C., Kaplan, N. and Main, M. (1984/1985/1996). *The Adult Attachment Interview*. Unpublished manuscript. University of California, Berkeley.

George, C. and Solomon, J. (1996) Representational models of relationships: Links between caregiving and attachment. *Infant Mental Health Journal*, 17(3): 198–216.

Harlow, H.F. (1958) The Nature of Love. *American Psychologist*, 13: 673–685.

Hesse, E. (2008) The Adult Attachment Interview: Protocol, Method of Analysis, and Empirical Studies. In J. Cassidy and P. Shaver (eds) *Handbook of Attachment: Theory, Research, and Clinical Applications* (pp. 552–598). London: The Guilford Press.

Hughes, D.A. (2011) *Attachment-Focused Family Therapy: The workbook.* New York: W.W. Norton.

Hughes, D.A. and Baylin, J. (2012) *Brain-based Parenting: The neuroscience of caregiving for healthy attachment.* New York: Norton.

Kennedy, H., Landor, M. and Todd, L. (2011) *Video Interaction Guidance: A relationship-based intervention to promote attunement, empathy and wellbeing.* London: Jessica Kingsley Publishers.

Kobak, R. and Madsen, S. (2008) Disruptions in Attachment Bonds: Implications for Theory, Research and Clinical Intervention. In J. Cassidy and P. Shaver (eds) *Handbook of Attachment: Theory, Research, and Clinical Applications* (pp. 23–47). London: The Guilford Press.

Lieberman, A.F., Van Horn, P. and Ippen, G.C. (2005) Toward evidence-based treatment: Child–parent psychotherapy with preschoolers exposed to marital violence. *Journal of the American Academy of Child and Adolescent Psychiatry*, 44: 1241–1248.

Lieberman, A.F., Van Horn, P. and Ippen, G.C. (2006) Child–parent psychotherapy: 6-month follow-up of a randomized controlled trial. *Journal of the American Academy of Child and Adolescent Psychiatry*, 45: 913–918.

Lorenz, K.Z. (1935) Der Kumpan in der Umvelt des Vogels. *Journal für Ornithologie*, 83: 137–213 and 289–412.

Main, M. and Goldwyn, R. (1984) *Adult Attachment Scoring and Classification System.* Unpublished manuscript, University of California, Berkeley.

Main, M. and Goldwyn, R. (1998) *Adult Attachment Scoring and Classification System.* Unpublished manuscript, University of California, Berkeley.

Main, M. and Hesse, E. (1990) Parents' unresolved traumatic experiences are related to infant disorganized attachment status: Is frightened or frightening parental behavior the linking mechanism? In M.T. Greenberg, D. Cicchetti and E.M. Cummings (eds) *Attachment During the Preschool Years* (pp. 161–184). Chicago: University of Chicago Press.

Main, M., Kaplan, N. and Cassidy, J. (1985) Security in infancy, childhood, and adulthood: A move to the level of representation. *Monographs of the Society for Research in Child Development*, 50(1–2, Serial No. 209): 66–104.

Main, M. and Solomon, J. (1986) Discovery of an insecure-disorganized/disoriented attachment pattern. In T.B. Brazelton and M. Yogman (eds) *Affective Development in Infancy* (pp. 95–124). Norwood, NJ: Ablex.

Main, M. and Solomon, J. (1990) Procedures for identifying infants as disorganized/disoriented during the Ainsworth Strange Situation. In M.T. Greenberg, D. Cicchetti and E.M. Cummings (eds) *Attachment During the Preschool Years* (pp. 121–160). Chicago: University of Chicago Press.

Meins, E., Fernyhough, C., Wainwright, R., Clark-Carter, D., Das Gupta, M., Fradley, E. and Tuckey, M. (2003) Pathways to Understanding Mind: Construct Validity and Predictive Validity of Maternal Mind-Mindedness. *Child Development*, 74: 1194–1211. DOI: 10.1111/1467-8624.00601.

Mikulincer, M. and Shaver, P.R. (2012) An attachment perspective on psychopathology. *World Psychiatry*, 11(1): 11–15. DOI: 10.1016/j.wpsyc.2012.01.003.

Music, G. (2011) *Nurturing Natures: Attachment and Children's Emotional, Sociocultural and Brain Development*. Hove, UK: Psychology Press.

National Institute for Health and Care Excellence (NICE) (2012) *Social and emotional wellbeing: Early years*. Retrieved 07.28.2015 from https://www.nice.org.uk/guidance/ph40

National Institute for Health and Care Excellence (NICE) (2013) *Autism: The management and support of children and young people on the autism spectrum*. Retrieved 07.28.2015 from https://www.nice.org.uk/guidance/cg170

Perry, B.D. (2002) Childhood Experience and the Expression of Genetic Potential: What Childhood Neglect Tells Us About Nature and Nurture. *Brain and Mind*, 3: 79–100.

Pianta, R., Egeland, B. and Sroufe, L.A. (1990) Maternal stress in children's development: Predictions of school outcomes and identification of protective factors. In J.E. Rolf, A. Masten, D. Cicchetti, K. Neuchterlen and S. Weintraub (eds) *Risk and Protective Factors in the Development of Psychopathology* (pp. 215–235). New York: Cambridge University Press.

Pianta, R.C., Marvin, R.S., Britner, P.A. and Borowitz, K.C. (1996) Mothers' resolution of their child's diagnosis: Organised patterns of caregiving representations. *Infant Mental Health Journal*, 17(3): 239–256.

Rutter, M. (2008) Implications of attachment theory and research for child care policies. In J. Cassidy and P. Shaver (eds) *Handbook of Attachment: Theory, Research and Clinical Applications* (pp. 958–974). London: The Guilford Press.

Van IJzendoorn, M.H. (1995) Adult attachment representations, parental responsiveness and infant attachment: A meta-analysis on the predictive validity of the Adult Attachment Interview. *Psychological Bulletin*, 117: 387–403.

Van IJzendoorn, M.H. and Bakermans-Kranenburg, M. (1996) Attachment representations in mothers, fathers, adolescents and clinical groups: A meta-analytic search for normative data. *Journal of Consulting and Clinical Psychology*, 64: 8–21.

Van IJzendoorn, M.H., Goldberg, S., Kroonenberg, P.M. and Frenkel, O. (1992) The relative effects of maternal and child problems on quality of attachment: A meta-analysis of attachment in clinical samples. *Child Development*, 63: 840–858.

Van IJzendoorn, M.H. and Sagi-Schwartz, A. (2008) Cross-cultural Patterns of Attachment: Universal and Contextual Dimensions. In J. Cassidy and P. Shaver (eds) *Handbook of Attachment: Theory, Research and Clinical Applications* (pp. 880–905). London: The Guilford Press.

Van IJzendoorn, M.H., Schuengel, C. and Bakermans-Kranenburg, M.J. (1999) Disorganized attachment in early childhood: Meta-analysis of precursors, concomitants, and sequelae. *Development and Psychopathology*, 11: 225–249.

Vygotsky, L. (1978) Interaction between learning and development. In M. Cole, V. John-Steiner, S. Scribner and E. Souberman (eds) *Mind in Society: The development of higher psychological processes* (pp. 79–91). Cambridge, MA: Harvard University Press.

Wright, S. (2013) How do we prevent another Winterbourne? A literature review. *Advances in Mental Health and Intellectual Disabilities*, 7(6): 365–371.

Chapter 3

ATTACHMENT RELATIONSHIPS BETWEEN PARENTS AND THEIR CHILDREN: THE IMPACT OF 'THE LOSS OF THE HEALTHY CHILD'

Helen K. Fletcher

Bucks Community Learning Disabilities Team, Southern Health NHS Foundation Trust, High Wycombe, Buckinghamshire, UK

It is part of our biological conditioning to protect and nurture our children, meeting their needs physically and emotionally. This bond is both beautifully simple and amazingly complicated. For parents whose children have disabilities or chronic health conditions, the task of nurturing their child can be extremely challenging. Parents may be faced with an impossible task where their urges and efforts to protect and care for their child do not change the reality of the child's disability or health condition. This can lead to distress and disruption of the attachment and caregiving systems.

This chapter explains how attachment theory can be applied to families who have children with intellectual and developmental disabilities to help make sense of the difficulties they may experience. This will include discussion of:

- Parents' reactions to their child's diagnosis;
- How grief and loss can interfere with parents' caregiving abilities;
- The challenges of developing mutually positive and enjoyable interactions with young children who have intellectual disabilities and complex needs;

Attachment in Intellectual and Developmental Disability: A Clinician's Guide to Practice and Research, First Edition. Edited by Helen K. Fletcher, Andrea Flood and Dougal Julian Hare.
© 2016 John Wiley & Sons, Ltd. Published 2016 by John Wiley & Sons, Ltd.

- Connections between early attachment experiences of people with intellectual disabilities and their later expression of challenging behaviours;
- Working with families who present with ongoing complaints about services.

Case examples will be used to illustrate challenges faced by families and describe how these can present to professionals working in health, education and social care services. The chapter will also provide ideas for appropriate support and interventions for families following diagnosis and when they continue to experience distress related to their child's disability.

BECOMING A PARENT AND ANTENATAL SCREENING

The relationship between parents and their child begins as soon as they find out they are expecting a baby. They begin to think about what their baby will be like, how it will look and what kind of personality it will have. The widespread use of antenatal scans and tests means that parents have the experience of monitoring the health and development of their child from the first few months of pregnancy. The increasing accessibility and affordability of 3-D ultrasound scans means that many prospective parents have seen a 3-D image of their child's face and body *in utero*. Whilst these experiences may help parents to bond and connect with their developing foetus, such advances in technology also bring the possibility of finding out about health problems and disabilities well before the baby's due date. This offers the choice of whether to proceed with their pregnancy or consider a termination and also allows parents time to plan and prepare for their child's condition before the birth. However, the experience of pre-natal testing can have a profound impact on mothers-to-be, placing them at risk of experiencing symptoms of post-traumatic stress disorder, depression and anxiety (Horsch, Brooks and Fletcher, 2013). Therefore, mothers are likely to need a particularly high level of social and emotional support following diagnosis of a foetal abnormality during pregnancy.

Individuals who are born with intellectual disabilities (ID), physical disabilities and/or chronic health problems may find themselves searching or wishing for a 'cure' to get rid of their disability in order to lead a 'normal' life. In addition to their own distress and sense of being different, there can also be a deep sense of shame that they have caused their parents to feel disappointment and loss. For parents themselves, they have the complicated task of trying to protect and meet the needs of their child in addition to managing their own feelings of loss, distress and potential guilt at having either caused the disability or having been unable to prevent this and successfully protect their child (Lloyd and Dallos, 2006).

RECEIVING A DIAGNOSIS

> '...and it's not just a sentence, every word is important because you are hanging on to everything they say and you will remember every word that they say, it sticks in your mind. They need to really plan their sentences and their words because this is going to stay with you for the rest of your life.'
> Parent, Informing Families Focus Groups (The National Federation of Voluntary Bodies in Ireland, 2010)

Most parents report experiencing shock, disbelief and sadness when faced with the realization or news that their child has a disability or chronic health condition (Bowlby, 1980; Waisbren, 1980; Blacher, 1984; Marshak and Seligman, 1993). This has been described as grieving the loss of the healthy or 'perfect' child the parents were hoping to give birth to (Goldberg et al., 1995). The nature of the child's condition influences when symptoms are likely to be recognized and diagnosed. Children with Down's syndrome are usually diagnosed antenatally or within the first few weeks of their life, whereas other conditions such as hearing impairment, autism spectrum disorder (ASD) and global developmental delay may not be recognized until the child is older.

Delays in diagnosis can lead to increased levels of stress, as the parents usually suspect that their child has a problem and want a diagnosis so that they can access the best support and interventions. In such cases, receiving a diagnosis may bring positive emotions and relief to a family system, in particular for those families who have been aware of their child's difficulties and have been searching for a diagnosis and support for their child for some time (Dickman and Gordon, 1985). However, some parents are unaware of their child's difficulties and receive an unexpected diagnosis following referral by external agencies such as their general medical practitioner (GP) or nursery/school who have raised concerns about a child's development. Parents who have children with a pattern of uneven cognitive skills may experience increased difficulty understanding their child's condition and accepting its chronicity (Koegel et al., 1992). This is particularly relevant for parents who have children with ASD, where some of their skills and abilities may be average or above average, whilst other skills may be significantly impaired compared to their peers.

There has been much written about the experience of receiving a diagnosis of a child's chronic health condition or disability and the emotional impact of such news on the family. Helpful guidelines for good practice have been developed by The National Federation of Voluntary Bodies in Ireland *'Informing families of their child's disability: National best practice guidelines'*, based on published research and consultation with families. These provide a number of recommendations in addition to the suggestion that health professionals should receive specific training regarding giving diagnoses. These include:

- Family-centred disclosure in a private space with both parents present;
- Additional support to be offered after the appointment;
- Professionals to give clear information about the diagnosis and disability as well as realistic messages of hope;
- Professionals to behave in a sensitive and empathic manner;
- The offer of a follow-up appointment to discuss the diagnosis further;
- Information to be given about counselling and opportunities to meet other families with similar conditions.

> 'It's the toughest part of the job really. When you have experience you will prioritize this, because it's a big priority, because it's something that parents remember.'
> Consultant Paediatrician, Informing Families Focus Groups (The National Federation of Voluntary Bodies in Ireland, 2010)

In summary, although there is general agreement about the most helpful and unhelpful ways to receive a diagnosis, each family differs in the needs they have, rendering a prescriptive 'one size fits all' approach inappropriate. Rather, there is a need for health professionals to develop a relationship with families such that diagnosis can be discussed and explained over time, reviewed and revisited at different transitional points and reflected on with the wider family system in terms of the implications for the family and support needs.

ATTACHMENT THEORY AND REACTION TO DIAGNOSIS

Hornby (1994) and Holder (2000) reported that some parents appear able to resolve loss and trauma surrounding their child's condition fairly quickly whilst others continue to experience difficulties for many years. Marvin and Pianta (1996) proposed attachment theory as a useful framework within which to understand the process of resolving the loss and trauma associated with having a disabled child. Bowlby (1980) wrote extensively about grief processes following the loss of a close loved one and Marvin and Pianta (1996) proposed that Bowlby's theory is applicable whether the loss concerns actual death or intrapsychic loss of the expected healthy child. Bowlby suggested that resolution of grief may be associated with the extent to which parents are able to interact sensitively with their children and provide 'effective' parenting. Barnett et al. (2003) reported that parents go through a process of grieving for the loss of the healthy child they had hoped for before replacing the expectations they had with the reality of their disabled child. If parents are not able to develop an internal representation of their child's *actual* abilities rather than the *hoped for* abilities, then this may impede their ability to parent sensitively and develop a secure attachment with their child (Atkinson et al., 1999).

A group of researchers in the USA developed a measure to try and better understand parents' reactions to their child's diagnosis and how this relates to their attachment relationships. The Reaction to Diagnosis Interview (RDI; Pianta and Marvin, 1992a) assesses parents' resolution of the losses and trauma surrounding their child's diagnosis. It uses five questions to explore the parents' state of mind with regard to their child's diagnosis, how their feelings have changed over time and their beliefs about why they have a child with a disability. The responses are coded using a standardized procedure and parents are classified as resolved or unresolved regarding their child's condition (see Box 3.1), with studies indicating good validity and reliability (e.g. Morog, 1996; Pianta et al., 1996).

Parental resolution refers to the integration of parents' emotions and information regarding their child's disability within the parents' representational system of themselves, their child and their relationship with their child. Resolution is seen as a continuing process and it is expected that parents will re-experience periods of crisis, particularly around times of transition (Wilker, Wasow and Hatfield, 1981). The extent to which the parents' loss and trauma are resolved will vary over time depending on the child's and parents' circumstances. Parents who are unresolved continue to experience disorientation associated with grieving and have not yet integrated information about their child's condition without distorting reality. Pianta and Marvin (1992b) suggest that unresolved coping strategies may have a negative impact on the parent–child relationship, as such cognitive distortions could prevent the parents responding to their child in a sensitive, balanced way which best meets the child's needs. Walsh (2003) reported that mothers' interactions with their children were significantly associated with whether they were resolved with regards to their child's diagnosis of cerebral palsy or epilepsy but not whether they were resolved with respect to past losses/traumas relating to attachment figures.

It is important to note that Pianta and Marvin assume that there are some elements of being both resolved and unresolved in each interview and that this may change over time. The interviews are classified according to whether the parent shows more signs of being resolved or unresolved. Whilst providing a useful framework for assessing parents' responses to their child's diagnosis, the RDI can be criticized for using a categorical approach. Some researchers view categorical coding systems, as used on the RDI and Adult Attachment Interview (AAI; George, Kaplan and Main, 1984/1985/1996), as being overly deterministic and suggest using a dimensional approach instead (Dunn, 1993).

Fletcher (2004) interviewed 43 mothers of school-aged children with ID using the AAI and RDI and found that more than half (56%) were unresolved on the RDI. A concerning result was that high levels of psychological distress were reported by mothers (using a standardized

---

Box 3.1 Signs of Resolution and of Being Unresolved

Signs of resolution

Parents:

- Are focused on the present;
- Are able to identify changes in their feelings since the time of diagnosis;
- Indicate that they have moved on from their initial grieving to concentrate on the task of parenting their child;
- Have suspended their search as to why this has happened to their child;
- Are able to discuss their child's abilities accurately;
- Have coherent discourse;
- Talk about emotional experiences related to diagnosis in the past tense with an appropriate level of affect.

> ### Signs of Being Unresolved
>
> Parents may appear to:
>
> - Be 'stuck in the past';
> - Be emotionally overwhelmed;
> - Present with extreme anger towards professional services and systems;
> - Speak in a confused or incoherent manner, telling a story which is hard to follow or inconsistent;
> - Appear 'cut-off' from the pain and in denial of the impact of their child's condition;
> - Have difficulty focusing on the present;
> - Have difficulty moving on with current tasks of parenting;
> - Have not yet integrated information about their child's condition without distorting reality by:
>   - Minimizing or denying the child's true condition (cognitive distortions);
>   - Continuing to search for the reason that their child has a disability;
>   - Focusing too much on information to the exclusion of present-day realities (stuck in the past and preoccupied);
>   - Denying the pain and impact of the diagnosis on the parent (cut off);
>   - Displacing the pain and sadness to anger at the medical or educational systems.
>
> (Pianta and Marvin, 1992b)

measure of psychopathology), even for those who were resolved on the RDI, coded as autonomous/secure on the AAI and who reported having high levels of social support. There was no relationship found between the AAI and RDI in this study (contrary to the original hypotheses), which led to careful thought and discussion within the research team. However, it is likely that this reflects the fact that the attachment and caregiving systems, although linked, are not the same (George and Solomon, 2008). Therefore, having a child with an ID may overwhelm the parent's mental caregiving system and lead to lack of resolution even when the attachment system is functioning optimally. Walsh (2003) found a significant link between mothers' secure/autonomous classifications on the AAI, being resolved on the RDI and secure attachment of children with cerebral palsy. However, she did not find the same relationships in the group of children with epilepsy. She proposed that this could be due to the unpredictable nature of epilepsy, which is different to the more stable development of cerebral palsy. Surprisingly, Walsh did not find any relationship between being unresolved with respect to past losses and traumas on the AAI and being unresolved on the RDI. This led her to propose that trauma and loss surrounding the child's diagnosis appear to overpower the attachment and caregiving systems and reduce the impact of protective or risk factors associated with the mother's early attachment experiences.

In this research study, parents were significantly more likely to be unresolved on the RDI if they had a male child with ID, had experienced a higher number of recent stressful life experiences and reported receiving less social support from family members. Social support from non-family members was unrelated to resolution even for mothers who reported feeling well supported by a large social network. This suggests a particular emotional loss resulting from lack of supportive family members. The results of this research hold an important message for those working with families with ID because it was the *current* life situation of parents that was found to be related to resolution of diagnosis rather than *historical* attachment relationships (as assessed on the AAI). This provides hope that intervening to support parents with their grief and distress may improve the quality of relationships between parents and their children with ID, reducing the risk of later difficulties.

MODELS OF FAMILY GRIEVING

> You think you've accepted it all but I don't think, deep down, you've completely accepted it because you always, when they're younger, you always have this hope that when they get older they might grow out of it, or it's going to get better, it's going to get easier and it doesn't get any easier. I'm not sure it's going to get any better, it's just different to be honest...it's much harder when you've got a nine-year-old girl walking down the road screaming her head off or throwing a wobbly than it is to have a two-year-old sitting in a pushchair throwing a wobbly...and as you get older you realize that, in actual fact, you could have this adult of 30 on your arm screaming or throwing a wobbly and that's very difficult to come to terms with.
>
> Excerpt from interview with the mother of an eight-year-old girl with severe learning disabilities and autism (Fletcher, 2004)

Several different models have been developed to explain the grieving process that parents experience following the news that their child has an intellectual disability. Olshansky (1962) developed the term 'chronic sorrow' to describe parents' ongoing emotional state with regard to their child's disabilities. Such chronic sorrow was described as a normal reaction to having a disabled child that would change over time. Roos (1995) emphasized the importance of differentiating between chronic sorrow and *pathological or complicated mourning* in order to provide appropriate services and support. This distinction is particularly important, as chronic sorrow is not subject to resolution but must be viewed as a response to an ongoing loss that does not go away.

Some researchers have postulated that parents need to go through different stages of grieving for the loss of the healthy or 'perfect' child they had expected to give birth to before they are able to adjust to their child's disability (Bicknell, 1983). Such 'stage models' assume that parents' feelings of grief will eventually be worked through and replaced by acceptance of their child and resolution of their loss. Other researchers have criticized stage models and propose that resolution is an ongoing, developmental process related to life transitions (Blacher, 1984; Bruce *et al.*, 1994). Wilker *et al.* (1981) suggest that parents' unconscious expectations about their child's development are discrepant with their child's actual development. As a result, parents experience new losses and grief that require resolution as each key developmental milestone is not reached by their child. Korff-Sausse (1999) and Goldberg *et al.* (1995) suggest that resolution is a cyclical process that is affected by developmental transitions such as going to school, adolescence, leaving home/launching (Olson *et al.*, 1984). They state that it is unrealistic to expect families to completely resolve their mourning and that they may continue to re-experience grief at key, transitional points in the family life cycle.

Goldberg *et al.* (1995) described family therapy with families who had children with ID. They described the difficulties families had moving from one life cycle stage to the next. They hypothesized that each transition involves change and loss, which stimulates emotions experienced during previous episodes of grieving. They suggest that this provides families with the opportunity to re-grieve past losses in a more adaptive manner. Their case studies are an interesting illustration of the long-term impact of unresolved grief within families of children with an intellectual disability. They found similarities between the initial grief response experienced by parents and their later behaviour when re-experiencing/capitulating their grief. For example, they described one mother's angry response to the news that her daughter had an intellectual disability and how she reacted angrily to each successive loss within the family system. Goldberg and colleagues formulated that parents might be stuck at a particular life stage through trying to protect their children from the consequences of their intellectual disability. This can lead to difficulties in separating from their child, for example at school age or at the time when other children are leaving home. They also suggested that unresolved grief concerning the loss of the 'perfect' child may result in rigid relationships between children with ID and their parents. The aim of their family therapy is to introduce change in the family's current relationships, enabling grieving and transition to the next stage in the family life cycle.

Each family will respond differently to discovering that their child has an intellectual disability on account of their cultural beliefs about disability, ethnicity, religious beliefs, socio-economic status and broader social attitudes towards disability (Krauss-Mars and Lachman, 1994; Seligman and Darling, 1997; Miltiades and Pruchno, 2002). Although most research to date has focused on the experience of mothers, there may be important differences in the reactions of fathers and other family members which are, as yet, unexplored.

PARENTS' CAREGIVING ABILITIES

A number of studies have reported important differences in the interactions between mothers and their children with ID or premature birth compared to control groups of children (Nind and Hewett, 1994; Slonims *et al.*, 2006; Potharst *et al.*, 2012). These factors are important to consider, as it is likely they will significantly affect the development of mutually enjoyable interactions between children and their caregivers, potentially leading to difficulties in emotional attunement and attachment (see Box 3.2).

Parents who have children with ID may need extraordinary sensitivity to overcome the challenges their children have in expressing their attachment signals and respond appropriately to them (Schuengel and Janssen, 2006). This may partially explain the finding that young people with intellectual disability have increased incidence of insecure attachment relationships with their parents compared to non-ID peers (Vaughn *et al.*, 1994; Atkinson *et al.*, 1999; Ganiban, Barnett and Cicchetti, 2000). Some critics have suggested that the observed lower levels of secure attachment in people with ID are due to error in

> **Box 3.2 Interactions between Mothers and their Children Born with ID/Prematurely**
>
> - Children with ID are frequently less responsive to their caregivers and do not initiate interactions.
> - Children may be 'floppy' and have reduced control over gaze and vocalizations.
> - Mothers have increased difficulty understanding their infant's signals and have to work harder in interactions.
> - There can be a lack of mutual pleasure in mother–child interactions and poor interactive 'fit'.
> - Mothers may become overly stimulating and directive in their interactions with their child and less supportive of their autonomy.
> - Mothers may become more remote and less sensitive to their child due to lack of child-initiated communications.

measurement related to differences in expression of attachment signals (see Chapter 4 on assessment). However, Atkinson et al. (1999) demonstrated a link between attachment security and sensitive parenting in children with ID, making it unlikely that measurement error reflects the whole story.

Pianta and Marvin proposed that if parents are unresolved with regard to their child's diagnosis, this will affect their relationship with their child and their caregiving skills. To this end, they carried out a series of studies with mothers of children aged 15–50 months who had cerebral palsy and epilepsy, and found that resolved mothers were more likely to have secure attachments with their children and unresolved mothers were more likely to have insecure attachments with their children (Marvin and Pianta, 1996). Wachtel and Carter (2008) found that mothers of young children with ASD who were more emotionally resolved on the RDI were rated higher in their supportive and cognitive engagement during play interactions with their children. They engaged in more verbal and nonverbal 'scaffolding' to aid the child's attention and play and this led to greater reciprocity and mutual enjoyment.

Given that people with ID often require ongoing support from professional caregivers, it is important to consider that other family members and professional carers may also struggle with recognizing and responding appropriately to the child's/adult's attachment signals. This may be particularly difficult within education or care systems which have a high staff turnover and lack of time to develop emotional connections with individuals (see Chapter 8 for further discussion on this).

The importance of providing sensitive and attuned emotional responses to people with ID will now be discussed in relation to the risk of later developing behaviours which are described as challenging.

CONNECTIONS BETWEEN EARLY BEGINNINGS AND LATER CHALLENGES

As mentioned in Chapter 2, Bowlby (1969) hypothesized that the development of a secure relationship is dependent on a smooth enough interaction between the parents' caregiving behaviours and the child's attachment behaviours. The child's behaviour (e.g. crying) signals a need, the parent responds sensitively and swiftly, and restores the child to homeostasis. The child then continues with their play and exploration. Thus, the child learns that they can rely on their caregiver to understand and sensitively meet their attachment needs. They feel confident that their parent will be available and will allow contact and closeness as required by the child to comfort them. Under sub-optimal conditions, the parent or caregiver may delay their response, or dismiss the child's attachment behaviour. Here, the child learns to avoid expressing their attachment needs directly to their parents, and instead dampens them down, as this is the best way of maximizing proximity to their caregivers. This pattern of behaviour has been described as an 'insecure avoidant' attachment style. Other parents may respond inconsistently, leaving the child confused as to how best to maximize the chances of their parent responding to them. Here, the child may increase their attachment signals and may appear conflicted as to whether they desire closeness to their parent. This has been referred to as an 'insecure resistant' or 'ambivalent' attachment style. Where parents are consistently unavailable or respond in a frightened or frightening manner (e.g. abusive), the child is left feeling abandoned, isolated and alone, and this risks attachment disorganization (Solomon and George, 2008).

Research shows that parents of children with disabilities are at increased risk of experiencing mental health problems, particularly depression (Singer, 2006), and this negatively affects their emotional availability and ability to be a responsive parent. Given that unresponsive parenting is strongly associated with insecure attachment (De-Wolff and Van IJzendoorn, 1997), poor social-emotional development (Bornstein and Tamis-LeMonda, 1989), aggression and behavioural problems (Campbell, 2002), this means that children with ID may face a number of emotional and behavioural risks primarily related to the emotional distress their mothers are experiencing. Lower levels of child behavioural problems are associated with greater parent–child emotional reciprocity, co-responsiveness and cooperation in biological and adoptive parent–child dyads within the same family (Deater-Deckard and Petrill, 2004). This gives weight to the argument that it is crucial to offer support to families to improve the quality of their parent–child relationships to reduce the risk of behavioural problems emerging.

In summary, the studies published to date support clinical observations that problematic development of sensitive caregiving and secure attachment relationships in families of children with ID is associated with parents' emotional distress and their difficulties related to understanding the communications of their child. It is therefore essential for services to develop appropriate support and interventions for families following their child's diagnosis and at later points throughout their lives when challenges arise. Without such interventions, the cycle of grief, loss and attachment difficulties will be perpetuated, with the result that people with ID will continue to express their emotions in ways which challenge their communities and significantly limit their independence and quality of life. However, such an approach presents difficulties for professionals working within health, social care and education services where increasing pressure is placed on teams to offer time-limited interventions in order to share resources as fairly as possible. This chapter proposes that some family systems require ongoing support within a boundaried and carefully contracted care plan in order to prevent distress from being perpetuated throughout the system and to lead to the most positive outcomes for the person with ID.

FAMILIES WHICH PRESENT WITH ONGOING COMPLAINTS

When family-focused support is available, many families experiencing distress do not feel able or willing to engage in family therapy sessions. In the author's clinical experience, these families often have a high level of contact with paid carers and professionals from the local ID teams, which can result in stress being experienced throughout the system. Services are often inadequate and fail to meet families' needs, and a cycle of complaints can be created and perpetuated, with parents presenting numerous concerns or complaints. Professionals and carers may respond by developing their own narrative about the family complaining unfairly and being 'impossible to please'. Responses to complaints often fail to acknowledge possible grief and anxiety experienced by parents at their inability to protect their child from their disability, or disappointment that services are not able to 'fix' their child or find the cure. In this way, the wider system becomes stuck and static, with a lack of positive change and progress despite a high level of clinical contact between families and services. This clinical issue will be explored further using case examples to illustrate positive experiences of working with distressed families who present with ongoing complaints about services.

Case Example: Stephanie

Background: Mr and Mrs T, a white British couple, had adopted their daughter, Stephanie, as a baby and were not aware that she had an intellectual disability. At the time of referral, Stephanie was in her 50s and her parents were in their 80s and growing increasingly frail. Stephanie had spent the majority of her adult life in long-stay hospitals following breakdown of her residential placements due to her challenging behaviours. She had spent the past eight years in an inpatient unit and was finally being moved to a residential home following a local campus closure project directed by commissioners. Mr and Mrs T had always been very strong advocates for their daughter. The staff at the inpatient facility struggled with the frequency and intensity of contact Stephanie's family initiated and felt criticized and scrutinized. Stephanie visited her family home every fortnight and repeatedly asked when she was going to speak to her parents and go home. When she was unsettled she would destroy furniture, throw objects and hit and kick out. She would also shout and swear very loudly for sustained periods of time. Staff struggled with Stephanie's constant questioning about when she would speak to her family and visit them and her parents' repeated complaints about her care. They felt that Mr and Mrs T did not help Stephanie to become more independent from them because they called and visited her so often. They were also concerned that they did not set boundaries with Stephanie and 'spoiled' her, which they felt contributed to her challenging behaviours.

An appropriate home was found for Stephanie but staff were concerned because Mr and Mrs T seemed anxious. The staff felt that Stephanie would only settle in her new home if Mr and Mrs T were happy with it. The team stated that in order for the placement to be successful, Stephanie would need to see her new accommodation as 'her home' rather than her family home.

During the first meeting with psychology, Mr and Mrs T spontaneously talked about their experiences of adopting Stephanie and finding out about her disability. They were tearful and distressed talking about Stephanie's early life and their later guilt when they could not continue to look after her at home.

Formulation: Mr and Mrs T presented as being unresolved in their grief relating to Stephanie's intellectual disability and experiencing recapitulation of grief. The current intrapsychic 'loss' of Mr and Mrs T's child was related to her transition to her own home from the inpatient service. Mr and Mrs T's current reaction connected to their early experiences of loss related to Stephanie's diagnosis of an intellectual disability and the distress that they felt regarding this. Their caregiving style had always been to remain closely connected to Stephanie and to have frequent contact with staff to ensure she was well looked after and kept safe. This parental protection was experienced by staff as being intrusive and when Mr and Mrs T commented on things which had not been done, the staff felt they were complaining. This resulted in the staff team feeling disempowered and wishing to disconnect from Mr and Mrs T. The emotional and physical withdrawal of staff unfortunately led to increasing parental anxiety and frequency of contact/monitoring of care. Stephanie found it difficult to develop secure attachments with staff. She continued primarily to feel safe with her parents, depending on regular contact with them to manage her anxieties. This meant that she experienced high levels of anxiety when separated from her parents, which was communicated through behaviours others experienced as 'challenging'.

Intervention: Work with Stephanie centred on working closely with her support network including her family, carers and the professionals from the health and social services teams. It was important to build up trust and honesty with Mr and Mrs T and the carers, and to develop a formulation of Stephanie's difficulties which incorporated her disability, communication problems and attachment strategies. Within this, it was important to highlight the pattern of Mr and Mrs T becoming increasingly anxious when they felt pushed away by staff, which, in turn, led to increased contact. It was also important to encourage regular contact between the carers and Mr and Mrs T with sharing of appropriate information (which Stephanie would also tell her parents about independently). A central part of the work was holding regular, separate meetings with the carers to discuss the emotional impact of working with Stephanie and her family. This therapeutic space enabled the carers to discuss difficult events which had taken place and use the formulation to understand, reflect and consider ideas to help prevent the same issues happening in future.

During the discharge planning process, Mr and Mrs T were offered some psychology meetings to support them through Stephanie's transition to her new home. In particular, the aim was to generate a care plan which Mr and Mrs T would agree to regarding contact with Stephanie and visits home. One idea generated was to take Stephanie's furniture from her family room and move it into her new home, leaving her old room empty for a short period of time. It was hoped this would communicate to Stephanie that she was 'leaving' her family home and getting her own home.

Mr and Mrs T spoke honestly about their concerns about the transition plan, particularly the idea of Stephanie not visiting home for a few weeks and not having her furniture in the family home. It was incredibly painful for them to think about having a 'spare room'. However, they did agree to visit Stephanie in her new home for the first few weeks of her 'settling in' period rather than her coming to their home. After careful thought and discussion, they also agreed to move her old furniture into her new room to create a familiar environment. Mr and Mrs T reported that it had been 'very helpful' to meet with a clinical psychologist and have space to talk and think about their feelings and experiences as parents. They explained that they had never been 'emotional' people and had just coped by doing everything they could to fight for Stephanie's rights and those of other people with ID. They were surprised at how emotional they had felt but found it helpful when this was framed as being connected to a significant transition and 'letting go' of their daughter in her move.

Outcome: The psychology involvement continued following Stephanie's move to her new home and this provided much-needed continuity and containment. There were some significant concerns raised about Stephanie's challenging behaviours following her move, which led to threats of placement breakdown. However, after a number of network meetings, the placement stabilized. Holding regular professional network meetings led to a reduction in the need for crisis response meetings regarding Stephanie, although it has not seemed possible to close her case to the team as yet. It has been extremely difficult to maintain a consistent staff team to support Stephanie and a high percentage of staff are from agency services. Although the case continues to require an intense amount of support from the health professionals in the team, it is encouraging that Stephanie's placement has not broken down and she has now lived in her own home in the community for several years. Stephanie's carers report finding the psychology meetings helpful in allowing them to continue with their work, despite the fact that the difficulties they face continue.

The next case describes the experiences of a family with a young child at the time of her diagnosis, describing their reactions and the clinical work provided in order to support engagement with services.

Case Example: Grace

Background: Mr and Mrs M had six children under the age of ten years: four boys and two girls. They had come to the UK from Sudan as asylum seekers. Sadly, following this, Mr M died of an infectious disease, leaving his wife looking after their children with support from his sister and brother-in-law. Their two-year-old daughter, Grace, was later referred to the Child Development

Team (CDT) by her GP. She was developing well in her motor milestones but was not speaking and did not seem to understand what other people were saying to her. Following a comprehensive multi-disciplinary assessment, Grace was diagnosed with autism spectrum disorder (ASD). The CDT professionals involved shared the diagnosis with care, explaining the results at a meeting with only two professionals present (to prevent the family feeling overwhelmed), with an appointment slot of at least one hour to allow time for discussion, questions and a care plan to be agreed with support for Grace. A follow-up meeting was arranged at the time of the diagnosis and the family was offered a psychology meeting to talk further about the diagnosis and their reactions to this. The Specialist Health Visitor also shared information about the diagnosis and details of support groups and appropriate services which the family could access.

Grace's family were distressed by the diagnosis of ASD and in disagreement with the results of the assessments. They felt that Grace was able to do much more than reported by the professionals. They described Grace playing appropriately at home, being able to understand instructions and respond to prompts by her family, for example when asked to help with sweeping up in the kitchen. Mrs M and her brother-in-law felt that Grace was just delayed in her language development and that she would eventually catch up with her older siblings. After reading through the information about ASD, the M family were also concerned that if Grace had ASD that she had been 'given it' by something in the UK, as they believed that ASD did not exist in Sudan. Mrs M felt sure that the MMR vaccine would be to blame, as she had been told about this by a family friend who had a child with ASD. Mrs M stated clearly that Grace was nothing like her friend's child. She fluctuated in her discussions between feeling upset about Grace's difficulties and the meaning of them and anger at the health professionals who were giving the diagnosis. Mrs M had a strong Christian faith and had taken Grace to see faith healers on several occasions. She was looking to raise money to take her to the USA to see a famous spiritual healer and felt that this would lead to a cure.

Formulation: Mrs M's grief regarding Grace's difficulties and diagnosis led to her developing cognitive distortions whereby she minimized Grace's disability in order to protect herself from the unbearable loss she was feeling. Therefore, Mrs M and her family spoke about Grace's difficulties as being a delay in her speech and language which would get better with time. Mrs M also showed some searching behaviours where she continued to look for alternative diagnoses or reasons for Grace's difficulties and a cure for them. This helped Mrs M to be able to engage in active coping where she spoke to people and found out about different causes and cures for ASD. This led to active participation in fundraising within Mrs M's church community to raise money to travel to the USA. Alongside these coping mechanisms Mrs M and her family also appeared to be displacing their sadness and loss to angry reactions towards the medical systems in the UK for potentially 'giving' Grace ASD through her MMR immunizations.

Intervention (post-diagnosis): Mrs M said she was keen to have further clinical psychology meetings but could only meet at her house due to childcare responsibilities and travelling difficulties. Clinical psychology sessions therefore took place in the family home and were focused on discussing Grace's diagnosis and thinking together about her needs and the needs of her family. It was helpful to use externalizing language to talk about 'the diagnosis of ASD' to create a narrative which allowed for presentation of Western, scientific knowledge about ASD and African, spiritual understandings of Grace's difficulties. It took several meetings to build up a trusting relationship where Mrs M could start to think about the therapeutic and educational support Grace might need, alongside her spiritual needs. It was difficult at times to maintain appropriate boundaries, as Mrs M always offered food and drink and appeared quite puzzled when these offers were refused. Mrs M also extended an invitation to attend a faith healer's event, which led to a difficult conversation about professional boundaries. Although tensions were felt during such times of refusal, Mrs M continued to engage in the sessions and was always at home and ready for meetings on time. Although Mrs M continued to struggle with the diagnosis of ASD, she was able to talk instead about Grace's difficulties in communicating and playing.

Outcome: Mrs M and her family agreed to the idea of Grace attending a nursery for children with ASD where she accessed appropriate speech and language therapy and occupational

> therapy support. This was a relief, as there were concerns within the CDT that the family's difficulties acknowledging her needs may have prevented Grace accessing appropriate support and therapy. Her family was extremely pleased to see her make progress in her communication using the Picture Exchange Communication System (PECS) and she started to make limited eye contact with staff and other children. The teaching staff successfully used Grace's love of music and dancing (which had been observed at home during psychology meetings) to develop her communication skills. In this case, using an outreach mode of working with considerable travel time (30 minutes each way from the CDT) was essential in engaging with Grace's family, and it is unlikely that they would have engaged with the CDT and been able to agree a joint care plan without this model of working. At the end of the psychology work, Mrs M and her brother-in-law continued to state that they did not feel Grace had ASD. However, they were happy with the support she was getting at the specialist nursery and were engaging with professionals from health and education services and ensuring Grace's developmental needs were being met.

SUMMARY

As the above cases have shown, the distress parents experience regarding their child's disability can be powerfully present at different life stages. Evidence suggests that this grief and loss can have a wide-reaching impact, affecting mothers' emotional wellbeing, their ability to offer sensitive caregiving, the development of secure attachment relationships with their children and enjoyment in being a parent. Of course, it is important to stress that this is not always the case and research indicates that approximately half of the population of parents who have children with ID are resolved in their loss and trauma surrounding their child's condition. Resolved parents have been observed to have a higher number of secure attachment relationships with their children and greater reciprocity and mutual enjoyment with their children during play interactions. Research from non-ID populations links insecure and disorganized attachment styles with a number of emotional and behavioural difficulties in childhood and later adulthood. Although there is no compelling evidence of this in the ID population yet, there is no reason to suggest that this would be different. Indeed, for people who have a long history of showing challenging behaviours, experience of early trauma and abuse has been clearly documented (see Chapters 6 and 7 for further discussion).

It is important to remember that resolution of diagnosis has been found to be significantly associated with current or proximal life events such as recent stressful life events and lack of support from family, rather than states of mind with respect to past attachment relationships. This provides hope that offering appropriate clinical interventions and support to families can have a real and lasting impact on their well-being in the short and longer term. The following recommendations have been developed through reviewing the published literature and drawing upon clinical experience. It is hoped that these will provide a useful clinical map for professionals in their work with families with ID.

RECOMMENDATIONS FOR PRACTICE

1) **Containment and consistency**
   Families experiencing high levels of loss, grief and separation anxiety may need services to provide a highly containing and internally consistent model of care. Teams need to work together to prevent 'splitting' within the system, which places professionals at risk of being pulled into opposing positions, feelings of mistrust developing in families, frequent complaints being made and potential breakdown of placements for people with ID. As the above case examples demonstrated, working with these families can involve intensive and longer-term interventions. However, following initial engagement, contact can then be reduced in frequency as long as the system supporting the family meets regularly (even if only 6–12 monthly) and has the ability to be brought together earlier, as required.

2) **Creative engagement**
   There are particular risks associated with families who do not agree with concerns expressed by others about their child and who therefore may not engage with support and interventions intended to address these. In cases where families have different religious and cultural beliefs about disability and the possibility of spiritual cure, professionals need to consider outreach work and liaison with religious leaders in the community to engage and form a dialogue about disability and the child's needs. Without this model of

working, there is the real possibility that individuals with intellectual disabilities will have their needs neglected and that their wellbeing will be compromised.

3) **Family-centred diagnosis and support**
   Diagnosis needs to be given in a family-centred manner with support for families during their initial period of grieving and at later time points/transitions when their grief may re-emerge. It is important for people working in ID services to assess and determine whether parents need support for themselves from external services or whether their difficulties are directly related to their child's disabilities and, as such, need support from within specialist ID services. In many cases, families may need professionals from ID services to engage with them and then refer them on to adult mental health services, as appropriate.

4) **Attachment-focused formulation and intervention**
   Formulations and clinical interventions need to include attachment theory and relationships at their core, regardless of the therapeutic model which is being used to inform the clinical work.

Essential factors to consider:

- Parents' reactions to their child's diagnosis and their resolution of loss and grief.
- The family's culture and religious beliefs concerning disability.
- Experiences of early separations, losses or traumas of parents/carers.
- Intergenerational attachment styles of parents/carers.
- Parents' mental health and emotional distress.
- Social support available to parents from their own families/support for carers within their teams.
- Parent–child (or carer–service user) interactions and attunement.
- Need for training for parents and carers to increase their understanding of attachment behaviours and identify helpful ways to respond (possibly using video to review their interactions).

(see Chapters 6 and 8 for further discussion on this).

FINAL THOUGHTS

In the author's clinical experience, the families which evoke the strongest feelings of anxiety within the ID services are often those which are most distressed about their child's disability. Their expressions of love and grief through advocating fiercely for their child, closely scrutinizing their child's care and making complaints can be extremely challenging for carers and professionals to work with. However, experience has demonstrated that the models and approaches to working described in this chapter can lead to positive outcomes for individuals, families and the teams that support them. They are particularly useful in the promotion of effective joint working across multiple systems, which is paramount in ensuring positive outcomes for people with ID. An essential part of the work is to remain connected to the grief and loss experienced by parents and carers and to continue to support them in the incredible task they undertake every day.

REFERENCES

Atkinson, L., Chisholm, V.C., Scott, B., Goldberg, S., Vaughn, B.E. and Blackwell, J. (1999) Maternal sensitivity, child functional level and attachment in Down syndrome. *Monographs of the Society for Research in Child Development*, 64 (serial no. 258): 45–66.

Barnett, D., Clements, M., Kaplan-Estrin, M. and Fialka, J. (2003) Building New Dreams: Supporting Parents' Adaptation to their Child with Special Needs. *Infants and Young Children*, 16(3): 184–200.

Bicknell, J. (1983) The Psychopathology of Handicap. *British Journal of Medical Psychology*, 56(2): 167–178.

Blacher, J. (1984) Sequential stages of parental adjustment to the birth of a child with handicaps: Fact or artefact? *Mental Retardation*, 22: 55–68.

Bornstein, M.H. and Tamis-LeMonda, C.S. (1989) Maternal responsiveness and cognitive development in children. In Borstein, M.H. (ed.) *Maternal Responsiveness: Characteristics and consequences* (pp. 803–809). San Francisco, CA: Jossey-Bass.

Bowlby, J. (1969) *Attachment and Loss. Vol.1: Attachment.* UK: Pimlico.

Bowlby, J. (1980). *Attachment and Loss. Vol. 3: Loss, Sadness and Depression.* UK: Pimlico.

Bruce, E.J., Schultz, C.L., Smyrnios, K.X. and Schultz, N.C. (1994) Grieving related to development: A preliminary comparison of three age cohorts of parents with children with intellectual disability. *British Journal of Medical Psychology*, 67(1): 37–52.

Campbell, S.B. (2002) *Behaviour Problems in Pre-school Children.* New York: The Guilford Press.

Deater-Deckard, K. and Petrill, S. (2004) Parent–child dyadic mutuality and child behaviour problems: An investigation of gene–environment processes. *Journal of Child Psychology & Psychiatry*, 46: 1171–1179.

De-Wolff, M.S. and Van IJzendoorn, M.H. (1997) Sensitivity and attachment: A meta-analysis on parental antecedents of infant attachment. *Child Development*, 68: 571–591.

Dickman, I. and Gordon, S. (1985) *One Miracle at a Time: How to get help for your disabled child – From the experience of other parents*. New York: Simon & Schuster.

Dunn, J. (1993) *Young Children's Close Relationships: Beyond Attachment*. London: Sage.

Fletcher, H. (2004) *The loss of the healthy child: Exploring the relationship between mothers' early attachment relationships and their reaction to their child's learning disability*. Unpublished Doctoral thesis, UCL.

Ganiban, J., Barnett, D. and Cicchetti, D. (2000) Negative reactivity and attachment: Down syndrome's contribution to the attachment–temperament debate. *Development and Psychopathology*, 12: 1–21.

George, C., Kaplan, N. and Main, M. (1984/1985/1996) *The Adult Attachment Interview*. Unpublished manuscript. University of California, Berkeley.

George, C. and Solomon, J. (2008) The Caregiving System: A Behavioural Systems Approach to Parenting. In J. Cassidy and P. Shaver (eds) *Handbook of Attachment: Theory, Research and Clinical Applications* (2nd edition, pp. 833–856). London: The Guilford Press.

Goldberg, D., Magrill, L., Hale, J., Damaskinidou, K., Paul, J. and Tham, S. (1995) Protection and loss: Working with learning disabled adults and their families. *Journal of Family Therapy*, 17: 263–280.

Holder, J. (2000) *Parental adaptation to the diagnosis of a learning disability in their child: Associations with affective representations of parenting*. Unpublished Doctoral thesis.

Hornby, G. (1994) *Counselling in Child Disability: Skills for working with parents*. London: Chapman & Hall.

Horsch, A., Brooks, C. and Fletcher, H. (2013) Maternal coping, appraisals and adjustment following diagnosis of fetal anomaly. *Prenatal Diagnosis*, 33: 1137–1145.

Koegel, R.L., Schreibman, L., Loos, L.M., Dirlich-Wilhelm, H., Dunlap, G., Robbins, F.R. and Plienis, A.J. (1992) Consistent stress profiles in mothers of children with Autism. *Journal of Autism and Developmental Disorders*, 22: 205–216.

Korff-Sausse, S. (1999) A Psychoanalytical Approach to Mental Handicap. In J. De Groef and E. Heinemann (eds) *Psychoanalysis and Mental Handicap*. London: Routledge.

Krauss-Mars, A.H. and Lachman, P. (1994) Breaking bad news to parents with disabled children: A cross cultural study. *Child: Care, Health and Development*, 20(2): 101–113.

Lloyd, H. and Dallos, R. (2006) Solution-focused brief therapy with families who have a child with intellectual disabilities: A description of the content of initial sessions and the processes. *Clinical Child Psychology and Psychiatry*, 11(3): 367–386.

Marshak, L.E. and Seligman, M. (1993) *Counselling Persons with Disabilities: Theoretical and clinical perspectives*. Austin, TX: Pro-Ed.

Marvin, R.S. and Pianta, R.C. (1996) Mothers' reactions to their child's diagnosis: Relations with security of attachment. *Journal of Clinical Child Psychology*, 25(4): 436–445.

Miltiades, H.B. and Pruchno, R. (2002) The effect of religious coping on caregiving appraisals of mothers of adults with developmental disabilities. *Gerontologist*, 42(1): 82–91.

Morog, M.C. (1996) Trauma and its relation to working models of relationships: Attachment and loss in mothers of children with disabilities. *Dissertation Abstracts International: Section B: The Sciences and Engineering*, 57(8-B): 5537.

Nind, M. and Hewett, D. (1994) *Access to Communication: Developing the basics of communication for people with severe learning difficulties through intensive interaction*. London: David Fulton.

Olshansky, S. (1962) Chronic sorrow: A response to having a mentally defective child. *Social Casework*, 43: 190–193.

Olson, D.H., McCubbin, H.I., Barnes, H., Larsen, A., Muxen, M. and Wilson, M. (1984) *One Thousand Families: A national survey*. Beverley Hills: Sage.

Pianta, R.C. and Marvin, R.S. (1992a) *The Reaction to Diagnosis Interview*. Unpublished materials, University of Virginia.

Pianta, R.C. and Marvin, R.S. (1992b) *The Reaction to Diagnosis Classification System*. Unpublished materials, University of Virginia.

Pianta, R.C., Marvin, R.S., Britner, P.A. and Borowitz, K.C. (1996) Mothers' resolution of their child's diagnosis: Organised patterns of caregiving representations. *Infant Mental Health Journal*, 17(3): 239–256.

Potharst, E.S., Schuengel, C., Last, B.F., Van Wassenaer, A.G., Kok, J.H. and Houtzager, B.A. (2012) Difference in mother–child interaction between preterm-and term-born preschoolers with and without disabilities. *Acta paediatrica*, 101(6): 597–603.

Roos, S.G. (1995) Chronic sorrow: A living loss. *Dissertation Abstracts International Section A: Humanities and Social Sciences*, 55(11-A): 3645.

Schuengel, C. and Janssen, C. (2006) People with mental retardation and psychopathology. Stress, affect regulation and attachment. A review. *International Review of Research in Mental Retardation*, 32:, 229–260.

Seligman, M. and Darling, R.B. (1997) *Ordinary Families, Special Children: A Systems Approach to Childhood Disability*, 2nd edition. London: The Guilford Press.

Singer, G.H.S. (2006) Meta-analysis of comparative studies of depression in mothers of children with and without developmental disabilities. *American Journal of Mental Retardation*, 111: 155–169.

Slonims, V., Cox. A. and McConachie, H. (2006) Analysis of mother–infant interactions in infants with Down Syndrome and typically developing infants. *American Journal of Mental Retardation*, 111: 273–289.

Solomon, J. and George, C. (2008) The Measurement of Attachment Security and Related Constructs in Infancy and Childhood. In J. Cassidy and P. Shaver (eds) *Handbook of Attachment: Theory, Research and Clinical Applications* (pp. 383–416). London: The Guilford Press.

The National Federation of Voluntary Bodies in Ireland (2010) *Informing families of their child's disability: National best practice guidelines*. Retrieved 07.30.15 from http://www.informingfamilies.ie/about-the-project/support-and-training-materials.257.html

Vaughn, B.E., Goldberg, S., Atkinson, L. and Marcovitch, S. (1994) Quality of toddler–mother attachment in children with Down syndrome: Limits to interpretation of strange situation behaviour. *Child Development*, 65(1): 95–108.

Wachtel, K. and Carter, A.S. (2008) Reaction to diagnosis and parenting styles among mothers of young children with ASD. *Autism*, 12(5): 575–594.

Waisbren, S.E. (1980) Parents' reactions after the birth of a developmentally disabled child. *American Journal of Mental Deficiency*, 84: 345–351.

Walsh, A.P. (2003) *Representations of Attachment and Caregiving: The Disruptive Effects of Loss and Trauma*. Unpublished Doctoral thesis.

Wilker, L., Wasow, M. and Hatfield, E. (1981) Chronic sorrow revisited: Parent vs professional depiction of the adjustment of parents of mentally retarded children. *American Journal of Orthopsychiatry*, 51(1): 63–70.

Chapter 4

ASSESSING ATTACHMENT RELATIONSHIPS IN PEOPLE WITH INTELLECTUAL DISABILITIES

Samantha Walker[1], Victoria Penketh[2], Hazel Lewis[3] and Dougal Julian Hare[4]

[1] Socrates Clinical Psychology, Huddersfield, UK
[2] Lancashire Care NHS Foundation Trust, Preston, UK
[3] University of Liverpool, Liverpool, UK
[4] South Wales D. Clin. Psy. Programme, Cardiff University, UK

INTRODUCTION

In order to understand a phenomenon, it is necessary both to describe and preferably measure it in some way. Arguably, this need to describe and measure accurately is even more pronounced in the case of psychological phenomena such as attachment. The assessment of attachment has gone hand-in-hand with the development of models of attachment. One apparent consequence of this, as will be discussed, is that such assessments typically involve lengthy and detailed clinical or laboratory observations by experienced researchers. However, it can be very difficult, if not impossible, for working clinicians to assess attachment in this way, given the complexity and length of such assessment procedures, in addition to the cost implications of the necessary training. Therefore, this chapter will have a practical focus on the assessment of attachment in workaday clinical services for people with intellectual disabilities (ID), starting with a brief review of the clinical assessment of attachment in typically developing populations, an examination of the challenges and practicalities of undertaking such work with people with ID and recommendations for practice.

Attachment in Intellectual and Developmental Disability: A Clinician's Guide to Practice and Research, First Edition. Edited by Helen K. Fletcher, Andrea Flood and Dougal Julian Hare.
© 2016 John Wiley & Sons, Ltd. Published 2016 by John Wiley & Sons, Ltd.

ASSESSMENT OF ATTACHMENT IN CHILDREN

The development of specific tools for assessing individual differences in attachment began with Ainsworth's (1967; 1978) development of the *strange situation procedure*. This assessment tool continues to be used in research with a variety of different clinical groups. The procedure involves a controlled setting such as a laboratory or clinic in which eight scripted interactions, each of three minutes' duration, are presented. The child and their carer, usually the mother, are observed via a one-way mirror or CCTV by trained professionals. The series of interactions involves two separations and reunions of the child and carer under increasing levels of stress to the child, with the introduction of a stranger into the procedure.

Two aspects of the child's behaviour are observed, namely the amount of exploration (e.g. playing with new toys) the child engages in throughout and the child's reactions to the departure and return of their caregiver. Based on the coding of child responses in the strange situation procedure, Ainsworth *et al.* (1978) identified three attachment behaviour classifications:

- Type A, in which the child shows an insecure avoidant attachment style where the child is relatively disinterested in its caregiver or where they are, may have a lack of so-called 'stranger danger' behaviour and subsequently display relatively little distress when a carer leaves the room during the experimental process. Studies have shown that these children are still experiencing distress when their caregiver returns to the room, as demonstrated by increased heart rates (Sroufe and Waters, 1977) but do not openly display this anxiety.
- Type C, in which the child shows an insecure ambivalent/resistant attachment style where the child displays markedly high levels of vigilance regarding the caregiver's presence, with wariness of the stranger and intense distress when the caregiver leaves the room. Children with this classification are noted to have a marked protracted reunion, often with displays of anger and resistance during the reunion such that it is difficult for the caregiver to soothe them.
- Type B, in which the child shows a secure attachment style where the child has noticeable warmth towards their caregiver, is interested in the interactions and toys available and displays mild wariness of the stranger with upset displayed when the caregiver leaves the room but relief when they return. They are not resistant to the caregiver upon return and are quickly soothed and readily return to play and interaction.

Key differences between these attachment classifications are the reaction to the stranger, the amount and intensity of emotion expressed in the situation of stress and the ability of the caregiver to soothe the child after the distress and/or the requirement for soothing from the caregiver.

A fourth attachment classification, Type D, in which the child shows a disorganized or disorientated attachment, has been described subsequently (Solomon and George, 1999). The function of this classification is unclear and it may be an emergency behaviour observed when the child otherwise has Type A or Type C attachment classification but feels under intense threat or is flooded by anxiety. Type D is characterized by overt displays of fear, freezing and dissociation.

As well as its obvious strengths, such as its continuing ability to generate new research data and concepts, the strange situation procedure has several weaknesses, not the least of which is that it is not readily transferable to everyday practice. Moreover, the categories described are descriptions of behaviour seen in research settings with typically developing children and lack ecological validity as clinical measures. There are also the ethical implications of the procedure given that the child is deliberately exposed to a distressing and stress-provoking situation to which they are unable to assent.

The Dynamic Maturational Model: Associated Measures

A more recent development in the formal assessment of attachment style is Crittenden's (2005) Dynamic Maturational Model (DMM), which encompasses six assessments of attachment processes in children: *The Care Index for Infants, The Care Index for Toddlers, The Infant Strange Situation, The Preschool Assessment of Attachment, The School-aged Assessment of Attachment* and *The Transition to Adulthood Attachment Interview*. These are clinical tools to be used to guide therapeutic intervention and require users to be trained specifically in their use.

The first two assessment measures, *The Care Index for Infants* and *The Care Index for Toddlers*, can be grouped together and involve coding a three-minute video recording of a play interaction between the child and the caregiver. The recording is rated in terms of caregiver sensitivity, control and unresponsiveness as well as infant cooperation with the caregiver, compulsiveness, difficulty and passivity. The procedure for *The Infant Strange Situation* is essentially the same as the original Ainsworth procedure but is coded using the DMM model rather than the original ACB (D) model. *The Preschool Assessment of Attachment* also uses the strange situation procedure, but is modified to take account of the child being able to walk, talk and open doors and is likewise coded using the DMM model.

The School-aged Assessment of Attachment, which can be used with typically developing children aged 6–13 years, uses a story-telling method that introduces a real or imagined threat to the child but does not require the child actually to have experienced the situation. The child is required to tell a story about a picture depicting a potentially threatening situation or event, which include: *Going out alone, Being rejected by one's best friend, Moving to a new neighbourhood, Being bullied, Having father leave home, Running away* and *Mother going to hospital*. For each card, the child is asked to describe the sequence of events that lead to the specific situation, to describe the emotions they are experiencing and also the child's perspective of the emotions the characters in the story are experiencing to give an evaluation of the child's theory of mind. The child is then asked to think about reasons for what happened and ideas for what actions they might take in the future should the events unfold again. Thus, the assessment offers insight into the child's cognition (sequence of events described), affect (feelings described) and cognitive reflective thinking regarding themselves (through reflection of future actions and learning).

The Transition to Adulthood Attachment Interview is a structured interview used with 16 to 25-year-olds in which the adolescent is asked to think about the self-protective strategies they would use in certain threat-inducing situations, particularly those involving intimate romantic relationships. An important aspect of this assessment is that, as the informants are on the cusp of but have not yet attained adulthood, there is an understanding that earlier, childhood states of attachment and strategies may still be used.

ASSESSMENT OF ATTACHMENT IN ADULTS

Existing adult attachment assessment measures can be grouped into one of three categories, namely interviews and/or observation, self-report questionnaires or Q sorts, and the more widely used ones are shown in Table 4.1.

The *Adult Attachment Interview* (AAI) (George, Kaplan and Main, 1996; Hesse, 1999) uses an interview to explore self-reported childhood experiences with attachment figures, with the emphasis not on attachment behaviour but on how an adult thinks, feels and understands a

Table 4.1 Attachment scales

Measure	Attachment dimensions identified
Adult Attachment Interview (Main and Goldwyn, 1994)	Secure; Dismissing; Preoccupied; Unresolved
Peer Attachment Interview (Bartholomew and Horowitz, 1991)	Secure; Dismissing; Preoccupied; Fearful
Current Relationships Interview (Crowell, 1990)	Secure; Dismissing; Preoccupied; Unresolved
Adult Attachment Q sort (Kobak, 1993)	Secure/Insecure; Deactivating; Hyperactivating; Cannot Classify
Marital Q sort (Kobak and Hazan, 1991)	Reliance; Psychological availability
Adult Attachment Styles (Hazan and Shaver, 1987)	Secure; Avoidant; Ambivalent
Adult Attachment Scale (Simpson, 1990)	Secure; Avoidant; Ambivalent
Adult Attachment Scale (Collins and Read, 1990)	Closeness; Anxiety; Dependence
Adult Attachment Questionnaire (Feeney and Noller, 1990)	Security; Avoidance; Anxiety and Confidence; Discomfort with closeness; Preoccupation with relationships; Need for approval; Relationships as secondary
Relationship Questionnaire (Bartholomew and Horowitz, 1991)	Secure; Dismissing; Preoccupied; Fearful

situation and then how this information is integrated into their personal history. The AAI is therefore designed to examine *memories* of attachment relationships with attachment figures during childhood rather than to identify what actually occurred. It also assesses a person's ability to think about and reflect on these experiences. On the basis of the scoring of the interview, a person's state of mind with respect to attachment figures is categorized as Secure/Free/Autonomous (F), Dismissing of Attachment (D), Pre-occupied/Entangled (E), Unresolved with respect to Traumas (U) or Cannot Classify (CC). The AAI is regarded as the 'gold standard' in terms of assessment of adult attachment, with a large body of research demonstrating a relationship between secure autonomous AAIs in parents and security of attachment with their children on the *Infant Strange Situation,* demonstrating clear intergenerational attachment transition. However, the assessment relies on a long interview and coding process, with the examiner requiring extensive training to be able to carry out and code the interview. This has led to other assessment measures being developed that do not require such extensive training and which are quicker to administer. However, these measures have not exhibited the same convincing evidence base as the AAI. There are, therefore, costs and benefits of the different assessment approaches relating to the validity of the assessments versus the time and training required to administer and code the assessments which specifically explore internal working models of attachment.

Another attachment-based interview is the *Peer Attachment Interview* (Bartholomew and Horowitz, 1991). This interview protocol is scored by two independent coders who measure the comments made during the assessment against prototypic answers relating to Bowlby's original attachment theory (Bartholomew and Horowitz, 1991). This is a measure developed for use with adults and secure attachment is characterized here as the individual being comfortable in romantic and interpersonal relationships and valuing intimacy and autonomy equally. Preoccupied attachment is thought to be represented by anxiety and over-involvement in relationships. A dismissing attachment style is thought to be represented by over-autonomy and independence and a fearful attachment style is represented by distrust and fear of rejection in relationships.

Rating scales and questionnaires have been developed to assess attachment in adults. These generally ask the respondent to answer a predetermined set of questions. Generally, these assessment measures are shorter to conduct than interview measures and, as a result, may be seen as more accessible to clinicians and researchers (Crowell and Treboux, 1995). Two such scales are the *Relationships Questionnaire* (Bartholomew and Horowitz, 1991) and the *Adult Attachment Styles Scale* (Hazan and Shaver, 1987).

For the purposes of illustration, the *Relationships Questionnaire* (Bartholomew and Horowitz, 1991) assesses for attachment styles that are very similar to those described by the AAI scoring (Crowell and Treboux, 1995). Hence, the secure description describes someone who is comfortable in interpersonal and romantic relationships without concern about rejection. The dismissing style describes someone who emphasizes independence and self-sufficiency. The preoccupied style describes an individual who is preoccupied with intimacy and desires a great relationship but is anxious and rejecting as a result (Bartholomew and Horowitz, 1991).

Attachment assessments utilizing Q sort methodology (Stephenson, 1953) include the *Adult Attachment Q sort* (Kobak, 1993; Kobak *et al.*, 1993), which examines the relationship between emotional expression and regulation and attachment in a secure versus insecure framework by sorting a set of 100 descriptors. In the *Adult Attachment Q sort*, an individual's 'sorts' are measured against an exemplar sort. This sort is then classified as secure, dismissing or preoccupied on the basis of correlations with the exemplar, and software is available to facilitate this analysis.

CHALLENGES IN THE ASSESSMENT OF ATTACHMENT IN PEOPLE WITH INTELLECTUAL DISABILITIES

Although a range of assessment techniques have been developed to assess attachment in typically developing children and adults, it can be difficult to use such techniques with people with ID. In the first instance, many such existing measures rely on the ability to recall and reflect on childhood experiences, which may be affected by autonoetic memory functioning. The ability mentally to place oneself in the past, future or in counterfactual situations, analyse thoughts (Hare, Mellor and Azmi, 2007) and reflect on current adult relationships (Smith and McCarthy, 1996) may be significantly compromised in people with ID. Secondly, although there is some evidence that the same types of attachment observed in the typically developing population are seen in people with mild ID (Larson, Alim and Tsakanikos, 2011), it cannot be presumed that the attachment dynamics and behaviour are comparable across the range of people with ID. For example, Cicchetti and Serafica (1981) found that children with Down syndrome displayed attachment behaviour akin to typically developing children but there were important differences in affective responding, which was markedly slower and affected the ability of the caregiver to process and respond to the attachment behaviour.

Many extant adult attachment assessments have explicit or implicit assumptions about adult life and experience of romantic relationships (Hazan and Shaver, 1987) that may not apply to people with ID. For example, many adults with ID have limited opportunities to establish and nurture romantic relationships. On this basis alone, many existing adult attachment measures have limited utility with this client group.

The necessity of using information gleaned from third-party informants whilst assessing people brings further difficulties, given the high turnover of staff. Not surprisingly, many paid carers may find it difficult to report the attachment behaviours displayed by those they are caring for accurately (Schuengel et al., 2010). This may be due to their interpretation of the distress they experience in the face of potentially threatening behaviour (Hastings et al., 2003) but also due to their own emotional arousal and relational interactions in the face of apparent threat (Bailey et al., 2006). In addition, staff are often the primary focus of the attachment behaviours of people with ID (De Schipper and Schuengel, 2010), sometimes to an intense degree depending on both situation and syndrome (Wilde, Silva and Oliver, 2013).

A specific issue when assessing people with mild to moderate ID concerns the parameters of their cognitive abilities. When using interview measures with people who have a moderate ID, there is a documented tendency towards acquiescence and suggestibility on the part of the interviewee (Clare and Gudjonsson, 1995). This is found especially when using closed (Yes/No) questioning and inevitably compromises the use and integrity of many forms of interview and questionnaire-based assessment. This problem is further confounded by impaired memory function, especially in immediate and delayed recall, and poor performance on narrative recall assessments (Beail, 2002) in this population.

Despite this, face-to-face interviews about attachment dynamics have been developed and used with people with ID. For example, Larson, Alim and Tsakanikos (2011) used a verbal interview based upon the attachment categories described by Hazan and Shaver (1987) but acknowledged that the verbal format was limited and potentially confounding.

ATTACHMENT MEASURES DEVELOPED FOR PEOPLE WITH INTELLECTUAL DISABILITIES

Given the above critique, there have been attempts to develop measures of attachment behaviour specifically for use with people who have ID, and these are described below.

The *Self-report Assessment of Attachment Security* (SRAAS) (Smith and McCarthy, 1996) is a measure of attachment specifically developed for use with people with ID and takes self-reported comfort-seeking behaviour as an index of secure attachment. In developing the SRAAS, the researchers pointed to a body of research evidence that outlines that people with positive attachment experiences will tend to seek and then gain comfort from others in emotive and stressful situations. The researchers also looked at evidence that people with ID can explain their own personal experiences when supported to do so and that reliable and valid information can be gained when suitable methods of interview are employed. These methods include using grammatically simplified questioning, with the goal of increasing understanding, and multiple choice questions. The measure was designed to assess participants' current attachment experiences by looking at whether they sought comfort from a significant other when experiencing a range of negative emotions (miserable, worried and frightened) that are related to attachment security.

Reliability for the SRAAS was compiled through repeat assessment after ten weeks. Construct validity was explored through analysis of the relationship of this measure with other related theoretical constructs such as self-esteem and independence in the social environment, both at home and away from home. The SRAAS was developed with $N=31$ aged 20 to 54 years and both male ($N=14$) and female ($N=17$) participants. Ten of the original participants had Down syndrome and the others were reported to have ID of unknown aetiology. None had a diagnosis of autism spectrum disorder or autistic traits and all were living at home and had had no separations from the family home during childhood. On being presented with the negative emotion, participants were provided with three choices (a) tell somebody, (b) not tell anyone about the way you are feeling (cope on your own, avoid people, keep it to yourself) or (c) express the feelings in an uncontrolled way (throw things, scream, shout, hurt myself). Participants were also asked to provide an example of a time they felt the emotion in order to gauge the accuracy of their understanding of the question posed and also to give the assessors and participant guidance on further formulation of the response and to act as a memory aid. Smith and McCarthy (1996) reported that 41% ($N=12$) of the respondents were found to confide in others when they experienced two out of three negative emotions and were therefore deemed to be secure in their attachments. Consequently, 59% of the sample was categorized as insecure. Test/re-test reliability was at a good level (90%) and the SRAAS scores were not correlated with IQ scores.

Smith and McCarthy (1996) concluded that attachment processes in people with ID can be reliably and validly investigated using self-report with the SRAAS allowing the participant to be 'part of' the process of assessment. They found that the participants wanted to explain the reasons for their answers and to be understood by the assessors. This had the advantage of allowing the participant and assessor to develop a relationship from which the assessor could gain a higher quality of insight into potential attachment behaviours. However, there remains the difficulty of using such a measure with individuals who do not use verbal communication and who do not have adequate emotional language in order to express their feelings. The scoring criteria of the SRAAS classifies a response of 'no answer or changeable response' as indicating insecure attachment, although this may actually represent either an inability to understand the concepts or difficulty in formulating a coherent response due to memory and/or language impairments. The main advantage of the SRAAS is its clinical utility, as it allows for a quick assessment of understanding of emotional concepts as well as allowing an experienced clinician to develop an idiosyncratic understanding of the attachment. However, the lack of any assessment of its concurrent validity, that is, whether it is actually measuring attachment, remains a major weakness.

The *Adult Attachment Projective Picture System* (AAP) (George and West, 2001) is an interesting development in terms of assessing adult attachment via the use of pictures. As such, it does not rely on autobiographical memories of childhood experiences or evaluation of current relationships, both of which are likely to be problematic for people with ID. The AAP involves looking at and telling a story for each of seven pictures, six of which depict attachment-related scenes such as images of loss and separation, with one neutral image. The coding of responses involves the same descriptors of attachment as the AAI and aims to assess internal working models of attachment. The coding also examines intrusions of a personal attachment-based narrative into the stories and considers whether any aspects of the assessment appear overwhelming for the participant. The AAP has been used successfully with adults with ID (Gallichan and George, 2014) and is discussed in more detail in Chapter 10. However, similar to the AAI and the *Infant Strange Situation*, it requires extensive training in the administration and coding of the responses given, which may limit its use clinically for those working with people with ID.

The *Secure Base Safe Haven Observation* (SBSHO) (De Schipper and Schuengel, 2006; 2010) is a 20-item list of observations that are individually rated on a seven-point Likert scale, with higher scores indicating secure attachment behaviour. The SBSHO was developed from the Attachment Q sort (AQS; Waters, 1995) by taking specific items relating to secure attachment behaviours and then constructing further items to reflect attachment behaviour shown by children and adolescents with ID in stressful situations. The full list of items in the SBSHO is given in De Schipper and Schuengel (2010) and includes:

- This person looks at me when something exciting or dangerous is happening (in a situation like that, this person only starts to do something after he/she has searched for eye contact with me).
- I am able to comfort this person by paying attention and talking to him/her.
- This person uses me as a 'base' from which to explore the environment.
- When other people bother this person, he/she seeks contact with me.
- When this person enters the group, he/she immediately 'greets' me.

The AQS is a widely used and validated measure and forms the basis of the SBSHO. The authors have found that it has high internal consistency and moderate inter-informant agreement. The SBSHO was also found to have strong associations with the AQS when professional caregivers were asked to complete both (De Schipper et al., 2009). The authors of this measure outline its potential use within staff team changes, to highlight and aid connection between existing staff and clients when changes happen. This measure is quick to administer and was developed specifically with young people who have moderate to severe ID. As this is a third-party measure developed so that professional caregivers can complete the assessment, it allows for the assessment of attachment without the bias of language, cognitive ability or life experience factors. However, it does not give an account of the person's own thoughts about their attachment behaviours and interpersonal relations.

The *Manchester Attachment Scale – Third Party* (MAST) (Penketh et al., 2014) was similarly based on results from research that utilized Q sort methodology to identify a consensus about *secure* attachment in people with ID (Walker, 2009). The sixteen items considered to define secure attachment behaviour in people with ID were subsequently developed into an observational measure with the intention of providing a short, easy-to-use and quick assessment tool that requires minimal training to complete, with interpretation of the scores conducted by experienced clinicians such as clinical psychologists. The MAST requires an informant, such as a carer or professional, to rate the observable attachment behaviour of a person with ID on the basis of items including:

- The individual actively solicits comforting when distressed;
- The individual accepts carers' attention to others;
- The individual acts to maintain social interaction.

Each of the sixteen items that constitute the MAST are rated using a four-point Likert scale and a total score is calculated by summing the item scores (negatively worded items being reverse scored).

Penketh et al. (2014) examined the validity and reliability of the MAST, specifically in terms of internal consistency, test-retest reliability, face, concurrent and predictive validity, in order to assess to what degree the MAST measured secure attachment behaviour. A further aim was to assess whether the MAST was measuring attachment behaviour or whether it was simply measuring the quality of the relationship between staff–client dyads on a given day. To this end, the *Emotional Rating Scale* (ERS) was developed specifically to measure the perceived quality of the relationship and emotional closeness of the relationship between the individual staff member completing the MAST and the person with ID. The MAST was found to have adequate internal consistency and to be reliable over time and also to have reasonable concurrent validity with attachment-focused items from the *Edward Zigler-Yale Personality Questionnaire* (EZPQ; Zigler and Bennett-Gates, 1999) and the aforementioned SRAAS (Smith and McCarthy, 1996). Moreover, MAST scores were not significantly correlated with the ERS, indicating a degree of independence from relationship quality and level of emotional closeness.

The MAST has a number of strengths and limitations as a clinical tool. First, it has been designed purposefully as a measure of secure attachment for adults with ID, as secure attachment is arguably more consistently defined across the various models of attachment than insecure attachment. In addition, the MAST is further intended for use as a continuous measure of secure attachment within the context of idiosyncratic assessment and formulation and not as a tool to identify supposedly discrete forms of dysfunctional attachment, the validity of which are unknown. In terms of limitations, the MAST does not generate information about the individuals' own perspective on their attachment experiences or relationships. Normative data are currently being collected for different populations of people with ID using the MAST. A licence for using the MAST can be obtained from the University of Liverpool (A.Flood@liverpool.ac.uk).

STRENGTHS AND LIMITATIONS OF AVAILABLE MEASURES

A practical strength of the SBSHO, SRAAS and MAST is that they can be used as clinical tools and do not require extensive training to use. However, Penketh et al. (2014) found that direct care staff reported their knowledge of attachment theory was limited and therefore the interpretation of the MAST (and possibly the other measures of attachment) should be supported by clinicians with a good working knowledge of attachment theory so that a rounded understanding of the resultant behaviours seen can be formulated. A further limitation of the measures produced thus far is that they could neglect the 'voice' of the individual client concerned. As clinical tools, the measures need also to ask for the person's own experiences and opinions regarding their attachment relationships and history, which can be missed when third-party measures are employed. However, this then creates a circular argument with the biases and concerns regarding whether the attachment experiences, cognitive ability and language ability of the individual allow them to report their own life experiences accurately and succinctly, versus gaining a real and clear understanding of their attachment behaviours when concerns have been raised. It is therefore hard for researchers to develop such measures and why the authors here advocate that a toolkit of measures combined with clinical interview and information gathering from a variety of sources is preferred to assess attachment in ID. It should also be noted that there is much heterogeneity in the population of people with ID, which encompasses those with a mild disability through to people with much more severe disabilities as well as taking in the specific behavioural phenotypes associated with the many syndromes underpinning ID. As such, for some people, the use of the AAI may be appropriate, as they are able to understand the questions asked well, to give insightful answers and to recall and reflect on their experiences. For others, an observation-based measure is preferred, as they are unable to communicate their experiences well.

There seem to be similarities between the attachment measures described in their attempt to address and overcome the difficulties of assessment with this population of people. The AAP stands out from the SBSHO, SRAAS and MAST as being a distinct approach that utilizes face-to-face interviews with the person being assessed in order to explore the person's internal working models of attachment. The SBSHO, SRAAS and MAST use a third-party informant, which then offers a different insight into a person's presenting behaviours and may be more suited to those who have limited ability to express their experiences.

Crittenden (2005) indicates that a good measure of attachment is recordable, taps into more than one memory system, is standardized so that assessments are comparable and is validated by an evidence base. For people with ID this has not yet been achieved. Measures have been developed that have started to address this, but the 'validated evidence base' is an ongoing area of research. It may not be possible for people who have an ID to tap fully into more than one memory system, due to their cognitive limitations, and this is also an issue with the measures that have thus far been developed. However, positively, the measures have been shown to be comparable to other assessments available, and to other factors of emotional health thought to interact with attachment behaviours. Certainly, research and clinical use of the measures outlined should be tracked and entered into the pool of ongoing validation of these assessments.

AN ATTACHMENT TOOLKIT

As is discussed elsewhere in this book, attachment theory evidently has explanatory value in both research and, perhaps most importantly, in clinical work with people with ID. However, in order to apply such ideas and approaches to their full effect, it is necessary to be able to assess and describe attachment behaviours reliably and to consider the need for a range of assessment techniques. This chapter has reviewed the main assessment methods and their validity for use with people with ID but it is also necessary to consider the feasibility of assessments, especially when considering their use in clinical practice. One reason why attachment theory has had relatively little use in routine clinical work in this area may be the apparent high cost, in terms of both money and time, of training to use 'gold standard' attachment assessments. Therefore, a straightforward attachment 'toolkit' for clinicians and clinical researchers might comprise a number of different assessments of attachment security using, for example, a self-report interview, such as the SRAAS and an observational measure, such as the SBSHO or the MAST, alongside assessment of self-esteem and emotional wellbeing. Whilst there is evidence for the utility of using the AAP with people with ID, it is likely that the funding required to train in administration and coding of the assessment may impact on its adoption within clinical practice, at least in the short term.

It is important to emphasize that such assessments should not be used solely to inform the making of psychiatric diagnoses or in any other quasi-diagnostic manner in which they are the pre-determinants of subsequent treatment. Rather, it is important that such assessments are used in the context of formulation (Johnstone and Dallos, 2006) about the clinical difficulties as presented and experienced by the person with ID (Ingham, Clarke and James, 2008). Frameworks for and examples of formulation-based clinical practice informed by the assessment of attachment security are, of course, presented in other chapters in this book. We have included a case example here to aid a more general understanding of the assessment process outlined in this chapter.

Case Example: Lisa

Lisa was 32 years old when she was referred to Clinical Psychology by her social worker. She had a mild ID and used verbal language to communicate. She lived alone with support workers visiting daily and volunteered in a charity shop twice per week, although the work placement was increasingly unstable. The referral noted increased self-isolation, low mood and occasional 'angry' outbursts towards support staff.

Lisa was initially keen to cooperate with the process of assessment and talked about feeling lonely and different to other people. Her relationships with support staff were reported to be consistently poor and she would sometimes refuse to answer the door or become verbally abusive when staff pursued an interaction. Staff described how during 'calm periods', they would think that they had started to build a positive relationship, only for her to become agitated again and they would then feel rejected and confused. The staff team could not agree on how to support Lisa and morale was extremely low. They described her as difficult to 'reach' and some staff thought that she enjoyed upsetting them. There was a high turnover of staff as a result. An assessment was therefore undertaken involving individual sessions with Lisa, observations of interactions between herself and staff, a review of her health and social care records, administration of the *Glasgow Depression Scale* (GDS-LD; Cuthill, Espie and Cooper, 2003) the SRAAS and the MAST. The aim was to develop a psychological formulation to help the staff understand Lisa's presentation.

Lisa described herself as 'quiet' and 'friendly'. Although keen to meet with the clinician, she tended to become quiet when asked about her feelings, or responded with the phrase, 'I'm OK.'

She would describe herself using the phrases that support workers used, such as 'Sue says I need to cheer up'. Her low scores on the SRAAS reflected her tendency to act out or inhibit talking about her feelings. She scored under the cut-off for clinical depression on the GDS, and denied feeling tearful or sad but reported that she felt tired during the day 'a lot' and also agreed that sometimes she 'was in a bad mood'. The MAST was completed with her support staff and the total score 25/64 indicated that she showed behaviours inconsistent with secure attachment. Her staff strongly disagreed with items such as 'the individual views self as worthwhile' and 'the individual responds at an appropriate level of intensity to other people' whilst agreeing with the item 'the individual is basically distrustful of people in general'. Lisa's staff team reported that she did not approach staff for reassurance when she was distressed and concurred that she rarely cried or expressed sadness verbally. This was supported by clinical observations and applied to both her relationships with the paid staff and her other, albeit limited, relationships outside of the staff team.

Staff rated Lisa as not maintaining social interaction, but the observations did indicate that she occasionally sought staff to talk to them. Subsequent observations of these brief interactions indicated that they had a tangible outcome for Lisa, such as ensuring she had support to shop for an item she wanted.

Although it had not been possible to meet Lisa's family, the review of Lisa's records indicated a long history of service involvement. Her mother was described as severely depressed and there were references to an 'impoverished emotional environment' and that Lisa's support needs were not being met at home.

On the basis of the assessment, a formulation was prepared. It hypothesized that, as a child, Lisa's caregivers had been preoccupied and found it difficult to provide consistent, sensitive care. As a result, Lisa had developed an insecure attachment pattern and she developed an internal working model (IWM) characterized by beliefs that the world is a dangerous place, that she has limited worth and that caregivers are not to be trusted. It was thought that Lisa developed a strategy of inhibiting her own emotional reactions as a way of potentially reducing experiences of rejection from her early caregivers. As she grew older, she did not feel secure in her relationships with any caregivers, and when they demonstrated overt care this made her feel anxious and under threat, which resulted in her withdrawing or occasionally becoming angry. Her caregivers, receiving few positive responses to their overtures, became frustrated with her, reinforcing her negative feelings about herself and her lack of trust in them.

An assessment by the Speech and Language Therapist indicated that although Lisa was verbally fluent, she had a limited emotional vocabulary. Moreover, she did not identify sad feelings and was confused when staff attempted to talk to her about her mood and encourage her to be more upbeat and active. Her patterns of interacting as an adult were hypothesized to be an adaptive response to her childhood experiences which maintained a sense of stability and security. In particular, her withdrawal and occasional aggressive behaviour towards staff resulted in them maintaining an emotional distance from her. This, together with limited access to social opportunities, resulted in loneliness and reinforced her internal working model.

Lisa did not wish to engage in individual therapy but agreed to the clinician sharing a simplified formulation with her staff team. This helped her staff team to understand why Lisa responded to them in the way that she did. They were encouraged to reduce their focus on helping Lisa to 'cheer up' and instead focus on finding ways of spending time with Lisa completing activities that she felt comfortable doing. A protocol was developed that allowed Lisa to communicate her wish to be alone without needing to become angry with staff. Her support staff were encouraged to recognize that rejection of support was not a personal rejection of them. The team leader shifted focus on daily outcomes to improving consistency in staffing over time. Lisa was gently encouraged to try new activities and attend events with the aim of increasing contact with other people, although staff were careful not to emphasize that she should try and enjoy herself or 'make friends'.

CONCLUSIONS

The development of evidence-based and formulation-driven clinical practice requires accurate assessment information as well as appropriate theories and models. Attachment theory has enormous potential to inform such practice and, to this end, the validity and utility of the various available instruments for assessing attachment in people with ID have been reviewed in the course of this chapter. There is clearly a need for further work in this field, especially on the concurrent validity of measures such as the MAST and the SBSHO, as well as scope for the further development of self-report measures, but there is now a 'toolkit' of assessments available for clinicians and it is hoped that this will, in turn, foster and facilitate further work that takes account of attachment dynamics and behaviour to the benefit of people with ID and their supporters.

REFERENCES

Ainsworth, M.D.S. (1967) *Infancy in Uganda*. Baltimore: Johns Hopkins University Press.

Ainsworth, M.D.S., Blehar, M.C., Waters, E. and Wall, S. (1978) *Patterns of attachment: A psychological study of the strange situation*. Hillsdale, NJ: Erlbaum.

Bailey, B., Hare, D.J., Hatton, C. and Limb, K. (2006) The response to challenging behaviour by care staff: Attributions of cause and observations of practice. *Journal of Intellectual Disability Research*, 50(3): 199–211.

Bartholomew, K. and Horowitz, L. (1991) Attachment styles amongst young adults: A test of a four category model. *Journal of Personality and Social Psychology*, 61(2): 226–244.

Beail, N. (2002) Interrogative Suggestibility, Memory and Intellectual Disability. *Journal of Applied Research in Intellectual Disabilities*, 15: 129–137.

Cicchetti, D. and Serafica, F.C. (1981) Interplay among behavioral systems: Illustrations from the study of attachment, affiliation, and wariness in young children with Down's syndrome. *Developmental Psychology*, 17(1): 36–49.

Clare, I.C.H. and Gudjonsson, G.H. (1995) The vulnerability of suspects with intellectual disabilities during police interviews: A review and experimental study of decision-making. *Mental Handicap Research*, 8: 110–128.

Collins, N.L. and Read, S.J. (1990) Adult attachment, working models, and relationship quality in dating couples. *Journal of Personality and Social Psychology*, 58(4): 644–663.

Crittenden, P.M. (2005) Teoria dell'attaccamento, psicopatologia e psicoterapia: L'approccio dinamico maturativo. *Psicoterapia*, 30: 171–182. http://www.patcrittenden.com/include/docs/attachment_theory_2005.pdf

Crowell, J. (1990) *Current Relationships Interview*. Unpublished manuscript, State University of New York at Stony Brook.

Crowell, J.A. and Treboux, D. (1995) A review of adult attachment measures: Implications for theory and research. *Social Development*, 4: 294–327.

Cuthill, F.M., Espie, C.A. and Cooper, S.A. (2003) Developmental and psychometric properties of the Glasgow Depression Scale for people with a learning disability. *British Journal of Psychiatry*, 182: 347–353.

De Schipper, J.C., Ploegmakers, B., Romijn, M. and Schuengel, C. (2009) *Validity of caregivers' reports of children's attachment behaviour in group care.* Paper presented at the conference of the European Association for Mental Health and Intellectual Disabilities, Amsterdam, The Netherlands.

De Schipper, J.C. and Schuengel, C. (2006) *Secure Base Safe Haven Observation list for child attachment behaviour.* Unpublished work, VU University, Amsterdam.

De Schipper, J.C. and Schuengel, C. (2010) Attachment behaviour towards support staff in young people with intellectual disabilities: Associations with challenging behaviour. *Journal of Intellectual Disability Research*, 54: 584–596.

Feeney, J. and Noller, P. (1990) Attachment style as a predictor of adult romantic relationships. *Journal of Personality and Social Psychology*, 58(2): 281–291.

Gallichan, D.J. and George, C. (2014) Assessing attachment status in adults with intellectual disabilities: The potential of the Adult Attachment Projective Picture System. *Advances in Mental Health and Intellectual Disabilities*, 8: 103–119.

George, C., Kaplan, N. and Main, M. (eds) (1996) *Adult Attachment Interview*, 3rd edition. Department of Psychology, University of California: Berkeley.

George, C. and West, M. (2001) The development and preliminary validation of a new measure of adult attachment: The Adult Attachment Projective. *Attachment & Human Development*, 3(1): 30–61.

Hare, D.J., Mellor, C. and Azmi, S. (2007) Episodic memory in adults with autistic spectrum disorders: Recall for self- versus other-experienced events. *Research in Developmental Disorders*, 28: 311–329.

Hastings, R.P., Tombs, A.K.H., Monzani, L.C. and Boulton, H.V.N. (2003) Determinants of negative emotional reactions and causal beliefs about self-injurious behaviour: An experimental study. *Journal of Intellectual Disability Research*, 47: 59–67.

Hazan, C. and Shaver, P. (1987) Romantic love conceptualized as an attachment process. *Journal of Personality and Social Psychology*, 52(3): 511–524.

Hesse, E. (1999) The Adult Attachment Interview: Historical and current perspectives. In J. Cassidy and P.R. Shaver (eds) *Handbook of Attachment: Theory, Research and Clinical Applications* (pp. 395–433). New York: The Guilford Press.

Ingham, B., Clarke, L. and James, I.A. (2008) Biopsychological case formulation for people with intellectual disabilities and mental health problems: A pilot study of a training workshop for direct care staff. *The British Journal of Developmental Disabilities*, 54(1): 41–54.

Johnstone, L. and Dallos, R. (eds) (2006) *Formulation in Clinical Psychology: Making sense of people's problems.* London: Routledge.

Kobak, R.R. (1993) *The Adult Attachment Interview Q-Set.* Unpublished document, University of Delaware.

Kobak, R.R., Cole, H., Fleming, W., Ferenz-Gillies, R. and Gamble, W. (1993) Attachment and emotion regulation during mother–teen problem-solving: A control theory analysis. *Child Development*, 64: 231–245.

Kobak, R.R. and Hazan, C. (1991) Attachment in marriage: Effects of security and accuracy of working models. *Journal of Personality and Social Psychology*, 60(6): 861–869.

Larson, F.V., Alim, N. and Tsakanikos, E. (2011) Attachment style and mental health in adults with intellectual disability: Self-reports and reports by carers. *Advances in Mental Health and Intellectual Disabilities*, 5(3): 15–23.

Main, M. and Goldwyn, R. (1994) Adult attachment rating and classification system. Manual in draft Version 6.0. Unpublished manuscript, University of California at Berkeley.

Penketh, V., Hare, D.J., Flood, A. and Walker, S. (2014) Attachment in Adults with Intellectual Disabilities: Preliminary Investigation of the Psychometric Properties of the Manchester Attachment Scale – Third Party Observational Measure. *Journal of Applied Research in Intellectual Disabilities*, 27(5): 458–470.

Schuengel, C., Kef, S., Damen, S. and Worm, M. (2010) People who need people: Attachment and professional caregiving. *Journal of Intellectual Disability Research*, 54: 38–47.

Simpson, J.A. (1990) Influences of attachment styles on romantic relationships. *Journal of Personality and Social Psychology*, 59: 971–980.

Smith, P. and McCarthy, G. (1996) The development of a semi-structured interview to investigate the attachment related experiences of adults with learning disabilities. *British Journal of Learning Disabilities*, 24: 154–160.

Solomon, J. and George, C. (1999) *Attachment Disorganization*. New York: Guilford Publications.

Sroufe, L.A. and Waters, E. (1977) Attachment as an Organizational Construct. *Child Development*, 48(4): 1184–1199.

Stephenson, W. (1953) *The Study of Behavior: Q-technique and its Methodology*. Chicago: University of Chicago Press.

Walker, S. (2009) *Attachment in adults with intellectual disabilities: The development and preliminary validation of a new criterion Q sort scale*. Unpublished ClinPsyD. thesis, University of Manchester, United Kingdom.

Waters, E. (1995) Appendix A: The Attachment Q-Set (Version 3.0). In E. Waters, B.E. Vaughn, G. Posada and K. Kondo-Ikemura (eds) Caregiving, Cultural, and Cognitive Perspectives on Secure-Base Behavior and Working Models: New Growing Points of Attachment Theory and Research. *Monographs of the Society for Research in Child Development*, 60: 234–246.

Wilde, L., Silva, D. and Oliver, C. (2013) The nature of social preference and interactions in Smith–Magenis syndrome. *Research in Developmental Disabilities*, 34: 4355–4365.

Zigler, E. and Bennett-Gates, D. (eds) (1999) *Personality Development in Individuals with Mental Retardation*. Cambridge: Cambridge University Press.

Chapter 5

AUTISM SPECTRUM DISORDER AND ATTACHMENT: A CLINICIAN'S PERSPECTIVE

Ewan Perry[1] and Andrea Flood[2]

[1] Central Manchester University Hospitals NHS Foundation Trust, Manchester, UK
[2] University of Liverpool, Liverpool, UK

INTRODUCTION

Unlike many other neurodevelopmental disorders, autism spectrum disorder (ASD) is often not recognized or diagnosed until mid-childhood. However, there is evidence that the diagnosis can be made reliably as early as two years old (Moore and Goodson, 2003) and in the authors' clinical experience, families often report having been concerned about their child's development from the first few months of their life. Atypical patterns of social cognition and interaction are a core feature of ASD. Their emergence during early childhood coincides with the 'sensitive period' for the development of attachment relationships, which Bowlby stated occurred for most babies before the age of six months but which may sometimes continue into the child's second year of life (Bowlby, 1969). Attachment theory is considered to be a universal developmental theory, however there are important questions to be posed about the way in which it applies to children with ASD whose social communication and interactions are known to be different from children without ASD. Specifically, one needs to consider whether ASD impacts on the development of attachment relationships, how attachment can be assessed in children and adults

---

Attachment in Intellectual and Developmental Disability: A Clinician's Guide to Practice and Research, First Edition. Edited by Helen K. Fletcher, Andrea Flood and Dougal Julian Hare.
© 2016 John Wiley & Sons, Ltd. Published 2016 by John Wiley & Sons, Ltd.

with ASD and whether attachment theory is useful and applicable to clinical work with this population.

The idea that people may experience difficulties in communication and social relationships as a direct result of atypical neurological development has developed significantly over the past 30 years. Observations of the pronounced social differences in the children studied by Kanner (1943) and Asperger (1944) led to clinical case descriptions that have shaped the current understanding of ASD. Early aetiological theories inappropriately implicated parents in the pathogenesis of their children's difficulties. In the 1960s, Bettelheim popularized the 'refrigerator mother' hypothesis, which proposed that autism was the result of insensitive and cold parenting (Bettelheim, 1967). Although this has been disproven, many families were negatively affected by the idea, which led them to fear having somehow caused their child's ASD. In the late 1970s, Wing and Gould's study in Camberwell, London (Wing and Gould, 1979) marked a new era in the understanding of child development, and the concept of the autistic spectrum began to emerge. ASD is currently defined by the early onset of atypical patterns of social communication and repetitive patterns of behaviour, interests or activities. It is now widely understood to be a neurodevelopmental disorder with a heterogeneous range of causes including genetic susceptibility (see Pickles *et al.*, 2000; Constantino *et al.*, 2006).

The chapter begins with the rationale for exploring the attachment relationships of individuals with ASD. This is followed by a brief description of early social development in children diagnosed with ASD and a review of research which has sought to establish whether attachment theory in its current form is applicable to children with ASD and their caregivers. The chapter briefly considers factors that may influence attachment relationships before focusing on the practical application of theory in clinical practice. Case examples are provided to illustrate some of the key points.

THE IMPORTANCE OF ATTACHMENT IN PSYCHOLOGICAL WELLBEING

In Chapter 2, Fletcher and Gallichan described the theoretical underpinnings of attachment theory and the importance of early relationships in influencing psychological wellbeing in children with a neurotypical developmental profile (Green and Goldwyn, 2002). Research suggests that attachment plays an important role across the lifespan, influencing psychological functioning as an adult, including patterns of emotional regulation (Mikulincer and Shaver, 2007), vulnerability to low mood (Carnelley, Pietromonaco and Jaffe, 1994) and adaptation to stressful life events (Maunder *et al.*, 2006).

Many young people with ASD experience profound difficulties with mental health (Simonoff *et al.*, 2008) and, in particular, difficulties with emotional regulation (Samson, Huber and Gross, 2012). The evidence that early attachment relationships and later emotional functioning are linked in the general population provides a strong argument for exploring whether the same relationship exists for individuals with ASD. This may have important implications for long-term wellbeing and the type of intervention and support plans that best meet an individual's needs. It is worth noting that many other factors, such as sensory and information-processing differences (Green and Ben-Sasson, 2010), stress (Gillott and Standen, 2007) and access to employment opportunities (Walsh, Lydon and Healy, 2014) are already known to be associated with the wellbeing of individuals with ASD. Furthermore, co-occurrence of an intellectual disability (ID) in those with ASD is another potentially significant influence on long-term outcomes. Thus, attachment is considered as one of a number of factors that require attention in understanding an individual's presentation.

EARLY SOCIAL DEVELOPMENT AND AUTISM SPECTRUM DISORDER

Although diagnosis is frequently delayed (Crane *et al.*, 2015), there is evidence that the early social development of children eventually diagnosed with ASD may be different to their neurotypical peers. Research has used retrospective video analysis to assess this possibility, with the findings indicating differences in social development between very young children later assessed as having ASD and children assessed as developing typically (for a review, see Barbaro and Dissanayake, 2009). In particular, a reduced tendency to orientate to social stimuli, which is characterized by an infant's response to their name being called or things being pointed out to them, has been noted (Werner *et al.*, 2000). The presence of a co-presenting ID does not appear to account for this difference (Osterling, Dawson and Munson, 2002). The failure to orient to social stimuli has been suggested as one of the earliest and most basic impairments in ASD and is hypothesized to be a key developmental precursor to later-emerging difficulties in both social and communication domains (Dawson et al., 1998).

Recent research using 'sibling studies' has supported the findings of earlier video analysis research. These studies compare the development of infants thought to be at a higher risk of developing ASD, by virtue of already having an older sibling who has been diagnosed with ASD, to age-matched infants without this profile. Infants later diagnosed with ASD have been rated by their parents as less cuddly and less likely to smile than typically developing infants during caretaking and play in their second year (Clifford et al., 2013). In addition, differences in patterns of social monitoring (Chawarska, Macari and Shic, 2013) and in play interactions with caregivers (Wan et al., 2013) have been demonstrated.

ATTACHMENT AS A PSYCHOLOGICAL CONSTRUCT IN ASD

In the 1980s, researchers began to explore whether similar attachment behaviours were expressed by children with ASD compared to typically developing peers. The initial studies indicated that children with ASD do respond preferentially to their caregivers compared to a stranger. They spend more time directing social behaviours towards their caregiver and will seek close proximity with them following a separation. These behaviours are not found to be significantly different from typically developing children of a younger age or children with developmental delay but no ASD (Sigman and Ungerer, 1984; Sigman and Mundy, 1989). Children with ASD also use their caregiver as a secure base and engage in exploratory behaviours, as described by Ainsworth and Wittig (1969), when not under threat. The presence of a stranger results in an increase in attachment behaviours and a decrease in exploratory behaviours (Dissanayake and Crossley, 1996), and specific patterns of separation and reunion behaviour are also similar for typically developing children compared to children with ASD or Down's syndrome (Dissanayake and Crossley, 1997). Just over half of children with ASD are securely attached, whereas this figure is 65% in neurotypical children (Van IJzendoorn, Schuengel and Bakermans-Kranenburg, 1999; Rutgers et al., 2004).

Few researchers have explored patterns of attachment in adults with a diagnosis of ASD. In a small exploratory study, Taylor, Target and Charman (2008) piloted the use of the Adult Attachment Interview

(George, Kaplan and Main, 1985). The proportion of securely attached adults with ASD was lower than in the general population but similar to that of general clinical samples, whilst insecure-avoidant attachment styles were over-represented.

Studies in the neurotypical population have repeatedly shown that caregivers with secure internal working models of attachment are most likely to have children who are securely attached (Van IJzendoorn, 1995). Children with ASD who have securely attached caregivers are more likely to have increased functional and relational skills, including: the ability to initiate communication with caregivers using reciprocal smiles and vocalizations; the ability to engage in social problem solving (for example, guiding caregivers to things they want help with); and more advanced imaginative thinking, symbolic play and verbal communication (Seskin *et al.*, 2010). Furthermore, in the same study, the caregivers rated as secure were better at encouraging the development of their children's reflective functions and symbolic play.

Despite the obstacles posed by impairments in communication and social functioning, there is evidence that many caregivers of children with ASD are able to connect with their child and establish a sensitive parenting style that promotes secure attachment (Koren-Karie *et al.*, 2009). This is more likely to happen if caregivers are insightful (i.e. able to report what is going through their child's mind) and have come to terms with their child's diagnosis (Oppenheim *et al.*, 2009; 2012). Better psychological wellbeing resulting from increased social support has also been found to be important (Kim and Kim, 2009). The limited research in this area is not all consistent though, and Van IJzendoorn *et al.* (2007) have questioned whether children with ASD have a biological limitation that prevents them benefitting from typically sensitive parenting and requires instead a more directive style with an emphasis on non-verbal methods.

One of the challenges for researchers attempting to understand the relationship between attachment and ASD is that it frequently co-presents with other developmental difficulties, particularly ID. Rutgers *et al.* (2004) found that increasingly severe ASD symptoms partly accounted for lower attachment security in children with ASD compared to those without, but most of the difference was explained by the degree of ID. More recent research supports the view that severity of ID is a better predictor of differences in attachment behaviour than ASD symptoms (Grzadzinski *et al.*, 2014). This may reflect the challenge of accurately classifying attachment behaviours of children with ID, particularly those with additional physical disabilities and impaired verbal communication (see Chapter 4 for further discussion). The development of complex internal working models of attachment is also likely to be affected (Rogers, Ozonoff and Maslin-Cole, 1991), perhaps due to associated limitations in the development of the concepts of self and other (Yirmiya and Sigman, 2001). Naber *et al.* (2007) suggest that children with ASD are less able to develop the behavioural and emotional patterns necessary for consistent, organized attachment behaviours.

In summary, there is a growing body of evidence indicating that attachment as a psychological construct is applicable to people with ASD. Children with ASD and their caregivers can and do form observably secure attachments despite their neurodevelopmental difficulties. Many caregivers are able to attune to their child's needs and, equally importantly, the presence of ASD in itself does not necessarily inhibit a child's ability to signal their needs sufficiently clearly for synchrony to occur. Likewise, children with ASD can present with insecure attachment patterns, and co-presenting ID may increase this risk.

ASSESSMENT OF ATTACHMENT IN CHILDREN AND ADULTS KNOWN TO HAVE ASD

The range of formal measures to inform assessment of attachment in children and adults already diagnosed with ASD is very limited, particularly when there is a co-presenting ID. The strange situation (Ainsworth *et al.*, 1978) has been used successfully with children diagnosed with ASD, up to a chronological age of 69 months (Willemsen-Swinkels *et al.*, 2000). Minor changes were made to the standard protocol (as described in Chapters 1 and 4) in order to reduce potential distress to the child. Although many studies have used the strange situation successfully, their ecological validity with children with ASD has been questioned. Rutgers *et al.* (2007) have queried whether the difficulties adapting to change that are well documented in children with ASD may mean that their responses are actually triggered by unexpected changes in their environment rather than separation and reunion with their caregiver *per se*.

The Attachment Q-sort (Waters, 1995) has also been demonstrated to have good utility and ecological validity for children with ASD aged 12 to 72 months (Pechous, 2001; Brauner, 2003). Both the strange situation and the AQS assessment require training or specialist supervision, which necessarily limits their utility in everyday clinical practice. For older children, The Security Scale (Kerns *et al.*, 2001) may be a useful adjunct to an assessment. This is a self-report measure designed to elicit a child's perception of security in their relationship with their mother and it has been used to differentiate between secure and insecure attachment in research studies involving school-age children with ASD who do not have ID (see Bauminger, Solomon and Rogers, 2010).

Preliminary research suggests that the Adult Attachment Interview, which relies on verbal descriptions and recounted memories of an individual's attachment relationship with their parents (George, Kaplan and Main, 1985), is valid for adults with ASD who do not have an ID. However, subscales which 'code' for anger, passivity and lack of memory may reflect aspects of ASD rather than attachment (Taylor, Target and Charman, 2008). Given that adults with ASD appear to have specific difficulties with autobiographical memory (Skirrow *et al.*, 2015), any retrospective clinical assessment of attachment with this group should be approached with due caution. For clinicians primarily working with young people and adults with both ASD and ID, there are currently no evidence-based structured assessment protocols or methodologies.

There may be occasions when clinicians are primarily concerned with differentiating ASD from attachment disorders, particularly in the course of contributing to diagnostic assessments. Discussion of this is beyond the scope of this chapter, however, interested readers may wish to read Moran (2010) and Davidson *et al.* (2015).

Given the paucity of easily accessible measures, clinicians using an attachment-informed approach are required to integrate their broader understanding of psychological theory and models underpinning both attachment and ASD in their formulations and clinical work. The specific neurodevelopmental strengths and limitations associated with ASD, and where relevant an ID, should always remain a core feature of formulation. The aim is to connect historical and current information to develop an understanding of the individual's internal working model of relationships and pattern of affective functioning.

There is a risk for individuals with ASD that any difficulties they experience are incorrectly attributed solely to their diagnosis. This process of 'diagnostic overshadowing' occurs when the diagnosis takes a dominant position in the clinician's thinking about the way an individual behaves, feels and thinks in response to certain situations. Emerging empirical research into the development of symbolic play in children with ASD highlights the potential for diagnostic overshadowing, as attachment security has been found to be a better predictor of symbolic play than severity of ASD, despite the commonly held belief that deficits in symbolic play are related primarily to ASD (Naber *et al.*, 2008; Marcu *et al.*, 2009). This indicates the importance of considering both ASD and attachment when developing formulations relating to clinical problems experienced by people with ASD and their wider systems.

ASD AND ATTACHMENT IN CLINICAL PRACTICE

The suggestions below have been developed, based on the authors' clinical experience, as a guide to utilizing attachment-informed assessments, formulations and interventions with people with ASD. The evidence base about the stability of attachment patterns in individuals with ASD and the extent to which they influence relationships with other caregivers is particularly underdeveloped. This presents a predicament for the practising clinician, who may be working with individuals with complex relational histories, including breakdown of relationships in early childhood, but who is also mindful of remaining appropriately cautious given the paucity of research. Clinical interviews and direct observations are both extremely useful in informing hypotheses about an individual's pattern of attachment. In order to utilize attachment theory effectively in clinical work, it is important to understand the adaptive nature of an individual's attachment strategies, recognizing that patterns of attachment and emotional functioning may change over time, depending on the circumstances of a person's life (Waters, Hamilton and Weinfield, 2000).

Clinical Interview

Taking a developmental history that includes information about relationships can help elucidate patterns of emotional and behavioural functioning that are relevant to attachment. Depending on the individual's circumstances, it may be possible to meet with their parents to ask about their experiences of relating to and being with their son or daughter, and the journey this has followed. The clinician needs to remain mindful that individuals with ASD may express their emotions differently and this should not be interpreted as a sign of insecure attachment. It may be that an expression of emotion is

Box 5.1   Topics to Include in Clinical Interviews

- Early development and emerging interpersonal difficulties (possibly attributed to the person's ASD), particularly regarding response to soothing and later support-seeking behaviours in times of distress or anxiety.
- Mood, anxiety and emotional regulation, including interpersonal triggers, how the person communicates their emotional needs and stabilizers to fluctuations in mood.
- The attributions that caregivers make about behaviours, insight, intellectual ability and emotional functioning (particularly those that minimize the person's experience of emotions or thought processes in response to external events).
- How the individual has managed departures and reunions, both on a daily basis and over longer periods of time. How the person makes sense of endings, particularly when long-standing relationships end. This may include family members, paid staff and relationships with peers and co-tenants.
- The reaction to a diagnosis of ASD (and, if relevant, ID) – discuss themes of loss, grief and coming to terms with the diagnosis (see Chapter 3)

appropriate to the situation but is communicated in an unusual way due to an individual's ASD. See Box 5.1 for suggested topics to include in clinical interviews.

Clinical Observation and Assessment of Current Presentation

Spending time with an individual in environments both familiar and unfamiliar to them can be invaluable in collating relevant information. It is useful to consider the questions shown in Box 5.2 during observations.

During an assessment, it is important to consider how an individual's ASD symptoms manifest. Individuals may communicate preference for other people in non-typical ways. They may, for example, involve them in stereotyped behaviours or, when anxious, engage with people in a functional way (asking for a preferred item or activity) rather than openly asking for comfort or support. Changes in

> **Box 5.2 Questions to Inform Clinical Observation of Attachment Strategies**
>
> - How does the person interact with people around them?
> - What expectations do they appear to have of these interactions?
> - If supported by staff, how does the person respond to support staff beginning and ending shifts, or taking longer absences from work?
> - Does the person show a strong preference for a particular caregiver? Does this cause any difficulties or concerns?
> - How do they seek support from others during times of distress, anxiety or discomfort? Do individuals around them recognize support-seeking behaviours? Does the person develop trust in those who support them and respond positively to reassurance in unfamiliar situations?
> - How does the person respond to events which would be expected to be highly distressing for them? Do they communicate an emotional response or appear outwardly unaffected?

behavioural profile and 'exceptions' to usual patterns may be significant and should be explored. For example, an individual with ASD may routinely interact with staff in a predictable way focused on practical outcomes, however when particularly anxious, they may start to interact in a way that also increases proximity or maintains contact for longer than usual periods of time.

When working with staff teams, it is important to establish the stability and longevity of relationships. It is unreliable to develop working hypotheses based on the interactions between an individual and staff members who do not know each other well. It is also important to bear in mind that many individuals who are supported by services experience frequent, unplanned ruptures in key relationships. Periods of acute distress, or alternatively reduced affect, may be reported when this occurs. It is important to hold this experience in mind when considering how an individual responds to endings and losses, as both reported preoccupation and non-recognition of loss may be related to these experiences. As when assessing individuals without ASD, it is important to recognize that individuals may be distressed when they lose contact with important people in their life. This distress may manifest in idiosyncratic ways and may be interpreted as increased anxiety or feeling 'more stressed' by the staff team. Typically, a period of distrust of new staff may be expected, which slowly changes over time and with increased contact and continuing support.

Working with Young People as they Transition to Adulthood

It can be helpful during the assessment and formulation process to consider developmental expectations and changes within the family lifecycle. The transition into adulthood, in particular, can be a stressful time for families supporting young people with ASD, as they adjust to the changing demands, expectations and roles of a different legal and cultural framework. Approximately 85% of individuals with ASD present with cognitive and/or adaptive impairments that limit their ability to live independently, leading to the possibility that they will need some measure of care or assistance from their parents and families for the duration of their lives (Volkmar and Pauls, 2003). At a time when most young people are becoming increasingly independent as adults, parents are acutely aware of the particular emotional and behavioural needs of their son or daughter with ASD. They recognize that others could be confused by their son or daughter's presentation and, in the context of impaired social and communication functioning, may not recognize distress cues or the meaning behind particular behaviours. The wider world may view their child as an adult with ASD or 'special needs', but parents may still be relating to their son or daughter as if they are, at least in part, much younger. Separations, such as those that occur when a young person with ASD moves out of the family home, can be experienced as if they were happening to a very young child who is not equipped with the skills to make sense of and adapt to the separation, which heightens anxiety. It may be experienced more as a rejection by both parties and the ensuing increase in attachment behaviours can sometimes be attributed solely to ASD rather than understandable distress in response to the loss of family contact and the safety and comfort of their family home environment.

Situations that fit the above description can leave some parents feeling pulled in two directions. On one hand, they respond to their son or daughter's early level of emotional development, including the need for a primary attachment figure to be emotionally and often physically present to reduce their anxiety. On the other hand, they may not be able, or willing, to be emotionally available all the time and may be attempting physical separation or development of their child's independence from them. A young adult with ASD can struggle to understand these different parental positions, particularly as their sense of self and other is likely to be impaired (Skirrow et al., 2015). In some cases, circumstances enforce a separation in the absence of the typical developmental processes that allow parent and child to work together towards preparedness for independence.

Early Attachment-related Trauma and Loss: Working with Staff Teams

Many children and young people with ASD move to residential or supported living placements having experienced positive, nurturing relationships both prior to and during the transition. However, there are also children and young people with ASD who have experienced neglect or abuse during their early years and frequent changes in caregivers. These young people can present with emotional and behavioural needs that staff teams find particularly challenging to understand and support.

Although many paid carers are skilled in using person-centred approaches with young people with a history of disrupted attachments, there tends to be an inherent bias within services to conceptualize themselves as meeting the needs of either 'children who are looked after' or as an ID or ASD specialist service. Training provided to staff then tends to fit within this model of care, and the individual's problems are often conceptualized within the pre-existing framework of the service. It is vital that during the assessment process, the clinician considers the inherent expertise in the service and identifies 'missing elements' so that staff are enabled to make better sense of an individual's history and support needs and not attribute all the behaviours to a particular cause.

Where possible, a collaborative approach to formulation (see Ingham, 2011), informed by historical information as well as what occurs 'in the moment' prior to and during incidents, is preferred. In practice, it can be helpful to develop the formulation over a number of meetings, to enable the team to reflect on earlier discussions. A balance must be struck between avoiding over-simplistic reasoning and overwhelming the system with complex information and multiple hypotheses. The questions listed in Box 5.2 can be used to begin conversations about the person's attachment needs and their relationships with the staff team. Encouraging curiosity about the person's experiences of being cared for, often by multiple caregivers, can generate insight into how that person might experience relationships now.

Referrals for challenging behaviour should include a functional assessment (NICE, 2015) identifying the immediate antecedents and consequences, which should be integrated into the broader formulation. The intervention plan should be mapped to the formulation, with a likely focus on changing contingencies that occur in response to interpersonal behaviours and expressions of anxiety or distress. Interventions may also focus on supporting the individual to develop their own emotional regulation skills. The approach described in Chapter 8 may be useful when considering the interactions between staff and the individuals they support.

Services often use overly simplistic reward-based behavioural interventions which are likely to be ineffective in meeting the attachment needs of individuals with ASD. In the authors' experience, reward-based interventions pursued in the belief that they will reinforce preferred behaviours can have a contradictory effect, triggering fear of failure and 'loss' of the reward. They also have the potential to undermine relationships with caregivers, with the 'nurturer' becoming associated with distrust or unpredictability. This can create a rupture in established relationships and increase attachment behaviours, which may be misinterpreted by caregivers as 'challenging' or 'manipulative' behaviour, creating a cycle of increasingly coercive interactions. Identification and monitoring of anxiety and attachment behaviours can be helpful in demonstrating whether this is a particular concern, and staff can then be supported to develop an alternative intervention.

The case examples below illustrate the principles discussed above and provide detailed descriptions of attachment-informed work with people with ASD.

Case Example: Isa

Isa was 26 years old and had been living in supported accommodation for two years. He had a moderate learning disability and had been diagnosed with ASD when he was 11 years old. He moved to supported accommodation suddenly after physically assaulting his mother whom he lived with at the time. Following the move, he became highly anxious before visiting her. When anxious, Isa attempted to headbutt walls, picked at dry skin on his hands and held his breath for short periods whilst vigorously swaying back and forth. His self-harm sometimes necessitated treatment at the local hospital's Accident and Emergency department.

Isa sometimes expressed an idealized view of his relationship with his mother but at other times said she was cruel and did not listen to him. He was often preoccupied with seeing his mum and asked repetitive questions about visits. However, when they were together, he became agitated and sometimes angry with her. Isa closely monitored his mother's mood and behaviour. His mood changed very suddenly in response to perceived changes in his mum, which often led to attempts to 'control' her.

During the interview with his mum, she explained that when he was two years old she had left the country to care for a relative. Isa went to live with another family member, although they did not know each other well and the move was arranged at short notice. His communication regressed when he returned home and Isa found it hard to separate from his mother following their reunion. They developed an interdependency that reduced the frequency of separations from each other. Isa became increasingly controlling of his mother and she often felt unable to live up to Isa's idealized expectations and would react with frustration and disengage from him. At other times she did what she could to conform to his expectations. Isa's mum appeared to find it difficult to 'pitch' her interactions and expectations to his developmental level, resulting in him feeling confused and his mum frustrated. The assault and subsequent move to supported accommodation reinforced Isa's preoccupation with the idea that his mum had rejected him and most of their subsequent interactions ended with an escalation of anxiety and a 'replaying' of the original traumatic separation. Isa's exaggerated affect was most obvious in situations in which he felt under threat. This 'threat' did not necessarily need to be physical, but often reflected a perception that others may be anxious about his behaviour or emotional state.

Isa's staff team believed that his self-injury, repetitive questions, preoccupation and aggressive behaviour were the result of ongoing changes in environment and routine since moving to supported accommodation. An attachment-informed formulation provided an alternative way of understanding the difficulties and it was used to reframe patterns of behaviour that occurred each week. Weekly joint sessions including a reflecting team discussion were held over a 12-month period with Isa, his mother and staff. The sessions helped identify the setting conditions and triggers that led to tension between them, such as Isa's negative preoccupations about rejection and his mum's style of communication when she became frustrated. A visual timetable was developed to show when Isa could call or visit his mum. Visits were also shortened and Isa's mum put less pressure on him to do things out of his 'comfort zone', which made it more likely that they ended positively. Towards the end of the intervention period, they were having regular, unsupervised time together and both felt more positive about their relationship. Isa's mum stated that it had been important for her and Isa to have the experience of talking about difficult feelings in a supportive setting that helped make it less overwhelming.

Case Example: Leah

Leah was 19 years old when she was referred to the Clinical Psychology service by her support team, who requested input regarding her 'challenging behaviours'. Leah had a severe ID and ASD. She did not use verbal communication and her repertoire of intentional communication was very limited. She lived in a supported living service with three other young people.

The team described frequently occurring interactions with Leah during which she would scratch, pinch or 'catch skin' of staff members with her nails. During some of these incidents, Leah would become highly distressed or agitated and attempt to hit, kick and bite staff. However, if staff withdrew physically, she would follow and continue to attempt to hurt them. Staff members were unable to predict the events occurring; neither could they reassure Leah when they did. The frequency fluctuated, with at least two of the more intense incidents happening each week. The team had completed a basic functional assessment and behaviour support plan, but this had not been effective and there had been an increasing tendency to focus on reactive interventions. They were concerned that Leah was becoming increasingly isolated, as she would choose to sit away from staff members and engage in repetitive behaviours such as rocking and picking the skin on the backs of her hands. When staff approached her, she frequently engaged in the behaviours described. At times Leah would come towards staff and smile or sit next to them, but she would then appear to feel overwhelmed and again engage in the behaviours.

The assessment involved a file review, an interview with Leah's long-term foster mother, Mrs Carr, and observations of Leah being supported by her staff team. The team was already recording incidents using the service's agreed protocol, which involved recording any situation in which staff members were injured. However, they were not recording incidents in which Leah's anxiety did not escalate or she ended an interaction without engaging in the behaviours described. Thus, the protocol was adapted to collate this additional information. The team also started to record Leah's mood.

Leah had been placed in the care of the local authority before the age of four months, following evidence of neglect. She had lived with three foster families, the final one of these being a long-term placement. Mrs Carr described how, during the first few weeks of her placement, Leah had been very withdrawn, but that the pattern described by her staff team slowly emerged and became constant throughout the remainder of the placement. Despite the enduring nature of the final placement, there had been frequent periods of 'crisis' and Leah's social worker reflected that her foster family was often unable to meet her emotional needs. Mrs Carr stated that she had felt 'unsupported' by the local authority that had placed Leah in her care.

During the observations, it became evident that Leah was constantly vigilant in the company of others. Her interactions with others were functionally driven and there was rarely a sense of social enjoyment. She was largely socially passive and appeared unable to end interactions with other people except by hurting them. Her mood tended to be flat, with occasional periods of being intensely distressed without an obvious trigger. She did not seek comfort on these occasions.

Leah had experienced an early breakdown in her primary relationship with her birth family, followed by an unprecedented number of carers during planned and unplanned placements throughout her childhood. She did not have the opportunity to experience a secure base and would have been unable to make effective predictions about her caregiver's behaviour. She had not been able to develop early relationships that allowed her to feel safe in interactions with other people. Therefore, it had become adaptive to be hypervigilant in relation to interactions with others.

In the context of unpredictable care and her own social communication difficulties, hurting people became a way of both starting an interaction and escaping, either from a demand or from a social situation. As Leah grew older, those looking after her became aware of her behaviours to others and were less nurturing and prone to reject her if she hurt them. By the time she reached adulthood, a cycle of behaviours had been established that allowed Leah to maintain physical distance from others, and thus reduce the likelihood of rejection. However, it also meant that she had become less engaged in activities and experienced long periods of time without positive contact. She became increasingly reliant on stereotyped and repetitive behaviours to fill her time. Staff members were anxious about working with her as they feared being hurt, which reinforced her pattern of hypervigilance. When staff did interact, Leah learnt that engaging in one of the behaviours described brought the interaction to an end. She did not appear to have an alternative way of ending unwanted interpersonal contact. Interactions with staff were associated with increased arousal and fear, rather than a sense of joy or having her needs met.

Initially, a collaborative formulation was developed with the staff team, informed by information gathered during the assessment process. The purpose of this was to develop an empathic understanding of Leah's childhood experiences to enable team members (who had predominantly negative attributions) to develop more balanced beliefs. The team was also offered support from an experienced behavioural support team advisor on how to manage the most intensive incidents. Protective clothing was offered for a brief period to reduce the team's reluctance to be physically close.

Work was done to help Leah 'make sense' of her world, using environmental manipulation to better communicate routine daily elements. A 'now and next' strip was used to communicate immediate plans. In addition, symbols were introduced to mark the beginning and end of interactions and activities. The team began to use a 'sign' for finished at the end of every interaction, in order to model a way of ending social interactions. Leah was encouraged once again to take an active role with staff in completing elements of tasks, such as choosing and preparing her evening snack. The team was encouraged to be creative in developing sensory-based activities for Leah, to which she responded well.

It was important to help Leah develop more positive experiences of interacting with others and tolerate people in her 'space'. Staff members began to spend very brief periods of time with her, using touch, song, movements and 'interesting objects' to promote engagement. It was emphasized to staff that the interactions should be ended whilst 'successful', to reduce the likelihood of Leah using a non-preferred behaviour to end the interaction. Staff approached Leah frequently each day, monitoring her response to their initial approach, continuing only when her non-verbal behaviour indicated acceptance and retreating before any non-preferred behaviours were observed. Initially, these interactions lasted only a few seconds.

The effect of the interventions over a nine-month period was to reduce the frequency of the 'lower level' behaviours and the intensity of the most difficult-to-manage incidents. Staff reported increased confidence in managing the more intense situations when they did occur. Leah's relationships with the team improved markedly, with staff demonstrating obvious pleasure during interactions, and conversations reflecting a more balanced view of working with her. Leah's foster mother remarked on how much happier Leah had become.

The key aspects of the intervention were that Leah was learning that people were reliable and could be trusted to behave in predictable ways. This reduced her anxiety and need for hypervigilance, thus freeing her up to engage in a wider range of activities (albeit still restricted). In addition to this, Leah was experiencing emotional reciprocity in key relationships with staff members and appeared to be developing a sense of herself as someone of value who staff members could enjoy being with.

Summary of Clinical Recommendations

The above cases illustrated key aspects of integrating attachment theory within clinical work with individuals with ASD. The following recommendations have been developed as a helpful guide for clinical practice.

- Ensure ASD symptoms do not overshadow attachment issues or the importance of relationships for people with ASD.
- Consider the person in their social environment and their key relationships with others.
- Remain mindful that an individual's emotional and relational functioning may not be in synchrony with their cognitive development and adaptive functioning.
- Ensure attachment is understood as an adaptive process within a family/care system.
- Use visual communication systems which incorporate information about people. This may include where key people are, when they will be back and who is allocated to work with an individual.
- Provide interventions which have the potential to meet both attachment and ASD-related needs. This may include the provision of visual and/or written information about relationships, including the use of social stories (Gray and Garand, 1993), video interaction guidance to aid social and emotional relationships (NICE, 2013) and/or intensive interaction (Hewett *et al.*, 2011).

CONCLUSION

Parenting a child with ASD presents families with its own unique set of challenges. As with typically developing children, early secure attachment is important in helping children with ASD to realize their full potential (Oppenheim, Sagi and Lamb, 1988). Conversely, insecure attachment may increase the likelihood of emotional and behavioural difficulties, particularly in the context of interpersonal relationships, later in life. Further research is required to understand fully the extent to which attachment influences wellbeing across the lifecycle in individuals with ASD.

One of the major challenges facing clinicians is how to translate findings in the research literature into clinical approaches which consider the attachment needs of individuals with ASD. This chapter has described how attachment theory might offer an additional perspective to existing approaches when assessing, formulating and intervening in clinical issues that are commonly presented to services. It is argued that in order to provide the appropriate support, it is helpful to move away from diagnosis-led attributions about an individual, towards a richer appreciation of their interpersonal history and functioning. Regardless of whether presenting difficulties are primarily underpinned by features specific to ASD, attachment experiences or other psycho-social influences, individuals with ASD need support that helps contain their anxieties, meets their emotional needs and offers opportunities to develop enduring relationships with others.

REFERENCES

Ainsworth, M.D.S., Blehar, M., Waters, E. and Wall, S. (1978) *Patterns of Attachment*. Hillsdale, NJ: Erlbaum.

Ainsworth, M.D.S. and Wittig, B.A. (1969) Attachment and the exploratory behaviour of one-year-olds in a strange situation. In B.M. Foss (ed.) *Determinants of Infant Behaviour*, Vol. 4, pp. 113–136. London: Methuen.

Asperger, H. (1944) Die 'Autistischen Psychopathen' im Kindesalter. *Archiv fur Psychiatrie und Nervenkrankheiten*, 117: 76–136.

Barbaro, J. and Dissanayake, C. (2009) Autism Spectrum Disorders in infancy and toddlerhood: A review of the evidence on early signs, early identification, and early diagnosis. *Journal of Developmental and Behavioral Paediatrics*, 30: 447–459.

Bauminger, N., Solomon, M. and Rogers, S.J. (2010) Predicting friendship quality in autism spectrum disorders and typical development. *Journal of Autism and Developmental Disorders*, 40: 751–761. DOI: 10.1007/s10803-009-0928-8.

Bettelheim, B. (1967) *The Empty Fortress: Infantile Autism and the Birth of the Self*. The Free Press.

Bowlby, J. (1969/1982) *Attachment and Loss. Vol. 1: Attachment*. New York: Basic Books.

Brauner, T.E. (2003) Efficacy of Attachment-Oriented Family Therapy Interventions for Children with Developmental Disabilities: An Exploratory Descriptive Study of Process and Outcome in a Therapeutic Preschool. *Dissertation Abstracts International: Section A: Humanities and Social Sciences*, 64: 1405.

Carnelley, K.B., Pietromonaco, P.R. and Jaffe, K. (1994) Depression, working models of others, and relationship functioning. *Journal of Personality and Social Psychology*, 66: 127–140.

Chawarska, K., Macari, S. and Shic, F. (2013) Archival Report: Decreased Spontaneous Attention to Social Scenes in 6-Month-Old Infants Later

Diagnosed with Autism Spectrum Disorders. *Biological Psychiatry*, 74: 195–203. DOI: 10.1016/j.biopsych.2012.11.022.

Clifford, S.M., Hudry, K., Elsabbagh, M., Charman, T. and Johnson, M.H. (2013) Temperament in the first 2 years of life in infants at high risk for autism spectrum disorders. *Journal of Autism and Developmental Disorders*, 43: 673–686.

Constantino, J.N., Lajonchere, C., Lutz, M., Abbacchi, T.G., McKenna, K., Singh, D. and Todd, R.D. (2006) Autistic social impairment in the siblings of children with pervasive developmental disorders. *American Journal of Psychiatry*, 163(2): 294–296.

Crane, L., Chester, J.W., Goddard, L., Henry, L.A. and Hill, E. (2015) Experiences of autism diagnosis: A survey of over 1000 parents in the United Kingdom. *Autism*. Advance online publication. DOI: 10.1177/1362361315573636.

Davidson, C., O'Hare, A., Mactaggart, F., Green, J., Young, D., Gillberg, C. and Minnis, H. (2015) Social relationship difficulties in autism and reactive attachment disorder: Improving diagnostic validity through structured assessment. *Research in Developmental Disabilities*, 40: 63–72. http://dx.doi.org/10.1016/j.ridd.2015.01.007

Dawson, G., Meltzoff, A.N., Osterling, J., Rinaldi, J. and Brown, E. (1998) Children with autism fail to orient to naturally occurring social stimuli. *Journal of Autism and Developmental Disorders*, 28: 479–485.

Dissanayake, C. and Crossley, S.A. (1996) Proximity and sociable behaviours in autism: Evidence for attachment? *Journal of Child Psychology and Psychiatry*, 37: 149–156.

Dissanayake, C. and Crossley, S.A. (1997) Autistic children's responses to separation and reunion with their mothers. *Journal of Autism and Developmental Disorders*, 27: 295–312.

George, C., Kaplan, N. and Main, M. (1985) The Adult Attachment Interview. Unpublished manuscript, University of California at Berkeley.

Gillott, A. and Standen, P.J. (2007) Levels of anxiety and sources of stress in adults with autism. *Journal of Intellectual Disability*, 11(4): 359–370.

Gray, C.A. and Garand, J.D. (1993) Social stories: Improving responses of students with autism with accurate social information. *Focus on Autistic Behavior*, 8: 1–10.

Green, J. and Goldwyn, R. (2002) Annotation: Attachment disorganisation and psychopathology: New findings in attachment research and their potential implications for developmental psychopathology in childhood. *Journal of Child Psychology and Psychiatry*, 43: 835–846.

Green, S.A. and Ben-Sasson, A. (2010) Anxiety disorders and sensory over-responsivity in children with autism spectrum disorders: Is there a causal relationship? *Journal of Autism and Developmental Disorders*, 40(12): 1495–1504.

Grzadzinski, R.L., Luyster, R., Spencer, A.G. and Lord, C. (2014) Attachment in young children with autism spectrum disorders: An examination of separation and reunion behaviors with both mothers and fathers. *Autism*, 18(2): 85–96. DOI: 10.1177/1362361312467235.

Hewett, D., Barber, M., Firth, G. and Harrison, T. (2011) *The Intensive Interaction Handbook*. London: Sage Publications.

Ingham, B. (2011) Collaborative psychosocial case formulation development workshops: A case study with direct care staff. *Advances in Mental Health and Intellectual Disabilities*, 5(2): 9–15.

Kanner, L. (1943) Autistic disturbances of affective contact. *Nervous Child*, 2: 217–250.

Kerns, K.A., Aspelmeier, J.E., Gentzler, A.L. and Grabill, C.M. (2001) Parent–child attachment and monitoring in middle childhood. *Journal of Family Psychology*, 15: 69–81.

Kim, E.S. and Kim, B.S. (2009) The structural relationships of social support, mothers' psychological status, and maternal sensitivity to attachment security in children with disabilities. *Asia Pacific Education Review*, 10: 561–573. DOI 10.1007/s12564-009-9043-y.

Koren-Karie, N., Oppenheim, D., Dolev, S. and Yirmiya, N. (2009) Mothers of securely attached children with autism spectrum disorder are more sensitive than mothers of insecurely attached children. *Journal of Child Psychology and Psychiatry*, 50: 643–650. DOI: 10.1111/j.1469-7610.2008.02043.x.

Marcu, I., Oppenheim, D., Koren-Karie, N., Dolev, S. and Yirmiya, N. (2009) Attachment and symbolic play in preschoolers with autism spectrum disorders. *Journal of Autism and Developmental Disorders*, 39(9): 1321–1328.

Maunder, R.G., Lancee, W.J., Nolan, R.P., Hunter, J.J. and Tannenbaum, D.W. (2006) The relationship of attachment insecurity to subjective stress and autonomic function during standardized acute stress in healthy adults. *Journal of Psychosomatic Research*, 60: 283–290.

Mikulincer, M. and Shaver, P.R. (2007) *Attachment in Adulthood: Structure, dynamics, and change*. New York: The Guilford Press.

Moore, V. and Goodson, S. (2003) How well does early diagnosis of autism stand the test of time? Follow-up study of children assessed for autism at age 2 and development of an early diagnostic service. *Autism*, 7: 47–63. DOI: 10.1177/1362361303007001005.

Moran, H. (2010) Clinical observations of the differences between children on the autism spectrum and those with attachment problems: The Coventry Grid. *Good Autism Practice*, 11(2): 46–59.

Naber, F., Bakermans-Kranenburg, M.J., Van IJzendoorn, M.H., Swinkels, S., Buitelaar, J.K., Dietz, C. and Van Engeland, H. (2008) Play behavior and attachment in toddlers with autism. *Journal of Autism and Developmental Disorders*, 38: 857–866.

Naber, F.B.A., Swinkles, S.H.N., Buitelaar, J.K., Bakermans-Kranenburg, M.J., Van IJzendoorn, M.H., Dietz, C. and Van Engeland, H. (2007) Attachment in toddlers with autism and other developmental disorders. *Journal of Autism and Developmental Disorders*, 37: 1123–1138.

National Institute for Health and Care Excellence (NICE) (2013) *Autism: The management and support of children and young people on the autism spectrum*. Retrieved 07 28 2015 from: https://www.nice.org.uk/guidance/cg170

National Institute for Health and Care Excellence (NICE) (2015) *Challenging behaviour and learning disabilities: Prevention and interventions for people with learning disabilities whose behaviour challenges.* Retrieved 07 28 2015 from: https://www.nice.org.uk/guidance/ng11

Oppenheim, D., Koren-Karie, N., Dolev, S. and Yirmiya, N. (2009) Maternal insightfulness and resolution of the diagnosis are associated with secure attachment in preschoolers with autism spectrum disorders. *Child Development*, 80: 519–527. DOI: 10.1111/j.1467-8624.2009.01276.x.

Oppenheim, D., Koren-Karie, N., Dolev, S. and Yirmiya, N. (2012) Maternal sensitivity mediates the link between maternal insightfulness/resolution and child–mother attachment: The case of children with Autism Spectrum Disorder. *Attachment and Human Development*, 14(6): 567–584. DOI: 10.1080/14616734.2012.727256.

Oppenheim, D., Sagi, A. and Lamb, M.E. (1988) Infant–adult attachments in the Kibbutz and their relation to socioemotional development four years later. *Developmental Psychology*, 24: 427–433.

Osterling, J.A., Dawson, G. and Munson, J.A. (2002) Early recognition of one year old infants with autism spectrum disorder versus mental retardation: A study of first birthday party home videotapes. *Development and Psychopathology*, 14: 239–252.

Pechous, E.A. (2001) Young Children with Autism and Intensive Behavioral Programs: Effects on the Primary Attachment Relationship. *Dissertation Abstracts International: Section B: The Sciences and Engineering*, 61: 6145.

Pickles, A., Starr, E., Kazak, S., Bolton, P., Papanikolaou, K., Bailey, A. and Rutter, M. (2000) Variable expression of the autism broader phenotype: Findings from extended pedigrees. *Journal of Child Psychology and Psychiatry*, 41(4): 491–502.

Rogers, S.J., Ozonoff, S. and Maslin-Cole, C. (1991) A comparative study of attachment behavior in young children with autism or other psychiatric disorders. *Journal of American Academy of Child and Adolescent Psychiatry*, 30(3): 483–488.

Rutgers, A.H., Bakermans-Kranenburg, M.J., Van IJzendoorn, M.H. and Van Berckelaer-Onnes, I.A. (2004) Autism and attachment: A meta-analytic review. *Journal of Child Psychology and Psychiatry*, 45: 1123–1134. DOI: 10.1111/j.1469-7610.2004.t01-1-00305.x.

Rutgers, A.H., Van IJzendoorn, M.H., Bakermans-Kranenburg, M.J., Swinkels, S.H.N., Van Daalen, E., Dietz, C. and Van Engeland, H. (2007) ASD, attachment, and parenting: A comparison of children with autism spectrum disorder, mental retardation, language disorder, and non-clinical children. *Journal of Abnormal Child Psychology*, 35: 859–870.

Samson, A.C., Huber, O. and Gross, J.J. (2012) Emotional reactivity and regulation in adults with autism spectrum disorders. *Emotion*, 12(4): 659–665.

Seskin, L., Feliciano, E., Tippy, G., Yedloutschnig, R., Sossin, K.M. and Yasik, A. (2010) Attachment and autism: Parental attachment representations and relational behaviors in the parent–child dyad. *Journal of Abnormal Child Psychology*, 38(7): 949–960.

Sigman, M. and Mundy, P. (1989) Social attachments in autistic children. *Journal of the American Academy of Child and Adolescent Psychiatry*, 28: 74–81.

Sigman, M. and Ungerer, J.A. (1984) Attachment Behaviors in Autistic Children. *Journal of Autism and Developmental Disorders*, 14(3): 231–244.

Simonoff, E., Pickles, A., Charman, T., Chandler, S., Loucas, T. and Baird, G. (2008) Psychiatric disorders in children with autism spectrum disorders: Prevalence, comorbidity, and associated factors in a population-derived sample. *Journal of the American Academy of Child and Adolescent Psychiatry*, 47(8): 921–929.

Skirrow, P., Jackson, P., Perry, E.P. and Hare, D. (2015) I collect therefore I am: The role of autonoetic consciousness in collecting and hoarding behaviour in Asperger syndrome. *Clinical Psychology and Psychotherapy*, 22(3): 278–284. DOI: 10.1002/cpp.1889.

Taylor, E.L., Target, M. and Charman, T. (2008) Attachment in adults with high-functioning autism. *Attachment and Human Development*, 10(2): 143–163.

Van IJzendoorn, M.H. (1995) Adult attachment representations, parental responsiveness, and infant attachment: A meta-analysis on the predictive validity of the Adult Attachment Interview. *Psychological Bulletin*, 117: 387–403.

Van IJzendoorn, M.H., Rutgers, A.H., Bakermans-Kranenburg, M.J., Swinkels, S.H., Van Daalen, E., Dietz, C. and Van Engeland, H. (2007) Parental sensitivity and attachment in children with autism spectrum disorder: Comparison with children with mental retardation, with language delays, and with typical development. *Child Development*, 78(2): 597–608.

Van IJzendoorn, M.H., Schuengel, C. and Bakermans-Kranenburg, M.J. (1999) Disorganized attachment in early childhood: Meta-analysis of precursors, concomitants, and sequelae. *Development and Psychopathology*, 11: 225–249.

Volkmar, F.R. and Pauls, D. (2003) Autism. *The Lancet*, 362: 1133–1141.

Walsh, L., Lydon, S. and Healy, O. (2014) Employment and vocational skills among individuals with autism spectrum disorder: Predictors, impact, and interventions. *Review Journal of Autism and Developmental Disorders*, 1: 266–275.

Wan, M.W., Green, J., Elsabbagh, M., Johnson, M., Charman, T. and Plummer, F. (BASIS Team) (2013) Quality of interaction between at-risk infants and caregiver at 12–15 months is associated with 3-year autism outcome. *Journal of Child Psychology and Psychiatry*, 54: 763–771.

Waters, E. (1995) The Attachment Q-set. In E. Waters, B.E. Vaughn, G. Posada and K. Kondo-Ikemura (eds) Caregiving, cultural, and cognitive perspectives on secure-base behavior and working models. *Monographs of the Society for Research in Child Development*, 60: 247–254.

Waters, E., Hamilton, C.E. and Weinfield, N.S. (2000) The stability of attachment security from infancy to adolescence and early adulthood: General introduction. *Child Development*, 71: 678–683.

Werner, E., Dawson, G., Osterling, J. and Dinno, N. (2000) Brief report: Recognition of autism spectrum disorder before one year of age: A retrospective study based on home videotapes. *Journal of Autism and Developmental Disorders*, 30: 157–162.

Willemsen-Swinkels, S.H., Bakermans-Kranenburg, M.J., Buitelaar, J.K., Van IJzendoorn, M. and Van Engeland, H. (2000) Insecure and disorganised attachment in children with a pervasive developmental disorder: Relationship with social interaction and heart rate. *Journal of Child Psychology and Psychiatry*, 41: 759–767. DOI: 10.1111/1469-7610.00663.

Wing, L. and Gould, J. (1979) Severe impairments of social interaction and associated abnormalities in children: Epidemiology and classification. *Journal of Autism and Developmental Disorders*, 9: 11–29.

Yirmiya, N. and Sigman, M. (2001) Attachment in autism. In J. Richer and S. Coates (eds) *Autism: Putting together the pieces*. London: Jessica Kingsley Publishers.

Chapter 6

MAINTAINING THE BOND: WORKING WITH PEOPLE WHO ARE DESCRIBED AS SHOWING CHALLENGING BEHAVIOUR USING A FRAMEWORK BASED ON ATTACHMENT THEORY

Allan Skelly

Northumberland, Tyne and Wear NHS Foundation Trust, Newcastle upon Tyne, UK

> Instead of responding to the person, we typically respond to the behaviour...Most of what passes for assessment appears to be denial about the mutuality of our common condition.
>
> Herb Lovett

> Behaviour can be described as challenging when it is of such an intensity, frequency or duration as to threaten the quality of life and/or the physical safety of the individual or others and is likely to lead to responses that are restrictive, aversive or result in exclusion.
>
> *Challenging Behaviour: A Unified Approach*
> (RCP/BPS/RCSLT, 2007, p. 10)

Challenging behaviour as demonstrated by people with intellectual disabilities (ID) has long been understood to be a functional expression of underlying human needs that we all have (Emerson, 1995). The definition of challenging behaviour has also historically had a practical and conceptually clear focus. The ill-treatment of people at Winterbourne View Hospital in Gloucestershire, United Kingdom is depressingly reminiscent of no less than 18 other official inquiries into

---

Attachment in Intellectual and Developmental Disability: A Clinician's Guide to Practice and Research, First Edition. Edited by Helen K. Fletcher, Andrea Flood and Dougal Julian Hare.
© 2016 John Wiley & Sons, Ltd. Published 2016 by John Wiley & Sons, Ltd.

poor care of vulnerable patients, most of which have recommended more oversight and safeguards to ensure more compassionate care. Bush (2014) demonstrated that many of the findings of the Department of Health (2012) following the scandal of Winterbourne View were very similar to the findings of Howe et al. (1969) into Ely Hospital in Cardiff, UK some 43 years earlier. In the context of repeatedly forgetting the lessons of history, there is an almost total absence of regard to the importance of deep and enduring attachments in the psychological care of those receiving intensive or institutional responses to their behaviour. Bowlby himself had observed how orphans, deprived of early affection and placed in institutions, could become 'affectionless', and he noted the relatively high rate of early maternal separation in children who were caught stealing (Bowlby, 1951). Some psychologists (mostly of the behavioural tradition) at the time, and later, suggested that his findings could not be trusted, as they were largely based on observations of a single orphanage (Tizard, 2009). It has also been suggested that Bowlby failed to understand that children are resilient to primary maternal separation (Clarke and Clarke, 2008) and that institutional care has a role in the care of children and adults (Tizard, 2009). We would now say that a mixed genetic–environmental model is warranted (Bakermans-Kranenburg and Van IJzendoorn, 2011).

However, institutions in themselves do not provide loving care; people do. In this book, we do not contend that people are dependent on a single maternal love object in the first two years of life, as Bowlby originally thought. However, to cope with adversity and loss, resilience that is present in an individual must also be met with security, warmth and appropriate creative activity. While we are children, these conditions are delivered in the context of caring relationships. For people who have ID, such relationships, which are known to be protective for psychological health (Steele, 2002), may have to be provided in a more intense and prolonged way, even for a lifetime.

Currently, when people with severe impairment of intellectual functioning show behaviours that cause grave concern, community services do become more active. The primary approach in the UK is a behavioural analysis that posits the need for pleasure and avoidance of pain and proposes humane and non-punitive ways for the person to meet their needs without having to resort to challenging behaviour. In practice, few practitioners argue that other evidence-based approaches cannot be included to address behavioural problems in those with an ID, but many specialist support services and care providers use a model for intervention based on certain assumptions that have grown out of Applied Behaviour Analysis (ABA).

ABA privileges those features of the person's immediate environment considered to be 'triggers' (stimuli) and states that all behaviour is *functional* (i.e. meets an immediate underlying need), and that behaviour must be *reinforced* (rewarded) to increase in frequency or else it will become less frequent. Behaviour can also be made less likely to occur through *punishment* or aversive methods, and much of the evidence base for ABA was initially based on aversive methods such as use of a water spray, electric shock treatment, time-outs, and so on. Such overtly aversive methods have been found to be both relatively ineffective and ethically unacceptable and have given way to the use of Positive Behaviour Support (PBS), which has wide acceptance, partly because it seeks to minimize any restrictive practices, including aversion (see British Institute of Learning Disabilities Code of Practice, 2014). The change in attitude is apparent within the behavioural field itself (Baker and Shepard, 2005). Scandals about the mistreatment of people with ID may also have hastened the demise of punitive practices, although restraint remains over-used and is currently the subject of much concern, including at UK governmental level (Skills for Care and Skills for Health, 2014).

While clearly a progression from previous practice, few proponents of PBS/ABA appear minded to consider attachment behaviour in the terms described above, still less is there any coherent theory of relational outcomes within PBS, which remains focused on symptom reduction, though it has now included placement maintenance and measureable 'quality of life' within its main goals. While commendable, the maintenance of strong emotional bonds with significant others is not a main focus of outcome research in ID within the behavioural tradition. However, symptomatic change, such as reduction in risk or frequency of behaviours, may vary with improvements in relationship functioning, and indeed behaviour disturbance and worsening of relationships may not even be separate outcome factors (Skelly and D'Antonio, 2008; Skelly, Collins and Dosanjh, 2014).

Attachment theory, although based on empirical work, grew from the Object Relations School of psychoanalysis, which is entirely independent of ABA and the wider behavioural psychology tradition. However, the integration of these two approaches is of great potential value to people receiving the challenging behaviour label, and indeed some evidence of added value in adopting both approaches is emerging (Došen, 2001; Janssen, Riksen-Walraven and Van Dijk, 2003; Sterkenburg, Schuengel and Janssen, 2008; De Schipper and Schuengel, 2010).

This chapter will describe a method of working with referrals for challenging behaviour by developing a containing relationship with the primary caregiving individuals, with particular consideration as to the attachment behaviour of the client and how this affects their caring task. A case example is presented in order to demonstrate the key features of an intervention based on behavioural and attachment principles, including:

- Assessment of behaviour and how it may indicate insecurity and emotional needs;
- Developing a joint hypothesis about the underlying need met by the behaviour;
- Understanding the emotions communicated by the behaviour;
- Resisting 'ejection';
- Emotional 'holding' and 'containment';
- Retaining empathy;
- Ongoing commitment.

Case Example: Tom – Referral

Tom is 44 years old. He has very little language and has been diagnosed with autism and a profound ID. Tom speaks only to say a few phrases that are stereotyped (repetitive, the same intonation and without any obvious relevance to the context). Tom lives in his own home, with a support team who meet his care needs on a 24-hour shift basis.

Tom was referred to the Community Learning Disability Team for psychological help at the age of 40. The referral stated that he 'hits, kicks and grabs' at staff, and requested psychological input so that staff would know how to respond.

The Psychology team met with the staff and Tom. Tom was unable to consent to the psychological work and was seen in his Best Interests under the Mental Capacity Act (2005). The initial consultation held in the staff meeting was very fraught. Staff members were angry with each other and accused each other of 'giving in to his every whim' on the one hand, and 'being cruel' on the other. One member of staff in particular was singled out for criticism as being over-indulgent, even though this was the one person in the care team who never got physically hurt.

The behaviours seemed to occur in the early evening on arrival at home, and in the mornings after breakfast. Staff would prompt Tom to get on the bus to go to the day service. Most staff members ran the risk, at this point, of an assault, in the course of which Tom would run to them, kick, pull at their sleeves, vocalize in a stereotyped way and then run into his room. This caused delays in getting on the bus, but he would usually suddenly get on the bus and seemingly enjoy his day at the centre.

Prior interventions based on behavioural methods had some success in identifying that Tom found transition difficult and was using the behaviour to say 'no', and that he found being asked to leave the house unpredictable. However, staff found the proposed intervention, a visual timetable and simple communication via 'objects of reference' (a picture of a bus on a keyring), helpful only in that he would get on the bus more easily. Tom would still hit them on the way out and was reported to be more violent on his return. In the evenings he was even less responsive and staff felt that he was withdrawing and becoming depressed.

Staff also mentioned that they felt the previous Psychology intervention was very brief and they felt like the conversation had only just started when it was suddenly ended. One member of staff said that she felt 'dismissed'.

IMPORTANT CONSIDERATIONS IN CASES OF CHALLENGING BEHAVIOUR

Before thinking about a model of working with people such as Tom, it is important to name a number of themes that must be kept in mind.

'Reality Orientation' or Acknowledgement of the Person's Level of Emotional and Cognitive Development

When referrals are made to psychological services, there is often little consideration of the true developmental level of the person and what abilities they can be expected to have. Adults with severe or profound

ID are not children, but in terms of the progressive attainment of skills, by definition they tend to develop behaviours that would be expected to be seen in the first years of life, notwithstanding the strengths and weaknesses that can and do occur.

Emotionally connecting to the fact of very limited intellectual abilities can cause discomfort for care staff, professionals and family members and can seem like an insult or even a form of discrimination or prejudice. It is possible to address this by presenting a developmental model that normalizes the behaviour and places it in context, for example Mahler's separation-individuation (Mahler, 1968), or by using psychometric measurement that is accurate and valid, such as the Vineland Adaptive Behaviour Scales (Sparrow, Chichetti and Balla, 2005). Whichever method is used to explain the reality of the person's abilities, it must also be delivered in an empathic way, and with the express intent of accurately identifying what new learning is really fair to expect. In Tom's case, he was expected to get ready to go out as though he was a confident person without ID, without any separation anxiety from his favoured staff and to return without any residual anger towards those whom he felt to have pushed him away earlier in the day.

Bringing History into Mind

As will be apparent from the various contributions to this book, attachment patterns in behaviour, thought and emotion originate early in life, and the person's constitutional resilience will interact with the emotional responsiveness of their environment in infancy. In children with ID, one or both are often lacking, even necessarily so, for a wide variety of reasons, not least the impact of the arrival of the newborn child with a disability, and the effect of this on the parents (see Chapter 3).

One phenomenon that appears to co-exist with many cases of chronic challenging behaviour is the fragmentation of the person's history. No one, least of all the client themselves, holds a clear and integrated account of the person's history and how it may be related to the behavioural issues. This lack of a coherent concept of who the person is and their summative history is almost diagnostic of disorganized attachment and, clinical experience suggests, strongly indicative of emotional abuse or neglect. Some research is also supportive of this view, for example in a study of attachment style in the narrative of direct and indirect psychotherapy, Skelly, Collins and Dosanjh

(2014) found that some degree of physical, emotional or sexual abuse was always present in the narratives of those receiving treatment, with no exceptions. In those rated as 'disorganized' using a newly developed narrative tool (Skelly and Reay, 2013), the accounts lacked coherence from one session to the next, and alleged perpetrators were at times described in positive terms, while at other times vilified. This is sometimes described as 'vacillating object relations' by psychotherapists.

Case Example continued: The Continuing Presentation of Personal History

Tom was emotionally rejected by his birth mother when she noticed his dystonic floppiness in his first year. While contact was made again later, he spent a lot of his childhood in institutional care, where he was seen as undemanding and self-contained, locked into his repetitive behaviours with no apparent interest in others. He had a long history of aggression, usually explained and understood as 'attention seeking' or 'to get rewarded with food or drink'.

Tom's recorded history is one of 'incidents' of aggression that seemed to most people to be random or inexplicable. Clearly, attempts were made by services to remain focused on positive social outcomes in the face of his clear unhappiness and difficulties with communication. Records showed suspicions of bad treatment by other children at times when he was in local authority homes between failed foster placements, including a report of sexual abuse that was not proven or investigated fully.

His school history was one area described positively and with genuine affection in school reports. He was noted to be especially fond of one teacher who developed the 'intensive interaction' method in special sessions with Tom. This coincided with a period of general improvement in his school reports and a dropping away of incident recordings. However, at the end of his school career, this important relationship was not replicated in any subsequent settings. As with most children leaving school, the huge adjustment to be made in moving to adult placement was not addressed with the careful formation of new, intimate

> caring relationships, merely a few teatime visits to the adult home and a day centre, before a move that would have seemed very sudden and revolutionary to him.
>
> No work of any kind had been done with Tom focusing on his losses, which could not even be located in his case notes as an issue.

Realistic 'Dependency'

The expectation within specialist ID services is that of 'normalization', that is that people should be empowered to have as near as possible to a 'normal' adult life (*Valuing People Now*, Department of Health, 2009). This is often understood as living in a relatively small house with one's own bedroom, a job or day placement and a group of friends, voluntarily chosen. Quite rightly, we also expect an absence of neglect or abuse to be part of the ethos and practice of normalization.

A problem with the normalization approach is that people with ID, especially those who have experienced less than optimal early care, may struggle to reach the necessary levels of emotional maturity required to live a 'normal life', leading some to argue that normalization can be a problematic philosophy (Szivos, 1991).

Moreover, more severe levels of ID, such as Tom's, limit the ability of the person to function independently. A realistic understanding of personal and domestic skills can often be achieved, with a balance of new skill learning and care provision (assuming adequate funding). More difficult to achieve is an estimation of the level of emotional and social skill a person has attained, what they can realistically learn and what needs to be scaffolded or provided by others. Tom was not able, for example, to remember (in the sense of a formal understanding of the clock) that he would return at a set time to his home; indeed, he may not understand time well at all, or be able to estimate how much time has passed. He could not, therefore, be expected to be able to contain his anxiety when prompted to leave his comfortable living room.

Moving Past Conditioning Models

While the language of conditioning (e.g. 'boundaries', 'triggers', 'consequences', etc.) is widely used in care services, this is often imprecise, and the narrative that emerges in relation to someone's behaviour can sometimes lack a sense of the person's experience. Using conditioning models may inadvertently function to distance services, individuals and narratives from the deep emotional pain of working with people whose lives contain significant losses and impoverishment. Tom was understood, at the point of referral, as a man with undesirable behaviour that had some poorly understood reason, such as getting something from staff or manipulating them, but not as a man struggling with his history, development or emotional needs. Whether we see the lack of such an approach in cases like Tom's to be a sociological, theoretical or political lack, or even a form of psychological group defence (Stokes, 1994), it is essential that a shift of focus is made in working with people receiving the diagnosis of 'challenging behaviour'. It is not that they 'have challenging behaviour' as some routinely say, as one can 'have' an overactive thyroid, but that the behaviour is signifying something that is needed, and is currently lacking.

Changing the Language of Control to One of Understanding

One element of changing from a behavioural to an attachment-based narrative is to address terms such as 'management' and challenge these as a questionable application of positivist management science to patient care. As such, we recommend always substituting terms such as 'understanding' for 'management' and 'reflection' for 'supplying strategies'. This move from an unthinking, action-based and protocol-driven approach to a more reflective stance, where the underlying need for emotional containment is discovered or re-discovered, is, in our view, absolutely essential to successful work with behavioural issues.

A MODEL FOR WORKING WITHIN AN ATTACHMENT THEORY FRAMEWORK

Assessment: Behaviour, Security–Insecurity and Emotions

Clinicians are strongly advised to meet the person who is named in the referral even though it may be more likely that they will work with staff or a family carer as the main agent of change. Where possible, obtaining consent from the client to the work, making information as accessible as possible, will form essential ethical practice. The referred person should also be included in any decision making, even where they are deemed to lack capacity, taking into consideration their preferences and lifestyle.

Assessment may be formal and include behavioural technologies such as ABC (antecedent, behaviour, consequence) record forms, behavioural explorers, momentary or interval time sampling, and so on, and aim to achieve a functional analysis. A clear and measurable definition of the behaviour of concern, who tends to be present when behaviours occur, what time and other contextual factors such as noise, heat, and so on are very valuable in determining a baseline rate that gives everyone undeniable evidence of what is problematic.

However, it is of equal importance to assess carers' understanding of why behaviours occur, and the appraisals and theories they hold (Phillips and Rose, 2010). Sometimes carers will throw up their hands and state that they believe it 'just happens', based on a kind of deterministic organic cause that has nothing to do with how they act, or they become hopeless that anything they do will help it (Hastings *et al.*, 2003). A lack of belief that the behaviour can change contributes to a seemingly endless, stressful relationship. In these circumstances, it is more likely that they will eventually give up and the person will have to move. Such an outcome is necessarily unhelpful, not just because of the service implications such as finding it hard to remain local to the area of origin (Mansell, 2007) but also because it further breaks the person's attachments, compounding existing difficulties.

A key part of the assessment process is to introduce the idea of emotional security being central to psychological wellbeing. Introductory materials, such as an information sheet, that explain what can indicate insecurity are useful to hand out and serve to introduce the model without picking out specific issues with the case that can seem 'blaming'. In particular, the risks of insecurity can be mentioned in general terms within the research base. The model can also be introduced in simple, positive terms by giving 'five conditions for security': physical safety, emotional predictability, warmth, mutual enjoyment and shared exploration.

Developing a Joint Hypothesis About the Dominant Pattern of Behaviour

Assessment of behaviour should go hand in hand with a clear assessment and discussion of the person's reaction to separation and reunion with carers. This is an appropriate precursor to introducing the concept of emotional insecurity and attachment 'style', by which is meant a practical clinical concept that describes the person's behavioural responses in the *majority* of situations where personal proximity is uncertain (e.g. a stranger walks in, the carer walks out). The various forms of insecure attachment are described elsewhere in this book (see Chapter 2), but just starting a conversation at this point about insecurity and the importance of stability in the person's social universe is very important.

The joint hypothesis should be 'owned by everyone' involved in working with the behaviour: carers, professionals and others. It can be couched in behavioural, psychoanalytic or common-sense language, but should be consistent with the functional analysis and the principles of sound care that breed emotional security, safety, boundaries and fun. The use of punishment (e.g. time out, response-cost, overcorrection, etc.) or emotional withdrawal by the carer should be discouraged.

Examples of a joint hypothesis include that the person:

- Has a difficulty in accepting prompts that involve transition;
- Has an ongoing need for attention and social interaction during waking hours;
- Has a tendency to react as though earlier experiences of being attacked are about to happen again in certain situations;
- Prefers to be alone and to concentrate on their sensory needs.

Behaviour that is defined as challenging receives a hypothesis that is compatible with both the principles of operant conditioning and the principles of attachment theory. In our example above, difficulty in accepting prompts indicates that the person is unable to tolerate the other person signalling that they should engage in something else, that is, move on to the next activity or get outdoor clothes on in preparation for going out. This is also a symptom of an inability or unwillingness to allow others to have agency over one's behaviour. The prompts are perceived, at least some of the time, as stressful, attacking and unhelpful. In our example, this produces the person's internal attachment model of hostility. However, Tom's hostile, angry response to prompts is not just to ward others off, as for some staff, this was not experienced. Why should this be if prompts are always an unwanted stimulus?

In general, challenging behaviour meets underlying needs for (a) social interaction, an activity or basic need (food, drink, toileting), sensory feedback to the body and brain – *positive reinforcements* or (b) making something unwanted stop or go away – *negative reinforcement*. But equally, behaviours of concern are related to the person's tried and tested method of relating to others. So, in our example, the prompting, approaching person is fitted onto the attachment template, and there can be wide variation in whether the attachment behaviour is therefore produced, depending on the extent to which the individual is identified with this template.

The phenomenon of challenging behaviour is a product of interaction, that is, it is socially constructed. It must be perceived by the person 'receiving' it as problematic, or else it would not come to the attention of services. While some behaviours are widely agreed upon as challenging, for example aggression causing injury, others are less clear-cut and are not agreed upon, even within families or care teams. Therefore, challenging behaviour is something that occurs 'between' people. Often, challenging behaviour is conceptualized, initially, in the terms of the receiver (carer). The current carer may feel confused, as the person's behaviours are actually formed as part of the relationship with the original carer from the family of origin. For most, that is infant care by their mother or father. To some extent, then, it is possible that challenging behaviour occurs in response to an internal 'template of care', and may even promote unhelpful, but familiar, responses from the current carer. Psychotherapists sometimes refer to this as a 'transference' relationship, which is both familiar (and in one sense reassuring) and dysfunctional, because it would be more adaptive to respond to the actual care one is receiving now. Since each template is unique, idiosyncratic features can activate the template, such as hair colour, height, tone of voice, and so on.

Case Example continued: Introducing Attachment Concepts to Carers

The Psychology team introduced the idea that Tom was attached to his staff, with some attachments being more secure. The idea that attachment to another person is both helpful and a powerful instinct was also introduced. The Psychology team was keen to suggest that observing variation in the bonds to

> others, and in resilience to stress, is also natural. This validated the varying experiences of staff members and dispelled concerns that some were better staff members than others. It also indirectly raised awareness that we all have an attachment history.
>
> In further conversation with the care team, Tom became understood as struggling with feelings of hostility at separation from his care team. The staff member who was previously vilified for 'babying' him was found to hold some wisdom about his developmental level and his ability to cope with separation and reunion from his care team. The team allowed that the approach of more immediately understanding him, rather than upholding 'boundaries' more appropriate to someone with a higher level of understanding, was a better general approach, although some staff members could not change their approach, which they found distressing. However, reassurance that support from the Psychology team would be ongoing and not withdrawn was also found to be a relief.
>
> Tom continued in the current placement whilst exhibiting various behaviours, albeit more occasionally, that were now considered to be 'part of him', a phrase which seems to indicate acceptance.

Understanding Emotions and Resisting 'Ejection'

Staff teams and foster carers are people first and are as subject to stress and strain as everyone else. A carer may offer a safe, warm and enjoyable environment to a client who has demonstrated challenging behaviour for some time, and is quite practised in it and its pay-offs. This care may not result in the expected feelings of safety, enjoyment and freedom to play. The person may instead evoke feelings of severe hostility, emotional over-involvement, feeling controlled or inappropriately obsessed about. Working with people whose behaviour is fearful and disorganized is not easy and is often not well remunerated, still less valued.

Inevitably, working with people who have ID and traumatic relationship histories can lead to feeling hurt, drained, abused, sulked against or confused. This itself brings about one's own methods of coping based on one's own attachment templates. It is, therefore, important to mention the need for consideration of the emotional skills, support networks and care of professional and family carers.

After a clear assessment, psychological intervention should establish a resistance to 'getting rid' of the person in fantasy or as a real possibility. If the only solution seems to be to move, then the reality of what this will mean in terms of the emotional consequences for all involved should be considered.

The fantasy of ejection to a 'behaviour unit' or a 'new start' in another locality is a main driver of the multiple placement phenomenon, where the people who least need to start over again in their close relationships are forced to do just that. A further unhelpful idea is the 'yet to be learned behavioural skills', where a powerful new technique, vaguely defined as 'de-escalation', or 'mindfulness', and so on is going to remove all risk from the behaviour and render the person unproblematic. While these techniques can be substantial and evidence-based, it is unlikely that they can, alone, end the risk entailed in a challenging behaviour case.

Emotional 'Holding': Containment

There is a common-sense understanding that being physically held can provide comfort in times of stress or loss. Initially, babies will respond to the physical act of holding, but also to soothing communication and calm tones of voice. Later, there can be an emotional 'holding', which does not require physical holding, in the sense of perceiving that someone else understands your distress and empathizes with you. This is, in itself, a method of moderating extreme emotional distress. It may also indicate that the other person will help you practically if they can. In addition, this feeling of empathic understanding indicates that the other person is unlikely to be hostile or dismissive of your distress.

Holding in adult care contexts can therefore mean a physical act (e.g. a hug) or a psychological one (e.g. an empathic conversation), but it is essentially used here as a term that describes the use of one's own emotional skills to reduce the discomfort of another. This subsumes physical care if it is necessary, and it could be contended that effective physical care must always entail empathy, unconditional regard and genuineness towards the other person. It is not lost on those practising this approach that health and social care services require compassion from everyone that works within them, and we regret its loss in poor quality services (Skills for Care, 2014).

However, the person referred for challenging behaviour will often be hard to 'hold'. This does not refer to physical restraint, which is often an act of fear or of risk management, and may be experienced as aversive. By 'holding', we include any act or intended act of care that involves effectively receiving a person's signal of distress, keeping that in mind without retaliating or switching off from it, trying to understand what need is being signalled and responding to that calmly and effectively as much as possible. This process applies to the relationship between the psychological professional and the carer as much as to the carer–client dyad.

Staff Workshops

As can be seen in Table 6.1, staff workshops are a main pillar of intervention. These usually begin with an update and qualitative account of recent behaviour as well as a debriefing of carers or staff who may be physically injured or even traumatized. However, the main focus is to consider how the relationship of the client to the carer is progressing in terms of physical and emotional safety, enjoyment of each other and sufficient fun/stimulation. The hypothesis, couched in behavioural and/or attachment terms, is considered in terms of (a) how well the agreed changes in care could be implemented, and then (b) whether the hypothesis is supported or unsupported by the carer's experience. This inevitably leads to further discussion of the state of the relationship, any threat to its existence and any threat to its quality (warmth) and the enjoyment that can be shared. That is, the process is usually one of a pragmatic discussion, led by the psychologist, of the practical value of the intervention, followed by a deeper and more profound discussion of the person's current relationship to the carer. This is usually led by the carers. Finally, but less inevitably, early attachment experiences are discussed in relation to the current behavioural difficulties and current relationships; these conversations are less predictable in terms of who initiates them.

Table 6.1 A process of working with challenging behaviour referrals with an integrated positive behavioural/attachment approach

Process	Questions to ask	Clinical action
Referral	What is the behaviour? Is there a prima facae case for the diagnosis of Challenging Behaviour?	PRE-ASSESSMENT MAKING CONTACT AND CONTRACTING Indicating possibility of substantial and ongoing support if necessary to signal containment
Assessment	What is the topography of the behaviour? What is the frequency? Who does it happen with? Where and when? What are the beliefs of the carers as to why it happens? Do client behaviour/carer attitudes and beliefs indicate security, hostility or anxious attachment? What differences in view point are there?	FUNCTIONAL ASSESSMENT
	Is there a wish – even if presented as a risk or fear – that the person be gone? What physical and social resources do the carers have to hand? Are they contained by an understanding other (manager, supervisor, professional, family member)? Is there sufficient security in the carer to maintain the bond?	ASSESSMENT OF RELATIONAL ENVIRONMENT ASSESSMENT OF RISK TO CURRENT ATTACHMENTS

(*Continued*)

Table 6.1 (*Continued*)

Process	Questions to ask	Clinical action
	What is the person's level of cognitive functioning? Developmentally, when would such a skills profile be expected to develop (are there age equivalences)? What is the person's need for stimulation (social, sensory, 'fun')? What is the person's need for an available, warm and responsive other?	ASSESSMENT OF EXPECTATIONS OF EMOTIONAL MATURITY AND REALISM ABOUT THE PERSON
Intervention ⇨	How can a joint hypothesis about the behaviour be applied in a way that is meaningful and helpful? How can we express and explain negative or hostile feelings towards the person when they show the behaviour? How do we resist 'ejection' of the person from the placement? How can we 'hold' these feelings without impulsively responding to them when there is hostility? How can we retain empathy while under stress caused by the behaviour, sufficiently to maintain the bond?	PROVISION OF EMPATHIC UNDERSTANDING TO THE CARER NAME AND DEVELOP EMOTIONAL SKILLS AND ASPECTS OF PERSONALITY THAT HELP OR HINDER THIS

	Do the behavioural triggers need to be presented to the person? Why? Is there enough to do during the day? Is dealing with the behaviour a 'main activity' for the carer, or is it incidental to an otherwise busy day? Can a 'liked' consequence be presented for other behaviours that are desirable?	PROVIDING THE PRACTICAL INTERVENTIONS TO MANAGE BEHAVIOUR
	Have we reached an agreed support plan for the behaviour? Is there general confidence that the behaviour is understood and that there are new ways of thinking about it and acting towards it? Does everyone feel included and listened to? Can those not 'on board' be heard and acknowledged?	AGREE A SUPPORT PLAN
Review implementation	Are the features of the agreed plan – • Not implemented at all? • Partially? • More or less in full?	MONITOR IMPLEMENTATION PRIOR TO CONSIDERING OUTCOME

(Continued)

Table 6.1 (Continued)

Process	Questions to ask	Clinical action
Review outcome	Is this possible? It may not be, if implementation does not occur to a sufficient extent. Have ideas about ending the relationship with the carer/(placement) 'gone into remission?' Has the carer remained or improved in their empathic responding now they have a better understanding and containment? Were we wrong about the way we understood the behaviour? Do we need to go back to the start or change our view? Are the risks reduced? Is quality of life better? Can we look at this with a standardized tool?	MONITOR AND PRESENT OUTCOME TO ESTIMATE THE VALUE OF THE JOINT UNDERSTANDING (HYPOTHESIS)
Follow-up	Are there fewer symptoms on standardized assessments? Have the improvements been maintained? Is the relationship still pleasurable? Is the relationship more likely to remain for the medium term?	CHECK ADHERENCE TO IMPLEMENTING PLAN CHECK OUTCOME REMAINS GOOD
Closure	Can we say goodbye for the moment without causing excessive insecurity? Is relapse likely to follow closure?	FINAL REPORT AND EVALUATION OF THE CASE

> ### Case Example continued: Tom's Progress
>
> Tom continued to present with behaviours that could seem suddenly hostile and demanding, usually if he had a reason to be less tolerant (e.g. when he was unwell) and had returned from being out.
>
> Staff brought to an earlier workshop the fact that they get angry with Tom when he hits them. Some actually refuse to speak to him for a while and they have gained the manager's support to 'teach him that if he treats me like that it will have bad consequences for him'.
>
> Initially, the Psychology team argued the need for continued empathy and when discussing the case with each other, they dismissed the staff as 'unprofessional'. However, in supervision they were reminded that the staff members are receiving very threatening emotions and fear for their own safety, leading them to enact some understandable defences against the emotional trauma of working with Tom, and never feeling quite safe around him.
>
> In a later workshop, the Psychology team made a point of acknowledging that Tom was communicating hostility, and that staff would sometimes feel hostile to those who did not hear how difficult this work was, and also that their safety was a priority. Practical strategies became a focus of the session to keep them from physical harm, but the essence of this session was in the effective support of the staff by way of this focus. Their discomfort was understood and acted on, and therefore, the bond with the client was strengthened, with the side effect of a better bond with the Psychology team.

Retaining Empathy

It may appear to be self-evident to state that carers should remain compassionate and empathic towards people they are looking after, but it is perhaps more helpful to acknowledge that this is difficult in the best of circumstances. Processing painful emotions and helping people with emotional insecurity are core parts of this caring role. Moreover, there is also some risk to carers, both emotionally and sometimes physically. Retaining empathy is something that requires both a temperamental calmness and the mindful adoption of an attitude that behaviour problems are communicative, meet an underlying human need and are not necessarily inevitable. Further, the loss of empathy that sometimes occurs, often at the point of most concern about the client or others' safety, may occur unevenly, according to the personality of the carers. If there is more than one carer, this can lead to a form of 'splitting'. A related issue is that carers with good internal security may be able to tolerate negative emotions to a greater extent, but such differences between carers can lead to differing views of what they should be able to 'put up with'. If this leads to a divergence of opinion between carers, one or more carers may become a scapegoat, be seen as wrong-headed or even as the cause of difficulties. It is important to realize, together, that *this is a part of the case*. While people may have more or less extreme emotional experiences in the caring role, a feeling of being 'marginalized' or attacked by the views of others is to be understood as clinical information. A loss of empathy between any party (professional, carer or client) should be raised and discussed.

A truly joint hypothesis about behaviour follows the principles of attachment theory. That is, hypotheses should be created within discussions that are clearly informed, emotionally secure, with unremitting positive regard and with a clear stipulation that all views have value. The explanatory value of the hypothesis can then be tested as a joint venture that is not the view of one of the care network (e.g. the psychologist thinks the behaviour is based on insecurity, the psychiatrist believes it is due to a mental disorder, the speech and language therapist believes it is due to poor scaffolding of communication). It is imperative that, whilst real differences in expertise and experience need to be acknowledged, there are not 'different camps' that have opposing and unresolved ideas about why behaviour occurs.

The antidote to such splitting in a care team is always to set up ongoing conversations until views can be synthesized. Avoidance, at the level of not meeting, not having the conversations or at the level of extreme adherence to viewpoints, can be the negative factor to be removed.

Ongoing Commitment: Getting the Right Support and Protecting Time for Reflection

A formal plan of action with recommendations is not the end of the story and runs the risk of perpetuating a disjointed and episodic approach to challenging behaviour, which, in itself, can be problematic.

For example, Taylor, Oliver and Murphy (2011) found persistence of chronic self-injurious behaviour in 49 people with ID who were initially noted to show such behaviour in an earlier study by Oliver, Murphy and Corbett (1987), with 84% of the original sample continuing to self-injure after more than 20 years. Therefore, it is important for psychological services to remain available and develop long-term relationships with carers, as appropriate. This need not be inefficient, as the total number of contacts can be low, but it is important that psychological services do not project a 'get in–get out' mentality to those who need to hear that an agency is there for them for the long term.

Again, this need not be inefficient from a healthcare provision perspective, as intense observations, urgent support sessions for carers and workshops will give way to monitoring requiring low input from the psychological service, reviews at regular but relatively distant points and eventually discharge and follow-up. The whole process from referral to follow-up can take up to two years, and even then there is no expectation that help must not be requested at a later stage. Indeed, later life events such as bereavements can reasonably be expected to be associated with a new referral (MacHale and Carey, 2002). In our own experience, the commitment in terms of labour hours is often similar to that required by psychotherapy, with an average of 18 sessions from assessment to follow-up, varying between one and two hours' duration depending on the exact purpose. Tom's case, for example, took 23 sessions with a total of 41 hours committed.

Commitment must be two-way. Psychological services must be available to carers to contain difficulties that arise in the future, and carers must commit to the approach. So long as the person's challenging behaviour is understood as meeting an underlying human need, and that their emotional security is linked to the ability of the behaviour to be *contained* within the current care arrangements, it will be possible to cope with the risks involved.

Of course, no care arrangement can function without the right support at a practical and financial level. There must be sufficient financial resource to create a stable care environment, so that carers don't feel worried about their own circumstances. The person must have enough to do each day that is meaningful enough to regulate their sleep pattern, giving them a reason to get up in daylight hours and neither to over-eat to seek comfort nor under-eat due to excessive anxiety. If there are medical issues, such as epilepsy, or possible psychotic experiences, then these need to be considered not only in terms of the medical care required, but also in terms of potential side effects of medication on emotional state and the worry caused by being unwell. Existential issues can exacerbate underlying insecurity in a similar way to bereavement or anticipated loss.

Of course, life happens, and this will mean that challenging behaviour that is long established will tend to re-emerge at times of loss or major change. This includes when staff move on into new roles and at points of major transition, such as leaving college, closure of a day placement or a housemate moving out. Since, as the saying goes, 'grief is the price paid for loving', a person's security-seeking strategy will occur when they lose someone or something that they love deeply (Archer, 1998).

It is healthy that carers are accepted as experiencing satisfaction and dissatisfaction with psychological services on a varying scale. Hoping for a wonderful or magical transformation in the client is not realistic and may lead to feelings of failure and hopelessness. It is therefore helpful for carers to have a forum for the continued discussion of the emotional vagaries of their role. Support can come not only from psychological services, but other groups with reason to empathize, for example the Challenging Behaviour Foundation, the local Autism Society and similar organizations.

Psychological services should therefore hold onto hope that improvements can be made without simplistic ideas about 'cure', or belief in a cure-all technique or philosophy. In a sense, what should remain available is a continued offer of the respectful conversation described above.

Case Example continued: Tom, 18 Months On

Tom continues to be looked after by the same care team. Practical strategies such as the visual timetable, objects of reference and a high level of training in physical interventions (maintaining safe distance, escape and avoiding the use of hands-on restraint) are incorporated into his behaviour support plan.

His team meets the psychological service every three months and things are going so well that he may be discharged soon from the psychological service, on the understanding that a re-referral can be made at any time.

Other interventions have included psychiatric review and a reduction in an antipsychotic medication, a new day service involving a trip with an alternative care provider once a week and a review of his activity plan, taking out those things he seems to find boring.

Staff members believe that understanding Tom's insecurity has been the main intervention. They feel that they have a fuller understanding of his history and no longer see his behaviour as 'random' but part of an early coping strategy. Hoped-for improvements in his skill level have been relinquished, and he is accepted for the skill set he currently has; he is not required to 'become more independent in the toilet' or to 'become travel trained'.

It has been mentioned in the Psychology team's supervision process that communication is clear and smooth whenever problems arise. Staff will call the team, who arrange a call back and a new workshop, and this leads to new ideas in a relaxed, mutually supportive meeting in which staff and the Psychology team feel able to have a positive impact, even though some issues remain very difficult to resolve. While positive outcomes have been recorded in comparison with baseline to post-intervention frequency and severity recordings, staff satisfaction scales and a standardized measure (HoNOS-LD; Roy *et al.*, 2002), staff are still occasionally injured by Tom and can find their work emotionally draining.

REFERENCES

Archer, J. (1998) *The Nature of Grief: The Evolution and Psychology of Reactions to Loss*. London: Routledge.

Baker, P. and Shepard, J. (2005) The rebranding of behavioural approaches for people with learning disabilities and challenging behaviour. *Tizard Learning Disability Review*, 10(2): 12–15.

Bakermans-Kranenburg, M.J. and Van IJzendoorn, M.H. (2011) Differential susceptibility to rearing environment depending on dopamine-related genes. *Development and Psychopathology*, 23: 39–52.

Bowlby, J. (1951) *Maternal Care and Mental Health*. Geneva: World Health Organisation.

British Institute of Learning Disabilities (2014) *Code of Practice for minimising the use of restrictive physical interventions: Planning, developing and delivering training*, 4th edition. British Institute of Learning Disabilities publications.

Bush, A. (2014) *Challenging Behaviour: A Unified Approach; Implications for Psychologists post-Winterbourne*. Presentation to Advancing Practice: Annual Conference of the British Psychological Society DCP Faculty for People with Intellectual Disabilities, Llandudno, Wales, UK.

Clarke, A. and Clarke, A. (2008) Looking back: Discovering human resilience. *The Psychologist*, 21(12): 1084–1086.

Department of Health (2009) *Valuing People Now: A New Three Year Strategy for People with Learning Disabilities*. London: HM Government. www.orderline.dh.gov.uk

Department of Health (2012) *Transforming Care: A national response to Winterbourne View Hospital: Final Report*. London: DoH publications.

De Schipper, J.C. and Schuengel, C. (2010) Attachment behaviour towards support staff in young people with intellectual disabilities: Associations with challenging behaviour. *Journal of Intellectual Disability Research*, 54(7): 584–596.

Došen, A. (2001) Developmental–dynamic relationship therapy: An approach to more severely mentally retarded children. In A. Dosen and K. Day (eds) *Treating Mental Illness and Behaviour Disorders in Children and Adults with Mental Retardation* (pp. 415–427). London: APA.

Emerson, E. (1995) *Challenging Behaviour: Analysis and Intervention in People with Learning Difficulties*. Cambridge: Cambridge University Press.

Hastings, R.P., Tombs, A.K.H., Monzani, L.C. and Boulton, H.V.N. (2003) Determinants of negative emotional responses and causal beliefs about self-injurious behaviour: An experimental study. *Journal of Intellectual Disability Research*, 47(1): 59–67.

Howe, G., Adams, H.L., Cole, J., Davis, D.R. and Jenkins, G.E. (1969) *Report of the Committee of Inquiry into Allegations of Ill-Treatment of Patients and other Irregularities at the Ely Hospital, Cardiff*. London: HMSO.

Janssen, M.J., Riksen-Walraven, J.M. and Van Dijk, J.P.M. (2003) Effects of an intervention program to foster harmonious interactions between deaf-blind children and their educators. *Journal of Visual Impairment and Blindness*, 4: 215–229.

MacHale, R. and Carey, S. (2002) An investigation of the effects of bereavement on mental health and challenging behaviour in adults with learning disability. *British Journal of Learning Disabilities*, 30: 113–117.

Mahler, M.S. (1968) *On Human Symbiosis and the Vicissitudes of Individuation*. Minnesota, US: International Universities Press.

Mansell, J. (2007) *Services for people with learning disabilities and challenging behaviour or mental health needs*. London: Department of Health.

Mental Capacity Act (2005) *Code of Practice*. London: TSO.

Oliver, C., Murphy, G.H. and Corbett, J.A. (1987) Self-injurious behaviour in people with mental handicap: A total population study. *Journal of Mental Deficiency Research*, 31: 147–162.

Phillips, N. and Rose, J. (2010) Predicting Placement Breakdown: Individual and Environmental Factors Associated with the Success or Failure of Community Residential Placements for Adults with Intellectual Disabilities. *Journal of Applied Research in Intellectual Disabilities*, 23: 201–213.

Roy, A., Matthews, H., Clifford, P., Martin, D. and Fowler, V. (2002) Health of the Nation Outcome Scales for People with Learning Disabilities. *British Journal of Psychiatry*, 180: 61–66.

Royal College of Psychiatrists, British Psychological Society and the Royal College of Speech and Language Therapists (2007) *Challenging Behaviour: A Unified Approach*. Leicester: British Psychological Society. Retrieved 30.07.15 from http://shop.bps.org.uk/challenging-behaviour-a-unified-approach.html

Skelly, A., Collins, C. and Dosanjh, M. (2014) *Clinician-judged attachment narrative style and the course and outcome of psychodynamic therapy in people with intellectual disabilities*. Presentation to Advancing Practice: Annual Conference of the British Psychological Society DCP Faculty for People with Intellectual Disabilities, Llandudno, Wales, UK.

Skelly, A. and D'Antonio, M-L. (2008) Factor Structure of the HoNOS-LD: Further evidence of its validity and use as a generic outcome measure. *Clinical Psychology and People with Learning Disabilities*, 6(3): 3–7.

Skelly, A. and Reay, R. (2013) Quality of Early Relationships Rating Scale (QUERRS): A screening tool to aid psychotherapy assessment in people with mild to moderate learning disabilities. *Clinical Psychology and People with Learning Disabilities*, 11(1/2): 33–44.

Skills for Care and Skills for Health (2014) *A positive and proactive workforce. A guide to workforce development for commissioners and employers seeking to minimise the use of restrictive practices in social care and health*. Leeds: Retrieved 07.30.15 from http://www.skillsforcare.org.uk/Document-library/Skills/Restrictive-practices/A-positive-and-proactive-workforce-WEB.pdf

Sparrow, S.S., Chichetti, D.V. and Balla, D.A. (2005) *Vineland Adaptive Behaviour Scales*, 2nd edition. Pearson Clinical Assessment.

Steele, H. (2002) State of the art: Attachment Theory. *The Psychologist*, 15(10): 518–523.

Sterkenburg, P., Schuengel, C. and Janssen, C. (2008) Developing a therapeutic relationship with a blind client with a severe intellectual disability and persistent challenging behaviour. *Disability and Rehabilitation*, 30(17): 1318–1327.

Stokes, J. (1994) Problems in multidisciplinary teams: The unconscious at work. *Journal of Social Work Practice*, 8(2): 161–167.

Szivos, S. (1991) Consciousness Raising: An attempt to redress the more repressive aspects of Normalisation, but not its more positive ones. *Clinical Psychology Forum*, 33: 28–31.

Taylor, L., Oliver, C. and Murphy, G. (2011) The Chronicity of Self-Injurious Behaviour: A Long-Term Follow-Up of a Total Population Study. *Journal of Applied Research in Intellectual Disabilities*, 24: 105–117.

Tizard, B. (2009) Looking back: The making and breaking of attachment theory. *The Psychologist*, 22(10): 902–903.

Chapter 7

PSYCHOTHERAPY AND ATTACHMENT DYNAMICS IN PEOPLE WITH INTELLECTUAL DISABILITIES: A PERSONAL VIEW

Pat Frankish

Pat Frankish Psychology and Psychotherapy Consultancy Ltd, Gainsborough, UK

> **Case Example: Christine**
>
> Christine has been in and out of secure facilities for years. She sets fires in the community and they take her back into residential care. They offer her independent living, which works for a while, usually resulting in her finding a partner and a dog, then she sets another fire and it all starts again. She comes from a big family and has been in one sort of care or another since her mother died when Christine was 12 years old. She is the youngest in her family and several of her brothers also have intellectual disability.
>
> This case example will be referenced throughout the chapter.

INTRODUCTION

This chapter will provide a personal overview of what has happened in the provision of attachment-based psychotherapy for people with intellectual disabilities (ID) over the last 30 years. It will include

---

Attachment in Intellectual and Developmental Disability: A Clinician's Guide to Practice and Research, First Edition. Edited by Helen K. Fletcher, Andrea Flood and Dougal Julian Hare.
© 2016 John Wiley & Sons, Ltd. Published 2016 by John Wiley & Sons, Ltd.

descriptions of the approaches and models of understanding that have informed and helped my work.

People with ID have had access to psychotherapy for about 30 years (Frankish, 2013c). It was extremely difficult to begin to provide such services in a climate of behaviour modification, and equally to understand the significance of the role of the social environment regarding the onset and maintenance of behaviour. We can, to some extent, attribute some of the difficulty to Freud. It is commonly believed that he said that one could not conduct psychotherapy with someone of limited intellectual ability, whereas he stated that higher intellectual abilities were part of the profile of people with whom he worked. With the rise of Behaviourism in the 1960s and 1970s, it became the norm for behavioural approaches to be provided. At that time, institutional care was the majority provision for people with ID.

Even with the move to community-based services, which were often largely a movement of a particular group of people with ID from one facility to another, there was not much change in the way that people with ID were perceived by those caring for and supporting them. The first sets of community provision were 25-bedded hostels, followed by the development of 12- to 16-bedded small-group homes (Nelson and Beecham, 1993). Hence, the experience of people with ID continued to be that of living in groups and of having to behave in an appropriate way for group living conditions. There has always been, and continues to be, a small group of individuals who are not well served by this particular system. They are invariably labelled as people with challenging behaviour, although more recently, it has been accepted that they are people with complex needs and often histories of traumatic life experiences. As a consequence, it has become perhaps more appropriate to describe psychotherapy for these people as 'Trauma Informed Care'. Most of the available living arrangements for people with disabilities were, and still are, antagonistic to the development or maintenance of meaningful attachments.

Case Example continued

Returning to Christine, she has lived in most types of accommodation, from hospitals to 25-bedded hostels, where she did, in fact, establish a friendly relationship with a carer whom she still calls 'Mum'. Christine repeatedly travelled back and forth

> between the hospital, secure facilities and the community, never settling in any one place for long. She was in a 'step down' facility (15 beds) when I first met her.

THE RANGE OF APPROACHES

There is a distinction to be made between psychotherapy that is provided on an individual, one-to-one basis, psychotherapy provided on a group basis and a psychotherapeutic environment that is provided on an indirect basis with an organizational focus. What can be provided, and is provided, varies considerably according to the level of disability of the individual concerned. Organizational approaches are more commonly used with people with more severe disabilities. This is often because of a lack of verbal skills and the consequent difficulty of engaging the individual in one-on-one psychotherapy; on other occasions, this is a result of the difficulty in providing sufficient therapists. Providing a therapeutic environment may also be part of a wider package of care for someone who is traumatized and is receiving individual therapy as well. For Christine, all three approaches were needed. Whichever therapeutic approach is used, it is essential to take attachment needs into account.

INDIVIDUAL THERAPY FOR PEOPLE WITH MORE SEVERE DISABILITIES

Traditional assumptions advocate that it is simply not possible to engage individuals who do not speak, or speak very little, in talking therapy. Many therapists, including myself, challenge this assumption. People with limited cognitive and language abilities still have a range of emotions that need an opportunity for expression. This expression is frequently misconstrued as challenging and extreme behaviour. All behaviour has meaning and helping someone to express this meaning without these behavioural extremes is fundamental to person-centred care and the person's wellbeing.

My first experience of such work was many years ago with a non-speaking child. His extreme behaviours included kicking, spitting, refusing to be dressed or helped and stealing food. He was generally unable to express his feelings and emotions in an appropriate or effective manner. He was seen for ten sessions of one-on-one psychotherapy. As soon as the door closed and we were alone, I noticed his anxiety immediately reduced. He began to relate to me and attempted to show me through play (there was a box of appropriate toys and materials) what had happened to him. The meaning was clear: from the way he treated the toy versions of himself and me, I interpreted that he had suffered physical, sexual and emotional abuse, abandonment and rejection. He would throw toys, stamp on them, spit and such like. He had 'good spit' that he licked back up and 'bad spit' that he smeared over things. He had no sense of self-worth nor any understanding of what had happened to him. As he manipulated the toys in certain ways, an interpretation was offered to the child – during certain manipulations, he would make eye contact and relax a little, indicating that he had at least some understanding of the events that had occurred and knew that I did as well. If it was wrong, he continued with the above-mentioned behaviour until I got it right. The concept of 'right' seemed to hold some significance to him. Although the reasons as to why he presented these behaviours were not established, the intention of these sessions prioritized making the child feel *heard, accepted* and *cared for,* rather than reaching concrete conclusions. During the ten sessions, he became able to relate to others, allowed care staff to look after him and was largely more at peace with himself. This enabled him to eat, sleep and play, leading to a better quality of life. This positive response encouraged me to continue to explore this approach further. It was clear that developing a trusting relationship with me allowed him to translate this sense of trust to other relationships, thus enabling him to trust and rely on other individuals.

This initial exploration, and its subsequent positive outcomes, served as grounds to offer psychotherapy to a variety of other people with severe ID (Frankish, 1989). This branch of therapeutic work led to the development of measurement tools that could assist in evaluating the progress of people in therapy who cannot complete self-report measures. These tools are described later in the chapter. The available clinical evidence in relation to severely distressed behaviour suggests that it is caused by trauma in childhood (Sinason, 2010). Most of the adults referred for such treatment exhibit the same behaviour for many years. If they can be offered therapy earlier, it may help them, and reduce the number of people who are detained in secure forensic or challenging behaviour units in adult life. However, there is still a lack of published clinical evidence looking at whether children with ID and challenging behaviours are receiving appropriate trauma-informed care.

FEATURES OF THE THERAPY

The main rules of mainstream therapy still apply. The time and place need to be regular and protected. Much of the work is long term and sometimes takes a number of years (Jackson and Beail, 2013). The process begins with providing an environment, a secure base, within which attachment has a chance of happening. In my clinical experience, most people who have not had reliable attachment figures will engage in therapy and develop trust quite quickly, settling to work and making fairly rapid progress. Others, who have had no consistent attachment figures, will struggle and take a long time to trust their therapist, refusing, for example, to believe it when the therapist promises to return the following week. The most distressed do need to have daily attachment figures in their care staff as well as a therapist.

Once the initial relationship is established, the work progresses according to the history of the individual. Themes of abandonment and rejection are always present, normally as a consequence of traumatic experiences that are specific to the individual. For example, someone may have been traumatized by a hospital visit or a car accident, and others by sexual abuse and physical neglect. The horror that is imparted on the therapist can be difficult to withstand, and therefore good supervision and support are vital. It is likely that staff, in the past, have distanced themselves from what their service users have endured because of the risk of vicarious trauma and being overwhelmed. Even for professionals, it can often be difficult to hear about traumatic experiences and this has been documented throughout the provision of services for people with ID. The old long-stay hospitals were places of abuse in many cases, and there are still reported cases of non-speaking service users suffering more abuse than others. But even people who can speak may not be accepted as credible witnesses. Therapy strives to offer victims, and victims who have become perpetrators, a safe place to express their feelings regarding their trauma and attempts to help them find a degree of resolution that allows them to have a better quality of life. Therapists approach their work with the view that the past cannot be erased, but it can be reframed.

Traditional therapy requires that the therapist maintains an emotional distance, not putting anything of themselves into the therapy. This is often described using the phrase *maintaining a blank screen*. Undertaking therapy with people with ID is different because it uses an attachment-based model. It takes a more personal approach, requiring the therapist to communicate more compassionately and empathetically. Children and adults with ID may experience the blank screen as persecutory and it does not serve any therapeutic function. This can be challenging for therapists, especially if they are training primarily to work with neurotypical adults and then looking to apply their skills with people with ID. Most practising disability therapists have undergone additional training or found a supervisor who will support them in learning new skills and gaining the confidence to use them (Beail and Jahoda, 2012). Specific training to become a Disability Psychotherapist is essential when working with the most complex cases involving disability and trauma.

Therapist confidence may be negatively affected by the lack of feedback from the individual partaking in therapy. It is not uncommon for people to appear to get worse before they get better. Some people in early adulthood who are being listened to for the first time may experience a sudden outburst of suppressed emotion, and there may be a considerable amount of time before improvement is noted. Therapists often find themselves acting as advocates for their clients, fighting for them to be allowed to continue their therapy to resolution. As mentioned above, it can take a number of years. This is apparent in Christine's case. The trauma and distress she experienced, followed by the repeated patterns of *acting out*, consequently meant that several years of disability therapy were required before the number of incidents was reduced and significant recovery was noted. It is important for the therapist to accept that eradication of the expression of distress is not necessarily the aim, although it clearly is a good sign of improvement. The aim, rather, is to help the individual to live with what has happened to them and to recognize that the presence of triggers that prompt emotional episodes does not mean the traumatic event is happening again. As the client becomes more trusting in the therapist, they begin to develop trust in others, being able to use them as a secure base. Once that has happened they are on the way to being able to use more shared facilities and be more at peace with their lives.

Working therapeutically with people who have severe disabilities will always include some work with care-staff. Though often problematic, rules of confidentiality must be adhered to; it is sufficient to disclose to care staff merely that the therapy concerns past trauma relating to the family, school or previous care placement, for example. In order to avoid triggering emotional episodes, it is important to alert care staff to previous traumas. If this is the case, it is important to make the service user aware that the carer is adjusting the way they work to do so. Integrity of the process, as well as personal integrity, is critical. If the person lacks the capacity to consent to such information sharing, this can be done on a 'best interests' basis to provide appropriate care and support. However, careful thought should be given as to what is specifically required rather than sharing all such information.

EXAMPLES OF ISSUES AND HOW THEY ARE WORKED WITH

There is no doubt that the main issues that present in psychotherapy with people with ID are abandonment, rejection and cruelty. In the latter group, sex and violence feature heavily. Some people have been abused repeatedly by family or care staff, others have been subjected to traumatic attacks that may be a one-off but have had severe consequences. Rejection, adoption and even returning to care are other issues and thus the fear of, and actual, abandonment features frequently. There are also those specific experiences that anyone might find anxiety-provoking, like getting lost, or fear of something that was involved in a frightening experience that wasn't understood. I have worked with people who have been frightened by the sea, trains, cars, colours, epileptic seizures, siblings, hospital admissions and many more things. What matters is that the fear is recognized and accepted for its significance to the individual. A commonly occurring feature of distress is the absence of positive attachment figures to provide comfort and support.

I have worked with several psychotherapy service users, similar to Christine, who have developed patterns of serious self-harm, usually cutting, or have developed a negative relationship with food, following on from early emotional trauma. Their low self-esteem often means that they do not put any value on themselves. Delving into their history shows disturbed relationships in childhood, followed by inadequate institutional responses to their needs. Most have been receiving support from social care and have frequently accessed acute services such as Accident and Emergency hospital departments. They appear to be desperate for attention and affection but mostly receive irritation and criticism instead. The few individuals who do offer support to the service users are often rejected by those they care for, subsequently leading to feelings of frustration, which can be a negative experience for all involved.

Beginning therapy with people such as Christine can be difficult. They do not trust because they cannot trust. They will miss appointments, arrive late, leave early, refuse to talk, speak so quietly that you cannot hear and such like. These behaviours are designed to check that you care enough to keep going and that you will still be there next time. Only after this has been established will clients begin to talk about traumatic and sensitive events, both in their past and present. Gradually, the client will become more comfortable listening to the therapist's interpretations, which will consequently lead to appropriate resolution and reframing. It is not uncommon for it to take between three and six months of therapy before the client feels at ease enough to start the intervention work. Some people refer to this as pre-therapy (Prouty, 2001).

As most of these individuals will be living in supported care settings, it is important to gain their permission to share some things with their support staff. This is in order to enable them to change the way they behave and for them to work together with the client in the best way. Some clients will present visible signs of distress without recognizing what they are or why they are triggered. If staff can be taught to recognize the signs, they can help by redirecting or engaging in conversation. Once there is a sense of shared endeavour, there is more rapid progress. If trust is established and then broken, serious breakdowns can occur. When a breakdown of trust does happen, it is vital for the carer to apologize and express to the client the significance this will have. The individuals involved must openly discuss the incident so the client is reassured that this is not necessarily the catastrophe they perceive it to be and can be learned from. Over time the incidents become less frequent and recovery much quicker. The individual becomes more competent in looking after themselves and processing the distress, without being left feeling helpless.

The therapist must establish a relationship based on trust and reliability. We need always to maintain appropriate professional boundaries in relation to things outside of the therapy, whilst simultaneously remaining approachable and personable. Being with the client during a time of distress or an emotional episode enables them to have a positive therapeutic experience. Recognizing and accepting that there are people who have always been vulnerable because of their disability and, on top of this, have suffered extremes of emotional trauma, is hard, and vicarious trauma needs to be recognized and worked through in supervision. It is everyone working together that offers the best outcome (Beail, 2003, 2013; Beail *et al.*, 2005, 2007).

TRAUMA-INFORMED CARE – THE NECESSARY ELEMENTS

Through taking account of the attachment dynamics and the need for a secure emotional base, it has been possible to arrive at a comprehensive model of trauma-informed care. My own research has informed this approach, together with my experience of working with both institutionalized people and those who have never been in an institution at all, across all age groups. My own work practice is now based primarily on this approach (Frankish, 2013a), and it was used with Christine, as described below.

The model incorporates four specific elements. The first is the provision of a secure physical living environment that is a safe base but not usually or necessarily a secure unit. Sometimes a secure unit is required to provide the external elements of security and safety. More usually, the safe base is an ordinary house in the community with a secure tenancy which allows for any breakages to be repaired rather than leading to eviction. Christine was fortunate to be living in a residential facility owned by a personal friend, who was able to be persuaded to accommodate this need.

The second element is a sufficient amount of staff to provide regular, constant and reliable contact with a trusted person in order to help create a safe emotional base. This often means the presence of a one-to-one staff member 24 hours a day, including a member of staff who 'sleeps in' the building. These two elements provide a substitute for the original security of maternal presence and affection. In Christine's case, the staffing level was adequate enough to provide this and they were willing to be trained so they were able to offer the level of attachment and emotional support needed.

The third element is provision of training and support for the staff. This ensures that they both understand what is required to provide the aforementioned safe emotional base, and that they receive the support needed to cope with any emotional stress they may experience after spending long periods of time with someone who is traumatized. Most care staff are paid very low wages, however policy has been implemented that guarantees that they are paid as much as can be afforded. Thus, staff members feel more supported and feedback indicates that they are willing to do the work as long as they feel valued. For Christine's staff, regular support meetings were held to make sure that this was the case.

The fourth element is individual psychotherapy for the traumatized individual. In order to ensure these four elements are synonymous with the individual's specific needs, it is essential that a further specific assessment is completed. For example, in Christine's case, the therapy lasted for eight years on a weekly basis. In that time she developed a sense of herself as a good enough person and moved on a step closer to living in the community.

ASSESSMENT FOR ATTACHMENT-BASED PSYCHOTHERAPY

The assessment process for attachment-based psychotherapy also includes four elements. A thorough history is beneficial where the information is available. Christine's history included emotional, sexual and physical abuse together with abandonment and loss of key people in her life.

The second is a measure of intellectual capacity. This can be a standardized assessment tool such as the *Wechsler Adult Intelligence Scale* (WAIS-IV; Wechsler, 2008), the *Wechsler Abbreviated Scale of Intelligence* (WASI-II; Wechsler, 2011) or *Raven's Standard Progressive Matrices* (SPM; Raven, Raven and Court, 2003). The aim is not to arrive at an IQ score but to get an indication of the flexibility of mind and intellect of the individual. Formal testing had been completed for Christine and this revealed that she was functioning at a mild level of ID. She persevered over many years to learn to read and write.

The third element is an assessment of the person's psychological wellbeing or mental health, and is usually measured using the *Brief Symptom Inventory* (Derogatis, 1993), but can also be assessed with other tools. If there is the possibility that psychotropic medication might be of benefit to the person, then this should be considered within the context of the multi-disciplinary team, although care must be taken to ensure that medication is not used for behavioural control or sedation. However, if medication has already been prescribed for behavioural control, it should ideally be reduced in the early stages of the new provision, assuming it has been possible to offer an intervention based on the model of meeting the emotional needs. Christine was already prescribed multiple medications and, though the psychiatrist could not be persuaded to take her off all of them, they were greatly reduced.

The fourth element would be some form of projective test. Projective tests are used because they remove the element of self-report. There has been much criticism of projective testing, but I was introduced to them early in my career and have used them consistently since. They provide information that is not available otherwise, and it has been possible to show that they measure change over time. There is a brief handbook, based on many years of clinical experience, on the use of the *House, Tree, Person* and the *Object Relations Technique* available from the website www.frankishtraining.co.uk. These tests indicated that Christine had significant emotional developmental delay, insecurity, low self-esteem and was functioning at an emotional level of a child of less than two years old. Her need for secure attachments was evident and had to be met if she was to make progress.

Object Relations Technique

There are three projective tests that I recommend for use for people with ID. They have been well tried and tested and there is some guidance available on their use with this population. The first of these, for use with people who are verbally able and can engage in interaction, is the *Object Relations Technique* (ORT), which was developed at The Tavistock Clinic for use with neurotypical adults (Phillipson, 1988). The ORT uses a set of pictures which are blurred and ambiguous. The individual is asked to say what they can see in the picture, what they think is happening and what they think will happen next. They can be prompted with questions during the test if necessary. The pictures have different numbers of people in them, and different levels of ambiguity. The responses to the pictures are analysed and an opinion formed about the level of object relations that the individual has reached and is functioning at (one person, two person, three person or group).

My clinical experience indicates that people who are functioning at a *one-person* level have had little experience of any safe attachments, will be very fragile with a fairly high risk of breakdown and may not be suitable for exploratory therapy. They would therefore be offered supportive or indirect therapy. Anyone who has not progressed from the one-person level has not had the benefit of an early attachment figure, which has impaired their sense of self. We have found that people who are functioning at the *two-person* level have trauma associated with the primary relationship with the mother or primary carer and may have a diagnosis of borderline personality disorder as well as ID. Their primary attachment will have been ambivalent or hostile. People who are functioning at the *three-person* level will have more oedipal issues, such as competition, jealousy and difficulty functioning in relationships where there are more than two people. They will have had difficulty detaching from their primary attachment figure.

People who are functioning at the *group level* will achieve a reasonable level of object relations and may be able to engage in group therapy. Most people with ID and complex needs, that is those with trauma in their history, will be functioning at a one- or two-person level. These individuals need a therapeutic environment as well as individual therapy or therapeutic support. The initial trauma will have occurred in the absence of secure attachment figures (see Fairbairn, 1954 and Shaw, 2002 for an overview and exposition of Object Relations Theory).

The House, Tree, Person Test

The second projective test that is used widely is the *House, Tree, Person* (HTP; Buck, 1948), which was also originally developed at The Tavistock Clinic for use with neurotypical children in therapy. The premise behind the HTP is that drawings which are done quickly with minimal thought will provide insight into the unconscious. I have used this test extensively and gathered a significant amount of unpublished data regarding its effectiveness in showing change over time. If the HTP is used for assessment purposes, it is vital that it is not used in the therapy, since this will negate its usefulness for reassessment at the end of therapy. A detailed description of how to do it is available (www.frankishtraining.co.uk). If the test is used incorrectly, the results become invalid. Despite being a fairly simple assessment, if used correctly, it is a potentially very useful tool. The exposing nature means it is of the utmost importance that the therapist respects and takes the drawings seriously, as to do otherwise could potentially cause embarrassment and subsequently a breakdown in trust.

The three drawings are looked at together as a collective, to see if they are of similar size on the paper, have a similar style of drawing – shaded lines or a heavy pencil stroke, for example – and to see if they look as though they fit together. If one drawing is clearly not synonymous to the drawing style of the others, it is an indication of disturbance in that area of development. If all of the pictures are disturbed in some way, that is an indication of the degree of difficulty that the person is experiencing. If someone is engaged in therapy for a long period of time, it is usual to complete the HTP at annual intervals. The test gives an indication of the individual's basic security, ego development and identity.

Sometimes the drawings show deterioration at the first retest, as the individual becomes more aware of their internal difficulties.

But the test at the end of therapy invariably shows improvement in all three areas. Although the work has not been published, the clinical evidence would suggest that people in therapy draw differently at the end of therapy, and that people not in therapy will draw the same drawings, after a period of time, as they did the first time.

All of the development demonstrated and elicited by the projective tests reflects the quality of the early childhood attachments. The development of object relations happens in the context of the primary attachment relationship. The development of the security, ego and identity shown in the HTP occurs in the context of this relationship. The choice of test depends on the ability of the individual to complete them. They are essentially assessing the same thing, namely the quality of the primary attachment to a significant other.

Observation and Measurement of Early Emotional Development Within the Context of the Primary Attachment Figure

In addition to the tests mentioned so far, there is a third approach which adopts an observational methodology. This is particularly useful for people who do not use speech to communicate. The observational methodology is designed to identify the stage of emotional development that the person has reached, so that an intervention can be planned that meets the needs of that emotional developmental stage. The stage model comes from the writings of Mahler, Pine and Bergman (1975/2008) and has been adapted for use with people with ID (Frankish, 2013b).

The research carried out regarding the reliability and validity of this methodology formed the basis of my doctoral study. Essentially, progression from one stage to another can only happen in the presence of a secure attachment figure who should ideally be present from the early developmental stages. However, where an attachment figure is provided later rather than earlier in life, progress can still be facilitated (Frankish, 1989; 1992). The research demonstrates that a valid and reliable assessment can be completed in 40 minutes, although it does take some practice before the therapist can carry out the assessment to the best standard. The test requires that the observer (who may be different to the therapist) observes for 20 seconds and then writes for 40 seconds continuously until 40 data points are reached. These are subsequently coded for the four different levels of emotional development.

Code 1 refers to the *differentiation stage*, which, in typical development, relates to the age range of a few weeks to about eight months old. This includes lots of self-referenced behaviours and an absence of sought contact. *Code 2* regards the *practising stage*, which relates to approximately seven or eight months to about fifteen months in typical development. This is a stage wherein the brain is developing rapidly and the child becomes able to do lots of different activities. The newly available behaviour is practised repetitively until it is mastered, and can serve as a catalyst for further learning of other behaviours. In average development this is a very rapid process as the child becomes able to roll, crawl, move about, pick things up, throw things and so on. For people with ID, this process may be interrupted and the child becomes stuck with certain behaviours. These behaviours are commonly referred to as *stereotypical* behaviours but, from the psychodynamic perspective, they are instead referred to as *practising* behaviours. This is fundamentally an umbrella term for all of the behaviours that are part of being stuck at a certain emotional level.

Code 3 concerns *rapprochement behaviours*. Rapprochement behaviours occur during the stage wherein interactions with other people begin and in typical development are present from approximately 15 to 24 months. The first signs of early rapprochement can be the word 'no', beginning to play passing games and actively seeking attention. Once someone has reached the early rapprochement stage it becomes possible to engage in some negotiation and lots of two-way interaction. Once rapprochement has become valued, the individual moves on to *Code 4*, which is *late rapprochement*. This involves further development of the two-way interaction and the beginnings of independence. Thus, an individual with ID who has reached the late rapprochement stage will, typically, be able to negotiate with others, undertake 'if–then' types of activities, answer questions and come up with ideas of their own about what they would like to do.

The end of the late rapprochement stage, if it is reached, is *individuation*. The child or adult with ID who is individuated can more readily modulate their emotional responses. They become able to engage with more people, to cooperate, to choose and to be able to use their cognitive ability usefully. When adopting a cognitive approach, the late rapprochement stage must first be reached (Prouty, 2001). Reaching the individuation stage is an indication that the individual in question can undergo group work and therefore this therapeutic approach may best suit them.

The above three approaches, the ORT, the HTP and the observations, arrive at the same information by different routes. They establish the level of emotional development that is to be worked with, which will be a reflection of the individual's attachment relationships and experiences.

Using the Assessment Data

Once the assessments have been completed, usually by the proposed therapist, it is possible to draw up a profile that informs the therapy and support package that the individual requires. Sometimes it is necessary to illustrate the point and to describe the differences between the person's emotional, cognitive and physical developmental age. So, for example, if someone is assessed as having an intellectual capacity at the mild ID level, but is living in a physical body that is 28 years old and is then found to have an emotional developmental stage equivalent to 18 months, it becomes easier to see why they may be having difficulty living in the environment within which they are meant to survive.

Winnicott (1965) spoke about the need for synchrony between physical, emotional and cognitive development and this is, to some extent, what is being captured here. What is known from clinical work is that if you address the person's emotional developmental stage and facilitate development in this area to a higher stage, there is an increase in the availability of their cognitive ability. This is linked to Winnicott's work on the impact of anxiety on learning. The implication is that more securely attached individuals are less anxious and therefore can learn more. In my own experience, I have known individuals to be moved from ID services to mainstream services after therapy as they have become able to function at the low average level of ability.

KEY FACTORS IN INTERVENTIONS FOR PEOPLE WITH MORE SEVERE INTELLECTUAL DISABILITIES

There are some key features of any intervention with someone who has arrested or delayed emotional development. One element is the availability of a reliable significant other (an attachment figure) and staff who are on a first-name basis with their clients. The client must constantly be in the presence of an attachment figure. Even when there is a shift change, the transfer from one member of staff to another must occur professionally and in the presence of the person being supported. This is similar to the way that one would make sure that a young child is handed over formally at nursery.

Although the needs of adults with severe ID are not the same as children who attend nursery, there are similarities. For example, the adult in question will not necessarily trust or remember the person who is leaving after they leave. To avoid a breakdown of trust, they must therefore be encouraged to believe that there will always be somebody there to support them. Details of previous losses are not usually provided, but their presentation may indicate that reliable attachment figures have not been present in childhood. In some instances, the client may have been fostered or adopted and in others the attachment figure may have died. During my time as a clinical psychologist, it has become evident that the more extreme cases of interrupted development are usually due to early childhood trauma and/or abuse.

The attachment figure does not have to work one-to-one with the person all the time but they must be available at *any* time, just like a mother would be available to a young child in the home. In situations where there are not enough staff to allocate on a one-to-one basis, it may be sufficient to allocate people by name to the staff in a group context. Thus, for example, in a hospital ward with sixteen clients and four staff, the staff would each be allocated four named people at the beginning of each shift. They would introduce themselves to the relevant clients saying 'I am your person for this shift' and then make regular contact with those individuals to meet their needs, asking them to approach the same person each time they have a need to be met. This is the nearest that we can sometimes get to the ideal. In situations where people are in single-person services with 24-hour staffing, they can be clear about who is there for them at any one time, with no ambiguity.

It is evident, from my own clinical work, that in order to facilitate the development of a safe, trusting relationship and to secure an attachment figure, in some cases 24-hour, one-on-one services are required without compromise. Though it is never possible to provide the same attachment figure all the time, there is always a substitute. In a single-person service, the staff meet on a regular basis to ensure that they are working to the same care plan and will use a communication book at all times. In Christine's care plan, six people were identified as her team. This meant that one of them was on duty at any one time, and they knew that they were there to attend to her needs. Christine knew who to go to if she needed something. This method was so successful that it was established as a pattern for other residents. The staff teams met regularly to confirm that they were using the same approach with each client. The regular meetings ensured each staff member was certain in what was expected of them and consequently saw benefits such as increased job satisfaction, decreased staff turnover and decreased incidents.

WAYS OF WORKING: STAGES OF EMOTIONAL DEVELOPMENT

The way that members of staff work with their clients depends on the stage of emotional development at which they are functioning. This clearly relates to their ability to attach and trust, but all people who are pre-individuation must know they have an emotionally safe base. Insecurely attached or non-attached people, in my experience, have difficulty trusting that their needs will be met. Some of them will be so impaired in their emotional development that they will function at the early stage of differentiation, which typically occurs in the first few months of life. They have no trust that their needs will be met, and will almost certainly be unable to articulate what their needs are. They may appear to be withdrawn and diagnosed as autistic, which demands additional considerations, but does not limit the suitability of this approach. In order to develop the ability to make contact with another person, it is necessary to put in place a contact programme. The aim here is to ensure that the interaction is not only relatively intense, but it is provided on a regular basis, perhaps in short bursts but over a long period of time. So it may not be an intensive interaction for a period of half an hour or an hour, but rather a short burst of interaction every half an hour or every hour. The time interval depends on the availability of staff who can carry out the programme. It is vital that the frequency of interval is maintained, so it must be set at a realistic level. Assuming that the staff available can maintain interactions with their clients every 30 minutes, the staff member must visit the individual every half an hour and should do or say something positive. At no point do they ask anything of the individual. The staff member, for example, may take a drink into the room, smile, make physical contact, carry out an activity and will definitely make emotional contact. At times it may be difficult to think of things to say or do, but it is sufficient to just touch the arm and smile, thus providing a sense of warmth. What happens then is that in a relatively short time, days or weeks, the individual starts expecting visits. As soon as this happens, and the client looks to see who is turning up at the expected time, it is possible to move to an intermittent time schedule and this will be more reinforcing. It is likely that individuals who are stuck at this stage will remain there for many years and never understand the significance, nor the point of, engaging with another human being. Therefore, the first time they even show a little interest in doing so can be very exciting.

> ### Case Example: Steven
>
> Steven was aged 18 when referred and spent all his time aimlessly wandering around the house and garden, not connecting to or engaging with anyone. He had spent most of his life in care and had never been settled with secure attachments. Initially, he didn't respond when approached but, when a structured schedule of contact was put in place, he began to respond after about ten days and started looking to see who was coming to him. After that he gradually became more connected and involved with other people, and went on to learn new social as well as practical skills, substantially improving his quality of life.

'Practising' follows and involves the development of activities, within the context of the relationship with the significant other. This may be the therapist, but is usually the direct support staff, who have become familiar and trusted. At this stage, the individual is still very self-referenced and not ready to engage in any give-and-take reciprocal behaviours. However, they are able to pay more attention to what is going on around them and do show signs of valuing the attention of their significant other. The availability of the named person is still a vital requirement at this stage. The practising stage corresponds to the age nine to fifteen months in a child who is developing without hindrance, the time of rapid development in vocal and loco-motor skills. It may be that someone with an ID has limited vocal and loco-motor skills. However, most people will have some ability to vocalize and move. At this stage, it is helpful to draw attention to whatever is happening in the immediate surroundings. So, for example, if walking along a road, red cars, green trees or a yellow tractor, stepping down from the curb, stepping up, walking through a gate and so on can all be pointed out. What is happening is encouragement for the individual to see the world in which they are living, to teach them to pay attention to people and to the surroundings and to begin to trust in the fact that some things are reliable (for an example of this sort of intervention, see Frankish, 1992).

The next stages of early and late rapprochement involve the development of relationships and the management of interactions, with the individual gradually taking more of a lead. So, in the early stages, the individual is beginning to express a preference, maybe saying or indicating 'no' or indicating a choice. They are beginning to recognize that they have some agency, they are not just responding. As the stages continue, taking about two years overall (Frankish, 2016), the degree of independence increases and the sense of self grows (Frankish, 1992).

CONCLUSION

People with ID who have experienced traumatic experiences relating to their early attachment figures necessarily require trauma-based care to relieve distress and improve their quality of life. Many people with ID have not been able to develop secure attachments in early life and have gone on to 'fail' in care provision because of their inability to attach and trust. In the absence of positive experiences, they become stuck at primitive stages of emotional development. Through compliance and saying the *right things*, those with higher cognitive abilities can sometimes hide this. This works until they are triggered by something, and then their distress overwhelms them. At this point the attachment need becomes more obvious and a therapeutic intervention becomes more possible.

Much of my own work has focused on how to identify the problematic issues for an individual. I have realized, after many years of practice, that the unconscious emotional state can be well hidden, especially when people have verbal language and know how to hide indicators. This is well accepted in people without ID but has not been granted the same prominence in ID services. Effective systems of measurement are crucial for identifying the right starting point of an intervention. An attachment-based intervention, whether it is individual therapy or something less direct, has been shown to be effective and should be accessible to everyone who would benefit from it. The clients whose attachment has been disturbed, absent or negative are usually those who have been misguidedly labelled *challenging* or *unmanageable*, thus exacerbating the problem. Identifying the issue and offering intervention at the right level is effective and necessary.

REFERENCES

Beail, N. (2003) What works for people with mental retardation? Critical commentary on cognitive-behavioural and psychodynamic psychotherapy research. *Mental Retardation*, 41: 468–472.

Beail, N. (2013) The role of cognitive factors in psychodynamic psychotherapy with people who have intellectual disabilities. *The Psychotherapist*, 53: 8–10.

Beail, N. and Jahoda, A. (2012) Working with people: Direct interventions. In E. Emerson, C. Hatton, K. Dickinson, R. Gore, A. Caine and J. Bromley (eds) *Clinical Psychology and People with Intellectual Disabilities* (2nd edition, pp. 121–140). Chichester: Wiley-Blackwell.

Beail, N., Kellett, S., Newman, D.W. and Warden, S. (2007) The dose effect relationship in psychodynamic psychotherapy with people with intellectual disabilities. *Journal of Applied Research in Intellectual Disabilities*, 20: 448–454.

Beail, N., Warden, S., Morsley, K. and Newman, D. (2005) Naturalistic Evaluation of the Effectiveness of Psychodynamic Psychotherapy with Adults with Intellectual Disabilities. *Journal of Applied Research in Intellectual Disabilities*, 18(3): 245–251.

Buck, J. (1948) The H-T-P technique, a qualitative and quantitative scoring method. *Journal of Clinical Psychology Monograph Supplement*, 5: 1–120.

Derogatis, L.R. (1993) *Brief Symptom Inventory*. Oxford: Pearson.

Fairbairn, W.R.D. (1954) *An Object Relations Theory of the Personality*. Oxford: Basic Books.

Frankish, P. (1989) Meeting the emotional needs of handicapped people: A pyscho-dynamic approach. *Journal of Mental Deficiency Research*, 33: 407–414.

Frankish, P. (1992) A psychodynamic approach to emotional difficulties within a social framework. *Journal of Intellectual Disability Research*, 36: 559–563.

Frankish, P. (2013a) Facing emotional pain – a model for working with people with intellectual disabilities and trauma. *Attachment: New Directions in Psychotherapy and Relational Psychoanalysis*, 7: 276–282.

Frankish, P. (2013b) Measuring the emotional development of adults with intellectual disabilities. *Advances in Mental Health and Intellectual Disabilities*, 7(5): 272–276.

Frankish, P. (2013c) The pain of difference. *The Psychotherapist*, 53: 1–3.

Frankish, P. (2016) *Disability Psychotherapy – Innovative approaches to trauma informed care*. London: Karnac Books.

Jackson, T. and Beail, N. (2013) The practice of individual psychodynamic psychotherapy with people who have intellectual disabilities. *Psychoanalytic Psychotherapy*, 27: 108–123.

Mahler, M., Pine, F. and Bergman, A. (1975/2008) *The Psychological Birth of the Human Infant: Symbiosis and individuation*. New York: Basic Books.

Nelson, A. and Beacham, J. (1993) *Costing Community Care PSSRU*. Canterbury, UK: University of Kent.

Phillipson, H. (1988) The use of ORT as a facilitation of motivational process: Some implications for a range of applications with special reference to subliminal activation of preconscious processing. *British Journal of Projective Psychology*, 33(1): 84–105.

Prouty, G. (2001) The practice of pre-therapy. *Journal of Contemporary Psychotherapy*, 31(1): 31–40.

Raven, J., Raven, J.C. and Court, J.H. (2003) *Manual for Raven's Progressive Matrices and Vocabulary Scales*. London: Pearson.

Shaw, M. (2002) *The Object Relations Technique: Assessing the individual (plates and manual)*. New York: ORT Institute.

Sinason, V. (2010) *Mental Handicap and the Human Condition: An Analytical Approach to Intellectual Disability*, revised edition. London: Free Association Books.

Wechsler, D. (2008) *Wechsler Adult Intelligence Scale – Fourth Edition (WAIS-IV)*. London: Pearson.

Wechsler, D. (2011) *Wechsler Abbreviated Scale of Intelligence – Second Edition (WASI-II)*. London: Pearson.

Winnicott, D.W. (1965) *The Maturational Processes and the Facilitating Environment*. London: Karnac Books.

Chapter 8

ADULT ATTACHMENT AND CARE STAFF FUNCTIONING

Carlo Schuengel[1], Jennifer Clegg[2], J. Clasien de Schipper[1] and Sabina Kef[1]

[1] Section of Clinical Child and Family Studies, Faculty of Behavioural and Movement Sciences, VU University Amsterdam, The Netherlands
[2] Institute of Mental Health, University of Nottingham, UK

Box 8.1 Excerpts from Adult Attachment Interviews with Care Staff Members

Excerpt from the adult attachment interview with a care staff member with an autonomous-secure mental representation of attachment:

> My own attachment, of course, when I was five, with my parents, also did help me. That's why also – I can empathize with the clients, as in: well, yes, I know how it is to not live with your natural people and to be brought up in a large group. So I think that has all some advantages.

Excerpt from the adult attachment interview with a care staff member with a dismissing-insecure mental representation of attachment:

> So, I don't want to say that I am very strict, because the difference is, when I am here at work, then I am much more eh, eh more disciplined, towards them. I am the one who decides when things go too far for me. When, for example, a resident asks for something

---

Attachment in Intellectual and Developmental Disability: A Clinician's Guide to Practice and Research, First Edition. Edited by Helen K. Fletcher, Andrea Flood and Dougal Julian Hare.
© 2016 John Wiley & Sons, Ltd. Published 2016 by John Wiley & Sons, Ltd.

> three or four times, I would say, 'I have given you the answer, that's that.' You know, it's over now and then I would not listen any more. And then it is really finished for me.
>
> Excerpt from the adult attachment interview with a care staff member with an unresolved mental representation of attachment:
>
> I think that it always – it will have influence – and that you always wish for doing things better than your parents, do it different than your parents – when you have your own children or the children you work with or the clients you work with…well, that you just – want to be a bit more caring than…I think that all of this has influence. On how one works now. I think it is very important how people look like, I think it's very important that they look clean. No, but eh, no, I think it's just very important, that, that just appearance is very important, how people look, I think, and well cared for. But I think that I have got that from home.

Care staff around the world make huge differences every day in the lives of people with intellectual disabilities (ID). Care staff provide support, advice and protection, and may scaffold the autonomous exploration and development of people with ID. By doing so, they enrich the network of meaningful social relationships that humans need to flourish (Uchino, Cacioppo and Kiecolt-Glaser, 1996; Schuengel et al., 2010). Similar to family relationships of young people with ID (Totsika et al., 2014), better quality relationships between care staff and people with ID have been linked with fewer challenging behaviours in services (Clegg and Sheard, 2002; Eisenhower, Baker and Blacher, 2007; De Schipper and Schuengel, 2010). In residential care, aggressive client behaviours have been found to be linked strongly with client–staff interactions, such as attention seeking and evasion of demands (McAtee, Carr and Schulte, 2004; Embregts et al., 2009). Despite the obvious relevance of a social relationship perspective on the quality of care provision for people with ID, the literature provides little guidance for training and supervision of care staff on the ways in which they manage their relationships with clients (Van Oorsouw, Embregts and Bosman, 2013). Crucial questions remain unanswered as a result. Do services stimulate and support care staff enough in building good quality relationships, and what are the most important limitations that care staff need to overcome (Hermsen et al., 2014)? How do relationships with clients affect care staff on a personal level? Do policies and service cultures always pull out the best of human qualities that care staff can give (Bell and Clegg, 2012)? The goal of this chapter is to make a case for including attachment among the perspectives that should be considered in research, policy and practice around client–staff relationships. The central message of this chapter is that in order to improve care interactions and relationships, attention is required to understand attachment processes in people with ID and attachment processes in care staff as well. Implications of the small body of research on this issue will be discussed with regards to: policy and quality control, service development and organization, care staff and clients.

THE ATTACHMENT THEORETICAL PERSPECTIVE

The British psychiatrist John Bowlby (1907–1990) theorized that attachment is an important aspect of human behaviour, affect, cognition, and personality across the life span. As an evolutionary adaptation to the inherent vulnerability of human infants, a behavioural system develops that plays an important role in regulating our sense of security. The attachment behavioural system directs us towards specific persons who are perceived as wiser, stronger, and (at that moment) more able to cope with the world, as well as willing to share their resources and wisdom with us. While this system is likely to be highly active in children, to the extent that many situations challenge their abilities to fend for themselves, the system is also supposed to be active in adults at times when life's challenges outstrip their perceived personal resources. The attachment behavioural system is conceptualized within control systems terms as an adaptive, self-learning system that incorporates feedback from the environment into internal working models or mental representations of the social environment (Bowlby, 1984). These mental representations are supposed to play an important dynamic role in development, as these representations influence perceptions and behaviours in new relationships and new settings, and are updated and differentiated through ongoing new experiences (Sroufe, Coffino and Carlson, 2010). Attachment is therefore relevant across social contexts, not just for the family of one's upbringing.

The prime demonstration of the salience of attachment across contexts and generations is provided by the robust finding that parents' own representations of attachment predict the quality of the attachment relationships with their own children (Van IJzendoorn, 1995). This so-called intergenerational transmission of attachment has been found to be partially mediated by sensitive responsive caregiving by parents of their children (Bernier *et al.*, 2014). The explanation is that parents' mental representations of attachment facilitate or hinder accurate perception of children's signals and needs and adequate responses to those needs. This is because the mental representations that parents may have developed in adaptation to painful and distressing caregiving experiences from childhood onwards may bias or limit parental sensitive responsiveness. Their own children will therefore also have to resolve the ensuing feelings of rejection, anger or distress and adapt their own mental representations and behaviour within the parent–child relationship.

The impact of adult mental representations of attachment was discovered by Mary Main and her colleagues (Main, Kaplan and Cassidy, 1985) by studying parents' responses to semi-structured interview questions about their relationships with their own parents within the Adult Attachment Interview (AAI; George, Kaplan and Main, 1996). Questions about such affect-laden experiences are challenging for a speaker in two ways. Because the listener is completely unfamiliar with the speaker's background, the speaker has to present the experiences and evaluations in a way that the listener can understand. If the relationships with attachment figures have been difficult and complex, the story that the speaker needs to tell will be difficult and complex as well. At the same time, the topic of relationships with parents and the actual memories that are retrieved may be affectively arousing, setting self-regulatory processes in motion. Efforts on both these challenges may conflict, which may lead to confusing or incoherent narrative, unsuccessful regulation of affect, or both. Few difficulties are expected for speakers who have not had conflicting, confusing and distressing experiences which need to be incorporated in their mental representations of attachment. Relatively few difficulties may also be experienced by speakers who have extensively re-examined and reprocessed their more complex experiences, for example as a response to corrective experiences in new relationships (e.g., when a person who grew up in an emotionally cold family becomes involved with a loving, responsive partner, or when a person engages in psychotherapy). The interview may prove more difficult for speakers who have had relatively complex or unfavourable experiences, and who may not or only unsuccessfully have worked through those experiences. The problems and faults within the resulting narratives have proven to be a rich and powerful window into the complexity of human social functioning (Main, Kaplan and Cassidy, 1985).

In order to subject mental representations of attachment to quantitative empirical study, Main and Goldwyn (1994) developed a formal scoring and classification system based on verbatim interview transcripts, which is now used worldwide by researchers. As a result, a burgeoning literature has developed on individual differences in attachment representations, as characterized by classifications into a number of adult attachment categories (see Bakermans-Kranenburg and Van IJzendoorn, 2009 for a review of studies including data from 10,000 participants using the AAI). Most narratives in these studies (58% in North American samples of non-clinical mothers; Bakermans-Kranenburg and Van IJzendoorn, 2009) indicate an *autonomous-secure representation*, which goes along with an open and realistic stance regarding the nature of their experiences and an open and valuing discussion of the importance of their attachment figures in their lives. *Non-autonomous dismissing representations* indicate a distance taken towards attachment and attachment experiences, often seen in idealization of relationships with parents, failure to recall concrete attachment experiences or negation of any possible hurt or negative impact of harsh or insensitive parenting. *Non-autonomous preoccupied representations* indicate a mental entanglement and involvement in conflicted relationships with attachment figures, as shown by current anger flaring up during the interview or vagueness surrounding ill-defined, negative experiences. Specific attention is paid to loss of attachment figures and experiences of traumatic abuse from attachment figures. Disorganization and disorientation in speaking or reasoning about these experiences go along with an *unresolved-disorganized representation of loss or trauma*.

The theoretical view espoused in this chapter regards the adult attachment categories of autonomous, dismissing, preoccupied, and unresolved representations as developing patterns of affective-cognitive processing of attachment cues. This view differs from the approach that is often taken in social psychology to cast personality differences in attachment terms, speaking about secure or anxious *individuals*. While the latter approach stresses relatively fixed social behaviours and relationship styles, the developmental approach in the Bowlby–Ainsworth tradition provides psychological depth in understanding how social relationships shape, and are shaped by, relatively specialized affective-cognitive substrates. An important implication is that the impact of attachment representations on social relationships may be changed by understanding such processes and changing the social context, which will be demonstrated in the next section.

ADULT ATTACHMENT AND PROFESSIONAL CARE

The strong and robust associations between parents' mental representations of attachment and the quality of their caregiving behaviour and relationships with their children have spurred investigations into other domains that also present people with attachment-relevant cues. For example, in residential care for adolescents with severe behaviour problems, adolescents perceived their assigned group worker as more psychologically available if workers had an autonomous-secure attachment representation rather than a non-autonomous representation (Zegers et al., 2006). Also, the nature of interventions and working alliances between mental health workers and their clients were associated with workers' attachment representations (Dozier, Cue and Barnett, 1994; Tyrrell et al., 1999). A recent study found that when psychotherapists had dismissing attachment representations, their clients were more likely to rate the therapeutic relationship as avoidant-fearful (Petrowski et al., 2013).

In a study on the effectiveness of CONTACT, a video-feedback intervention to improve the relationship between support staff and people with visual impairment and ID (Janssen, Riksen-Walraven and Van Dijk, 2003; Damen et al., 2011), the role of the attachment representation of staff was included (Schuengel et al., 2012). Staff participated in a video-feedback programme to improve the sensitivity of their responses to the sometimes difficult-to-read interactive behaviour of residential clients. Of the 51 care staff, 18% were male, and 65% had a higher vocational education degree. On average, staff members were 31.0 years old (SD 9.3) and had, on average, 8.6 years of experience in working with persons with disabilities (SD 7.5). The 12 clients in the study had a combination of visual and intellectual disabilities. Clients were between 13 and 54 years old (median 38 years). Seven clients were male. Severity of intellectual disability ranged from moderate ($n=2$), through severe ($n=5$) to profound ($n=5$). Five clients were partially sighted, the other clients were blind.

To study the effect of the intervention, an A–B design for single-case experiments (Barlow and Hersen, 1984) was used. Each client and his or her care staff completed a series of interaction sessions. During the baseline period, video recordings were made of the interaction situations with each of the participating staff members. Each staff member was videotaped and observed twice during baseline and no interaction coaching was given. During the intervention period, three recordings were made, resulting in two baseline recordings and three intervention recordings for each client–staff dyad. Five minutes of each videotape were coded, using scales to measure the quality of the interaction in the form of: frequency of giving confirmation to the client, responsiveness (giving a reaction to initiatives of clients), and affective mutuality (high, moderate, or low) (for more details, see Damen *et al.*, 2011 and Schuengel *et al.*, 2012).

The results showed that 28 staff members were classified as autonomous, 12 as dismissing, and 11 as preoccupied with respect to attachment. In addition, seven participants received a primary classification as unresolved with regard to loss or trauma. Multinomial tests did not reveal significant differences between the sample distribution of AAI categories and the distribution found for general population samples of parents reported in the meta-analysis by Bakermans-Kranenburg and Van IJzendoorn (2009). Care staff were no more nor less autonomous-secure with regard to their attachment representations than the general population and no associations were found between attachment classification and gender, age, or years of working experience of staff. However, caregivers with higher vocational training were more often classified with an autonomous attachment representation than caregivers with lower vocational training. Our CONTACT study also made it possible to clarify the linkage between attachment representations and the quality of the interaction and, even more importantly, the linkage with the intervention to improve the quality of the interaction between staff and clients (for detailed results, see Schuengel *et al.*, 2012). The unresolved classification was disregarded in the statistical analyses, due to the small number of care staff within this group.

With regard to the associations between attachment representations and the indicators used for quality of the interaction, two significant patterns emerged. Staff members with dismissing attachment representations less often responded to signals of their clients with a confirmation that they had perceived the signal, compared to staff members with an autonomous classification or staff with a preoccupied classification. This led us to question how the attachment representations of staff related to intervention effects regarding improving the quality of the interaction they were involved in. Interestingly, no differences on the intervention effect by attachment representation group were found for the concept of confirmation. A significant improvement in the use of confirmation in general was found for all attachment groups in this study. Hence, despite an overall increase after interaction coaching in the rate with which staff responded with a confirmation of receipt of the clients' signals, care staff with dismissing classifications continued to show such confirmation at a lower rate than care staff with autonomous and preoccupied classifications. The lower rate of confirmation among care staff with dismissing attachment representations points to a more 'distant' interactive style that might reflect a general strategy to minimize exposure to negative affect in relationships (Kobak *et al.*, 1993; Roisman, 2006).

A second indicator of high quality of the interaction between staff and clients was the percentage of client initiatives responded to by the staff member ('responsiveness'). In general, the video-feedback intervention improved the responsiveness. A significant interaction effect between attachment category and recording occasion was also found. Figure 8.1 shows a drop in responsiveness from the first baseline recording to the second, and an increase from the last baseline to the first intervention recording for the care staff with non-autonomous attachment, while care staff with autonomous attachment showed an increase from the first to the second baseline recording, remaining stable thereafter. In other words, while care staff with autonomous classifications improved without support before the video-feedback intervention had started, staff members with preoccupied or dismissing classifications only showed improvement *after* they had received

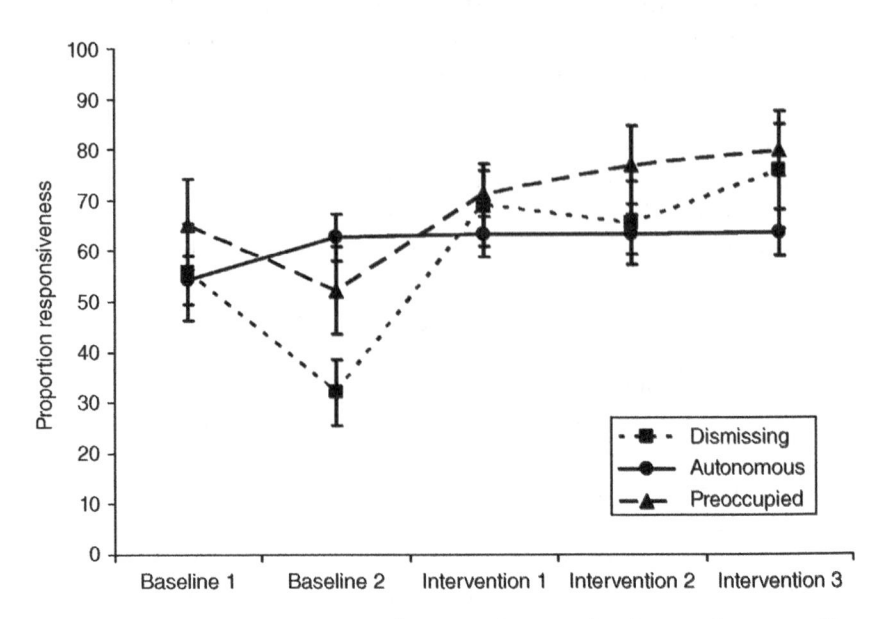

Figure 8.1 Mean proportions of responsiveness by interaction recording during baseline and intervention period for care staff in the three attachment categories.

interaction coaching. It is therefore encouraging that interaction coaching was effective in eliminating the emerging differences in responsiveness between care staff with autonomous and non-autonomous representations. However, the stronger dependency on the interaction coaching for non-autonomous staff might also make it more difficult to sustain their improvements in the long term.

A case example will now be used to describe the impact of the CONTACT intervention with a young boy called Tommie.

Case Example: Tommie

Tommie was placed out of his family home into a group home when he was ten years old, five years before the intervention. He had cerebral palsy and severe visual and intellectual disabilities, but generally few behaviour problems. He used some verbal communication, but his direct care staff had very little verbal interaction with him. They requested the CONTACT intervention in order to increase their verbal interaction with Tommie. They chose lunch time as an appropriate opportunity to video their interactions with him. After the intervention, the direct care staff evaluated the progress they had made in a group session. They concluded that the intervention helped them to learn that Tommie could understand simple messages within a relevant context, that they listened more and responded more and took conversational turns. They also reported gaining a better understanding of how Tommie's physical condition sometimes hampered communication, and that they became better in allowing Tommie more time to process cues and information.

It is recognized that supporting care staff through video-feedback interventions to interact with clients in ways that may be contrary to their natural inclination may cause psychological discomfort and strain for the staff. This study of video-feedback also explored staff's level of work experience and reported job satisfaction in relation to their attachment representation (Schuengel et al., 2010). Staff with a preoccupied attachment representation had a lower overall job satisfaction than staff with autonomous or dismissing attachment. Staff members with autonomous attachment were most satisfied about the work itself and their relationships with colleagues. Interestingly, the aspect that care staff members with dismissing attachment were most satisfied about was the autonomy that their job provided. Care staff with preoccupied attachment were most dissatisfied about the support they received from their colleagues and supervisors. They seemed to experience a misbalance between the support they provided their clients and the support they received from others.

This study provided evidence for the importance of attachment representations of staff working with vulnerable clients with visual and intellectual disabilities. Because of the importance of the relationships with staff in the lives of people with ID, care staff must be reliable, stable, and sensitive in their contacts. The above-mentioned results showed that care staff with non-autonomous attachment representations and, more specifically, care staff with dismissing representations need support and coaching to improve the quality of their interactions in working with children and adults with visual and intellectual disabilities. This support or coaching can ameliorate the at-risk character of the less-responsive interaction patterns in their natural social behaviour.

ADULT ATTACHMENT AND STAFF MANAGEMENT

Overcoming the effects of care staff's attachment representations on interactions with clients, as demonstrated in the CONTACT project, may be important but not sufficient in order to intervene in problematic staff–client relationships. In some cases, care staff may choose to continue with limiting confirmation of client signals as a strategy to avoid problematic overinvestment of clients in relationships with staff (Clegg and Sheard, 2002) and to discourage clients from becoming 'overly fond' of the staff member, which is reported as the most frequent challenging behaviour (Larson, Alim and Tsakanikos, 2011). Box 8.2 illustrates the strained interactions that may sometimes occur.

In attachment theory, the excessive attachment behaviours of some people with ID towards their care staff indicate a failure to develop an adaptive goal-corrected partnership with the attachment figure. Of the several possible pathways towards this relationship pattern, attention has focused on under-developed person permanence, especially for persons with intellectual and visual disabilities (Den Brok, Sterkenburg and Schuengel, 2012). A person who lacks person permanence and develops an attachment relationship is bound to be vulnerable to

> **Box 8.2 Excessive Attachment Behaviours**
>
> The person with ID searches for and talks about a particular member of staff, finds out about when she will be on shift, follows her around, including waiting outside the toilet for her to re-emerge, takes her photograph off display boards, and so on. These behaviours feel deeply intrusive and disturbing to the staff member. It feels as if the person is trying to crawl inside her skin. Incidents of aggression are easily provoked, as the person experiences intense jealousy when 'his' member of staff talks with a peer, particularly somebody similar who may be construed as a competitor. Having to work in locations away from the person makes the staff member feel, and resent feeling, that she is being prevented from doing her job properly.

anxiety during separations. To stimulate the development of person permanence and thereby to lessen anxiety when the attachment figure is out of sight or out of earshot, a mobile application was developed to facilitate communication independent of time and place. Care staff may employ these or similar strategies to lessen distress and attachment behaviour during separation, thereby not only increasing client wellbeing but also decreasing care staff burden.

As clinicians and researchers, we are all aware of policies that manifestly fail to limit turnover of direct care staff or that promote staff 'churn' so as to prevent special relationships developing between staff members and clients (De la Fosse and Baron, 1995; Leaf, 1995). There may even be attempts to justify such policies by reference to the anxiety that clients may experience around the inevitable separations and transitions that occur in non-family, professional care arrangements. Yet, this strategy has been implicated in the problems of people with ID intermittently over the years. King, Raynes and Tizard (1971) were the first to identify and express concern about up to 50 different staff caring for young children in any given week, an issue also raised by parents (Buntinx, 2008) and the current authors.

The concerns that managers and policy makers may have regarding support staff's lack of responsiveness to attachment behaviours of clients may be alleviated by attending not only to building secure relationships but also to the way in which such relationships are brought to a completion. Care staff may not only be a positive model for human connection, responsiveness and trustworthiness, but also for preparing and managing the disconnections that are inherent in any human relationship. Completing professional staff–client relationships in ways that promote emotional security and confidence in future relationships requires that care staff and clients are allowed time to prepare themselves and each other for such transitions. Within this transitional period, the security invested in the current relationship may be used to explore new relationships that may replace the current one (Schuengel and Van IJzendoorn, 2001). Such a display of respect for relationships that have been developed over time, whether close and enduring or perfunctory and limited, may generalize to other relationships that might be affected, for example with group members and neighbours during a residential move.

Awareness that their support contributes to the wellbeing of people with ID might be lower in care staff with non-autonomous representations (Schuengel et al., 2012). However, the intervention study of Schuengel and colleagues on video feedback indicates that there is the potential to make care staff more aware of their role in understanding and supporting people with disabilities. Furthermore, care staff appear to become capable observers of attachment behaviour in people with ID after a short 15-minute introduction to the Circle of Security diagram, which can be found on the Internet: circleofsecurity.net (De Schipper, Stolk and Schuengel, 2006; Hoffman et al., 2006; De Schipper et al., 2009). Hoffman and his colleagues developed their diagram for use with parents of non-disabled infants, who are portrayed wearing nappies. The principles depicted in the diagram are, however, also highly relevant to long-term care and support relationships with adults who have IDs.

See Boxes 8.3 and 8.4 for ideas to aid the introduction of the Circle of Security model of attachment to staff.

Attachment theory and research also suggest that there should be a focus on *all* staff members, because each staff member appears to contribute to the wellbeing of people with ID. Young persons with moderate to severe ID who showed secure attachment behaviour to more caregivers also showed less withdrawal and stereotypic behaviour (De Schipper and Schuengel, 2010). Although this association might be explained by client characteristics, the patterns of associations provided evidence that direct staff brought characteristics with them that influenced their relationship with each successive client. Second, the studies reported here have identified the role of support staff attachment representations and their engagement across varying groups of

Box 8.3 Topics for First Discussion of Circle of Security with Staff

- Explain how mature, competent adults help vulnerable individuals to grow and develop in two distinct ways: by encouraging them to explore the world and by being warm and responsive when they seek support.
- Explain that some people are able to do both of these well, but that most of us find one of them a bit easier than the other. Ask staff if they remember if their parents were more likely to encourage them to try new things and activities, or more likely to be warm and responsive when they approached them for comfort or reassurance.
- Ask staff to think about themselves and their colleagues at work. Ask if they are more likely than other people to encourage clients to try exploring new things and activities, or are they one of the available ones who respond warmly when clients approach?
- Discuss what it would be like to swap these different ways of working with a colleague who uses a different approach.

Box 8.4 Topics for Second Discussion of Circle of Security with Staff

- Explain that people with insecure attachments often *miscue* others about what they need.
  - Those who are very dependent on other people need sensitive encouragement to try some exploration, even though that seems to be the last thing they want.
  - Others may need emotional warmth to affirm that they are valued human beings, even though they seem unapproachable.
- Deciding not to follow the cues a person gives all the time has to be considered ethically, and done slowly and sensitively.
  - When people are preoccupied by getting their emotional needs met, they tend to 'tune out' the rest of the world, so may well find exploring something new very anxiety-provoking.
  - Similarly, people who have learned to avoid emotional closeness may need very low-key approaches to start with if they are not to feel overwhelmed by too much intensity of contact with staff.
- So it is worth staff taking the risk of interacting in ways that run counter to the person's cues if they do it carefully, thoughtfully and at low intensities, because it can initiate a radical improvement in the person's wellbeing.

people ranging from mild to profound ID with and without additional disabilities, suggesting that the framework of caregivers' attachment representation and behaviour applies to diverse services.

Taken together, these research studies suggest that management need not consider selective recruitment of support staff based on attachment representations, because staff with insecure attachments can become more flexible in the way they interact with their clients. Their specific attachment background may indicate that some ways of relating may go against the grain somewhat, but training, supervision and support can facilitate growth-promoting connectedness with clients who have ID.

ADULT ATTACHMENT AND PROFESSIONAL RISK AND RESILIENCE

In addition to direct linkages that may be found between care staff's own attachment issues and quality of care and interpersonal relationships with clients, adult attachment also has been found to influence other domains that affect the functioning of care professionals. Whilst a complete review of the adult attachment literature is outside the scope of this chapter, several findings will be highlighted that are particularly relevant to the quality of care staff's functioning with persons with ID.

Mental Health

The linkages between attachment representations and mental health are complex. Both constructs may contribute to adult functioning independently, and to a considerable extent. However, a meta-analysis of 200 studies ($N=10,000$ participants) found over-representations of non-autonomous attachment representations in samples of people with clinical psychological problems (Bakermans-Kranenburg and Van IJzendoorn, 2009). Preoccupied representations were over-represented among people with internalizing disorders, and in particular among people with borderline personality disorder. Preoccupied representations were also over-represented among partners involved in domestic violence. Depression was, however, associated with dismissing representations. People with dismissing representations may have a higher risk for suffering across a longer time, due to their reluctance to report their symptoms, despite the heightened severity of their symptoms in the eyes of professionals (Dozier and Lee, 1995). Given the psychological burden that carers often have to endure, including scenes of violence and human suffering, attention to attachment representations of staff may also be justified given their proneness to persistent mental health problems.

Support Seeking

Adult attachment representations are associated with seeking support within relationships, in marital couples (Crowell *et al.*, 2002) as well as in adolescent–parent relationships (Kobak *et al.*, 1993; Allen *et al.*, 2003). Adolescents with more autonomous attachment representations were perceived as seeking support more effectively (Zegers *et al.*, 2006). An Israeli study found that young adults with preoccupied representations were less satisfied with the support they derived from their parents, which provided an explanation for the difficulties they experienced in dealing with the stresses of entering military service (Scharf, Mayseless and Kivenson-Baron, 2011). Similarly, studies have found that the transition from home to college life was more difficult for young adults with preoccupied representations (Bernier *et al.*, 2004). Together, these findings provide grounds for speculating that some professional carers may seek and find support more effectively when faced with challenging situations at work because of their autonomous attachment representations. Failure to seek and find support may be especially detrimental for new care staff. With ever-limited training and supervision on the job, care staff with non-autonomous attachment representations may be less likely to seek out or welcome advice and help, which diminishes the opportunities for adjusting to the job situation, enjoying it and developing the necessary skills.

Mindset

Care staff working within services which exclusively use behavioural approaches may find that attachment-informed practice requires a different mindset. Although both approaches are firmly rooted in behaviourism as a psychological methodology (building theory on the basis of observable phenomena), behaviourism as a theory of functioning and behaviour change is exclusively based on learning principles whereas attachment theory is composed of tenets from ethology, evolutionary biology, cybernetics, systems theory, and psychodynamic theory. Put into practice, it may often appear as if attachment interventions focus on invisible phenomena such as bonds between people, and on the way past relationships affect the expectations each individual brings to meetings with new people. As a result, it may often not be transparent how researchers and clinicians within this orientation perceive attachment phenomena within case material (Clegg and Lansdall-Welfare, 1995). However, similar to the behaviouristic tradition, attachment-oriented scholars and practitioners train to become astute observers of interactive behaviours and astute readers and listeners of verbal behaviour in narrative form in order to infer quality of both attachment relationships and mental representations of attachment. This has two implications for clinicians working with care staff within an attachment framework. First, staff members will need help to understand this way of seeing their clients and work out how this influences any difficulties the client may have. In addition to this, they will also need ongoing support to maintain a grasp on this learning and find ways to combine this with existing protocols or behavioural therapeutic approaches already in place. Reminders in the form of Circle of Security diagrams have been shown to be helpful, but integrative approaches may also be developed (Schuengel et al., 2009).

Secondly, research indicates that the attachment histories of staff influence how open they may be to trying out new ideas, because security of attachment fosters exploration, learning and perseverance. For example, college students with dismissing and preoccupied representations reported the least positive dispositions towards learning (Larose, Bernier and Tarabulsy, 2005). Mothers with autonomous attachment representations showed an open and flexible mindset concerning the emotions they and their infants experience (DeOliveira, Moran and Pederson, 2005), while the general personality trait of openness to experience was found less among persons with dismissing attachment representations (Roisman et al., 2007). Since a mindset of openness to expressions of individuality of clients, appreciation of differences, and assuming that people might learn and change have been proposed as essential to personalized, high-quality care (Schuengel et al., 2010; Meppelder et al., 2014;), these positive personal qualities might be more strongly in need of stimulation and support among care staff who have non-autonomous attachment representations.

CONCLUSIONS

Relative to the external, structural forces that limit overall improvement of professional care for people with ID, the attachment representations of the care staff themselves might appear to be a relatively minor, secondary problem. However, research to date indicates that some of the efforts to improve care may be done more efficiently by identifying the care staff members who need such support the most. For example, relatively intensive and expensive video-based coaching from the CONTACT programme may be offered in a more differentiated way, so that it reaches the care staff with non-autonomous attachment representations who benefit the most (Schuengel et al., 2013). In an ideal world, efficient screening methods would perhaps exist to identify candidates for such interventions. Until that time arrives, we might employ the attachment theoretical framework as one of the tools for understanding some of the problems experienced by care staff who fail to deliver the qualities that people with ID require and deserve. The attachment theoretical perspective supports a fundamental trust in the opportunities for people, despite psychosocial liabilities developed over years, to learn and develop new response sets and inner understanding. This perspective may be an important component of the culture and climate of organizations that provide professional support for people with ID, promoting a mindset not only oriented towards social functioning of clients with ID, but also towards the capacity of care staff to change relationships with their clients for the better. Becoming aware of one's own vulnerabilities and limitations and those of others may be an important step towards sympathizing with the needs and vulnerabilities of even the most difficult clients with ID, and to recognizing how care staff can shape the interpersonal world of these clients.

REFERENCES

Allen, J.P., McElhaney, K.B., Land, D.J., Kuperminc, G.P., Moore, C.W., O'Beirne-Kelly, H. and Liebman Kilmer, S. (2003) A secure base in adolescence: Markers of attachment security in the mother–adolescent relationship. *Child Development*, 74: 292–307.

Bakermans-Kranenburg, M.J. and Van IJzendoorn, M.H. (2009) The first 10,000 Adult Attachment Interviews: Distributions of adult attachment representations in clinical and non-clinical groups. *Attachment & Human Development*, 11: 223–263.

Barlow, D.H. and Hersen, M. (1984) *Single Case Experimental Designs: Strategies for studying behavior change*, 2nd edition. New York: Pergamon.

Bell, B.G. and Clegg, J. (2012) An ecological approach to reducing the social isolation of people with an intellectual disability. *Ecological Psychology*, 24: 159–177.

Bernier, A., Larose, S., Boivin, M. and Soucy, N. (2004) Attachment state of mind: Implications for adjustment to college. *Journal of Adolescent Research*, 19: 783–806.

Bernier, A., Matte-Gagne, C., Belanger, M.E. and Whipple, N. (2014) Taking stock of two decades of attachment transmission gap: Broadening the assessment of maternal behavior. *Child Development*, 85: 1852–1865.

Bowlby, J. (1984) *Attachment and Loss. Vol. 1: Attachment*, 2nd edition. London: Penguin.

Buntinx, W. (2008) The logic of relations and the logic of management. *Journal of Intellectual Deficiency Research*, 52(7): 588–597.

Clegg, J.A. and Lansdall-Welfare, R. (1995) Attachment and learning disability: A theoretical review informing three clinical interventions. *Journal of Intellectual Disability Research*, 39: 295–305.

Clegg, J. and Sheard, C. (2002) Challenging behaviour and insecure attachment. *Journal of Intellectual Disability Research*, 46: 503–506.

Crowell, J.A., Treboux, D., Gao, Y., Fyffe, C., Pan, H. and Waters, E. (2002) Assessing secure base behaviour in adulthood: Development of a measure, links to adult attachment representations, and relations to couples' communication and reports of relationships. *Developmental Psychology*, 38: 679–693.

Damen, S., Kef, S., Worm, M., Janssen, M.J. and Schuengel, C. (2011) Effects of video-feedback interaction training for professional caregivers of children and adults with visual and intellectual disabilities. *Journal of Intellectual Disability Research*, 55: 581–595.

De la Fosse, F.J.C. and Baron, J. (1995) "In beweging kun je sturen …". In L.E.E. Ligthart, A.A. van de Voorde and F.L.H. De Keyser (eds) *Tehuis … thuis … tehuis: Geadopteerde jongeren in de residentiele zorg* (pp. 116–124). Oosterhout: FICE.

De Schipper, J.C., Ploegmakers, B., Romijn, M. and Schuengel, C. (2009) *Validity of caregivers' reports of children's attachment behaviour in group care*. Paper presented at the conference of the European Association for Mental Health and Intellectual Disabilities, Amsterdam, The Netherlands.

De Schipper, J.C. and Schuengel, C. (2010) Attachment behaviour towards support staff in young people with intellectual disabilities: Associations with challenging behaviour. *Journal of Intellectual Disability Research*, 54: 584–596.

De Schipper, J.C., Stolk, J. and Schuengel, C. (2006) Professional caretakers as attachment figures in day care centers for children with intellectual disability and behaviour problems. *Research in Developmental Disabilities*, 27: 203–216.

Den Brok, W., Sterkenburg, P. and Schuengel, C. (2012) Using mobile technology to support relationship development and emotional well-being: A case study. *Journal of Intellectual Disability Research*, 56: 680.

DeOliveira, C.A., Moran, G. and Pederson, D.R. (2005) Understanding the link between maternal adult attachment classifications and thoughts and feelings about emotions. *Attachment & Human Development*, 7: 153–170.

Dozier, M., Cue, K.L. and Barnett, L. (1994) Clinicians as caregivers: Role of attachment organization in treatment. *Journal of Consulting and Clinical Psychology*, 62: 793–800.

Dozier, M. and Lee, S.W. (1995) Discrepancies between self- and other-report of psychiatric symptomatology: Effects of dismissing attachment strategies. Special Issue: Emotions in developmental psychopathology. *Development and Psychopathology*, 7: 217–226.

Eisenhower, A.S., Baker, B.L. and Blacher, J. (2007) Early student–teacher relationships of children with and without intellectual disability: Contributions of behavioral, social, and self-regulatory competence. *Journal of School Psychology*, 45: 363–383.

Embregts, P.J.C.M., Didden, R., Huitink, C. and Schreuder, N. (2009) Contextual variables affecting aggressive behaviour in individuals with mild to borderline intellectual disabilities who live in a residential facility. *Journal of Intellectual Disability Research*, 53: 255–264.

George, C., Kaplan, N. and Main, M. (1996) *Adult Attachment Interview*, 3rd edition. Unpublished manual, University of California at Berkeley.

Hermsen, M.A., Embregts, P.J.C.M., Hendriks, A.H.C. and Frielink, N. (2014) The human degree of care. Professional loving care for people with a mild intellectual disability: An explorative study. *Journal of Intellectual Disability Research*, 58: 221–232.

Hoffman, K.T., Marvin, R.S., Cooper, G. and Powell, B. (2006) Changing toddlers' and preschoolers' attachment classifications: The circle of security intervention. *Journal of Consulting and Clinical Psychology*, 74: 1017–1026.

Janssen, M.J., Riksen-Walraven, J.M. and Van Dijk, J.P.M. (2003) Contact: Effects of an intervention program to foster harmonious interactions between deaf-blind children and their educators. *Journal of Visual Impairment & Blindness*, 97: 215–229.

King, R., Raynes, N. and Tizard, J. (1971) *Patterns of Residential Care*. London: Routledge.

Kobak, R.R., Cole, H.E., Ferenz-Gillies, R. and Fleming, W.S. (1993) Attachment and emotion regulation during mother–teen problem solving: A control theory analysis. *Child Development*, 64: 231–245.

Larose, S., Bernier, A. and Tarabulsy, G.M. (2005) Attachment state of mind, learning dispositions, and academic performance during the college transition. *Developmental Psychology*, 41: 281–289.

Larson, F., Alim, N. and Tsakanikos, E. (2011) Attachment style and mental health in adults with intellectual disability: Self-reports and reports by carers. *Advances in Mental Health and Intellectual Disabilities*, 5: 15–23.

Leaf, S. (1995) The journey from control to connection. *Journal of Child and Youth Care*, 10: 15–21.

Main, M. and Goldwyn, R. (1994) *Adult Attachment Scoring and Classification Systems*. Unpublished manual, University of California at Berkeley.

Main, M., Kaplan, N. and Cassidy, J. (1985) Security in infancy, childhood, and adulthood: A move to the level of representation. In I. Bretherton and E. Waters (eds) *Growing Points of Attachment Theory and Research* (pp. 66–104). Society for Research in Child Development.

McAtee, M., Carr, E.G. and Schulte, C. (2004) A contextual assessment inventory for problem behaviour: Initial development. *Journal of Positive Behavior Interventions*, 6: 148–165.

Meppelder, H.M., Kef, S., Hodes, M.W. and Schuengel, C. (2014) Mindset of staff supporting parents with intellectual disabilities: The association with working alliance and parental intentions to ask professional support. *Journal of Applied Research in Intellectual Disabilities*, 27: 341.

Petrowski, K., Pokorny, D., Nowacki, K. and Buchheim, A. (2013) The therapist's attachment representation and the patient's attachment to the therapist. *Psychotherapy Research*, 23: 25–34.

Roisman, G.I. (2006) The role of adult attachment security in non-romantic, non-attachment-related first interactions between same-sex strangers. *Attachment & Human Development*, 8: 341–352.

Roisman, G.I., Holland, A., Fortuna, K., Fraley, R.C., Clausell, E. and Clarke, A. (2007) The adult attachment interview and self-reports of attachment style: An empirical rapprochement. *Journal of Personality and Social Psychology*, 92: 678–697.

Scharf, M., Mayseless, O. and Kivenson-Baron, I. (2011) Leaving the parental nest: Adjustment problems, attachment representations, and social support during the transition from high school to military service. *Journal of Clinical Child and Adolescent Psychology*, 40: 411–423.

Schuengel, C., Damen, S., Worm, M. and Kef, S. (2012) Attachment representations and response to video-feedback intervention for professional caregivers. *Attachment & Human Development*, 14: 83–99.

Schuengel, C., De Schipper, J.C., Sterkenburg, P.S. and Kef, S. (2013) Attachment, intellectual disabilities and mental health: Research, assessment and intervention. *Journal of Applied Research in Intellectual Disabilities*, 26: 34–46.

Schuengel, C., Kef, S., Damen, S. and Worm, M. (2010) 'People who need people': Attachment and professional caregiving. *Journal of Intellectual Disability Research*, 54: 38–47.

Schuengel, C., Sterkenburg, P.S., Jeczynski, P., Janssen, C.G.C. and Jongbloed, G. (2009) Supporting affect regulation in children with multiple disabilities during psychotherapy: A multiple case design study of therapeutic attachment. *Journal of Consulting and Clinical Psychology*, 77: 291–301.

Schuengel, C. and Van IJzendoorn, M.H. (2001) Attachment in mental health institutions: A critical review of assumptions, clinical implications, and research strategies. *Attachment and Human Development*, 3: 304–323.

Sroufe, L.A., Coffino, B. and Carlson, E.A. (2010) Conceptualizing the role of early experience: Lessons from the Minnesota longitudinal study. *Developmental Review*, 30: 36–51.

Totsika, V., Hastings, R.P., Vagenas, D. and Emerson, E. (2014) Parenting and the behavior problems of young children with an intellectual disability: Concurrent and longitudinal relationships in a population-based study. *American Journal on Intellectual and Developmental Disabilities*, 119: 422–435.

Tyrrell, C.L., Dozier, M., Teague, G.B. and Fallot, R.D. (1999) Effective treatment relationships for persons with serious psychiatric disorders: The importance of attachment states of mind. *Journal of Consulting and Clinical Psychology*, 67: 725–733.

Uchino, B.N., Cacioppo, J.T. and Kiecolt-Glaser, J.K. (1996) The relationship between social support and physiological processes: A review with emphasis on underlying mechanisms and implications for health. *Psychological Bulletin*, 119: 488–531.

Van IJzendoorn, M.H. (1995) Adult attachment representations, parental responsiveness, and infant attachment: A meta-analysis on the predictive validity of the Adult Attachment Interview. *Psychological Bulletin*, 117: 387–403.

Van Oorsouw, W.M.W.J., Embregts, P.J.C.M. and Bosman, A.M.T. (2013) Quantitative and qualitative processes of change during staff-coaching sessions: An exploratory study. *Research in Developmental Disabilities*, 34: 1456–1467.

Zegers, M.A.M., Schuengel, C., Van IJzendoorn, M.H. and Janssens, J.M.A.M. (2006) Attachment representations of institutionalized adolescents and their professional caregivers: Predicting the development of therapeutic relationships. *American Journal of Orthopsychiatry*, 76: 325–334.

Chapter 9

HAVE A HEART: HELPING SERVICES TO PROVIDE EMOTIONALLY AWARE SUPPORT

Amanda Shackleton
Independent Clinical Psychologist, Derbyshire, UK

It is now well understood that early life attachments and care experiences can have a lifelong impact on emotional and relational functioning. However, this is still rarely considered when people with distressed or challenging behaviours present to intellectual disability (ID) services. This chapter describes a clinical approach which places central importance on thinking about emotional development and attachments. The ideas have been developed through training in Disability Psychotherapy and relate to working with adults with ID in staffed community living settings.

SETTING THE SCENE

Disability Psychotherapy draws heavily upon the ideas of theorists who understood that early care relationships are pivotal in emotional development. Winnicott (1964) described how the provision of reliable, containing, empathic, attuned care in the early years of life lays the foundation for future emotional health. He coined the term 'good enough care' to acknowledge that this process can never be perfect. Rather, this lack of perfect care, as long as the child has been emotionally 'held' and contained enough during its experience of being dependent on carers, will facilitate independence and emotional

---

Attachment in Intellectual and Developmental Disability: A Clinician's Guide to Practice and Research, First Edition. Edited by Helen K. Fletcher, Andrea Flood and Dougal Julian Hare.
© 2016 John Wiley & Sons, Ltd. Published 2016 by John Wiley & Sons, Ltd.

robustness. Mahler, Pine and Bergman (1975) described the phases of human emotional development leading up to 'psychological birth' or Individuation, at around three and a half years of age. At this point, the child has developed a 'sense of self', of being their own person separate from their carers, and can be apart from attachment figures without overwhelming anxiety. Bowlby's work (1979; 1988) emphasized the importance of early secure attachment relationships in providing a safe base to facilitate emotional regulation and the development of emotional management skills.

The above theorists stress that these early processes are a delicate interplay between children and their carers, with both partners being active initiators and participants. The presence of an ID can increase the vulnerability of this delicate process being disrupted or disturbed. This may impact on the child's ability to develop emotionally, as well as relate to, and form relationships with, other human beings throughout life. Fletcher (Chapter 3) describes the increased sensitivity required when parenting a child with ID who may have been less able to send clear attachment signals. She also identifies factors that can influence and be influenced by this process, particularly the family stress that can result from parenting a child with disabilities without adequate social and psychological support.

It is common in mental health services to find client personal histories revealing the presence of issues that have adversely affected an individual's attachment experiences and emotional development (Seager, 2014). There is no reason to expect this to be any less so in services for people with ID. In fact, given the increased likelihood of experiences such as time away from parental attachment figures due to alternative care or hospital stays, or in the case of older people, histories of institutional living, this client group may be even more vulnerable. In more extreme situations, McCarthy (2001) discusses the trauma, abuse and gross family dysfunction that have been experienced by some very distressed and challenging individuals. Overall, there are a myriad of reasons why people with ID may not have been able to avail themselves of care and nurture 'ingredients' needed to form secure attachments and for emotional development to occur.

Frankish (1989; 1992; 2013b) has applied Mahler's phases of emotional development to people with ID. She explains how individuals, through not being able to access all of the attuned, 'good enough' care ingredients needed to form secure attachments and progress in their emotional development, can become 'stuck' at one of the phases that occurs before Individuation. As a result, they still require attachment figures to help them to feel emotionally safe and secure as they have not been able to reach psychological separation. The ways in which they behave and relate to others may be typical for the emotional development phase they are at, but are deemed age-inappropriate or presumed to be part of their ID and therefore unchangeable. They may act in ways that are intended to get their emotional needs met, but which cause distress and are challenging for services to understand.

IMPLICATIONS FOR LATER LIFE

In typical service provision, with the emphasis on autonomy and independence, understanding that a person with ID may still be functioning at an early stage of emotional development and needing attachment and nurture is different to established ways of working. For the person whose emotional development is still at a pre-individuation phase and requires the emotional security and regulation of attachment figures, the drive towards autonomy may be at odds with their emotional needs.

People with ID may also present at services having been additionally traumatized by difficult life events, including low socio-economic position, social isolation, abuse and victimization (Quarmby, 2011; Emerson and Gone, 2012). If their emotional development is already compromised, they are unlikely to have developed the emotional resilience and skills to process and deal with these issues, which is further complicated by vulnerability to being taken advantage of and abused as they seek out nurture and attachments. Frankish (Chapter 7) describes the assessment of emotional development and Individuation. In terms of intervening and working with such clients, the basis of the approach to be described is giving the person, in conscious and sometimes concrete ways, an experience of those absent early emotional processes either via direct support staff and/or through individual therapy.

INCREASING EMOTIONAL SECURITY AND DEVELOPMENT THROUGH STAFF SUPPORT

Interventions guided by a Disability Psychotherapy approach are about constructing care experiences that aim to make the person feel emotionally safe, as well as giving them the necessary 'missing ingredients' to continue their emotional development. Frankish (2013a) describes the named worker system, where an individual is always supported by a 'core team' of six to seven staff so they always know the staff member supporting them. This number is small enough to ensure that the individual can begin to develop relationships with, and emotional attachments to, the staff. The staff themselves are also able to get to know the person they support well and deliver more 'attuned' support. Although attachments and emotional security are a basic human need, for individuals with limited or absent social or familial networks there is often no one other than staff teams to provide this.

The size of the team is large enough to ensure the person gets this support even when particular staff members are absent or leave the team, at which time a new core member can be introduced. From experience, it has been found that with a bigger core team, it is hard for the person to form attachment relationships with everyone. Once such a core team is established, group supervision with a focus on working practices and relationships can enhance the 'emotional security' of the individual and actively encourage attachment and emotional development.

Providing 'Good Enough' Care

Once a core staff group has been established, it can then provide care that is consistent, reliable, predictable, nurturing, contained and attuned. In other words, the very elements of 'good enough' early care necessary for emotional nurture and development which may have been unavailable in the client's early life.

Consistency is developed via the core group following the same procedures and guidelines to undertake care or support tasks with the individual. Staff reliability is not only about being physically present, but also about following through on promises and arrangements made with the individual, not letting them down regarding things that are expected, or making promises which cannot be met. Having a daily or weekly routine, developed with the person as much as possible, facilitates a sense of predictability. Warnings of staff holidays and breaks and reassurances of return are also really important. Many people in services may have lost previous attachment relationships, leaving them vulnerable to re-experiencing feelings of abandonment. Loss of staff, often with little warning, is a common experience for those who have lived in services (Mattison and Pistrang, 2004). Enabling a person to learn how to use a calendar in some form and providing necessary reassurance regarding staff return is central to promoting this basic sense of being able to trust other people. The above guidelines and practices are straightforward, but often neglected, aspects of care provision that support psychological as well as practical independence through the promotion of necessary interdependence.

Nurturing and Attuned Care

Nurturing and attuned care is an important, but sometimes absent, component of service provision, where emphasis is often placed on promoting skills and independence. This can sometimes be taken to the degree of staff being resistant to doing things pro-actively for an individual for fear of 'de-skilling' or 'spoiling' them. The acts of making a person a drink, doing chores for them if they are not feeling up to it or doing something nice for them are all basic human actions that help others to feel nurtured, cherished and cared for. Therefore, staff should be explicitly 'allowed' occasionally and as appropriate, to do these things for a person and to see this as an expression of nurturing care.

The staff team's ability to attune to clients can be enhanced by investing time in increasing their understanding of the individual's cognitive profile. Drawing upon assessments such as the Wechsler Adult Intelligence Scale (WAIS-IV; Wechsler, 2008) and the Test for Reception of Grammar (TROG-2; Bishop, 2003) can provide very useful information to help staff become more 'attuned' to an individual's difficulties and modify their support to 'fit' the person's cognitive needs better. Common issues are the need for staff to simplify and slow down their own speech and to be aware of information-processing issues, for example not overloading the individual as a result of overestimating a person's abilities.

Similarly, at a physiological level, understanding a person's arousal cycle (Breakwell, 1997), including awareness of triggers, indicators of increasing arousal and strategies to help the person de-escalate, is also an important part of staff being 'attuned' to the individual. This enables staff to be the person's 'emotional regulator' (Gerhardt, 2004) and provide containing care.

Services and staff should also be aware of important anniversaries for the person. These may be the birthdays of important people in their lives, when people have died or anniversaries of other traumatic life experiences. It is important to know these, as even for individuals who do not have a time concept, reminders can come from the rhythm of the seasons or key calendar celebration days such as Christmas.

Staff being prepared for and anticipating changes in distress or behaviour at these times can enable people to be better understood during these periods.

Boundaries

Being aware of boundaries is also very important in providing containing support. Caring staff can sometimes be tempted to 'go the extra mile' for clients and, with the best of intentions, may do things like giving out personal mobile numbers or taking clients to personal family occasions. Staff need to be helped to understand they are more likely to be able to deliver the attuned, consistent emotional care that an individual needs within the contained hours of a shift and are unlikely to be able to deliver it during a 2 a.m. phone call, unexpected visits at home or during calls whilst on holiday. The individual looking for attuned care at these times is not likely to get the response they are seeking, leaving them feeling rejected and distressed, which can lead to difficult behaviours, usually with negative consequences.

Physical contact between client and staff is often baulked at by services, meaning that people are deprived of touch, an important human need and the most basic form of early emotional regulation (Gerhardt, 2004). There are, of course, valid reasons why services are anxious about touch and many people, both staff and clients, find it aversive. However, there does need to be flexible thinking about what may be helpful for some people to promote emotional regulation, be it touch, a soothing voice or empathic body language. Such provision must necessarily consider what staff are comfortable with and ensure that everyone is safe. Again, staff may need to be 'given permission' that sometimes it is okay to deliver a normal human response to distress such as listening to someone, giving them a hug and then making them a cup of tea.

This section has highlighted how staff groups can be guided to deliver support that not only enables an individual to feel emotionally safe and secure, but also gives them the early life care elements which they may not have been able to receive. Once the person is feeling emotionally safer, specific activities can be undertaken with the named workers to enhance the client's emotional development (Frankish, 2013b). An example of the application of this approach is given in the case example about Mike.

Case Example: Mike

Mike has severe ID and was removed from his family into services as a child due to severe neglect and possible abuse. He was referred to Psychology services at the age of 25 years with a range of difficult behaviours that challenged services. The referral described aggressive outbursts during which staff had been injured. He also often ran away from staff during community activities, sometimes lying down on the pavement or in the road and refusing to move. Mike lived in a 24-hour staffed house with two other men. He sought staff attention constantly and if staff were with other clients, he would violently rock on the spot, flapping his arms and then run towards the staff member or person they were with, pushing one or the other out of the way. Initial information gathering highlighted that the behaviours had been present since childhood and many different approaches had been used in the past without long-term success. Consequently, staff felt very negative and hopeless about Mike and there was high staff turnover in the house.

Assessment and formulation: Part of the comprehensive psychological assessment with Mike was to assess his stage of emotional development using the procedure described by Frankish (2013b). This revealed that he was still at a very early stage of his emotional development and engaging in behaviours which were consistent with this, such as rocking, flapping and being in need of constant attention from staff (see Chapter 7 for further information on the stages of 'practising' and 'early rapprochement' related to the above behaviours). Due to his extremely deprived early emotional and attachment experiences, he appeared to have become 'stuck' in his development. However, as he had grown older, the expectations held by the service of him had become further removed from what he was capable of and needed at an emotional level. His behaviour was seen as challenging and inappropriate for his age, but could alternatively be understood as characteristic of his level of emotional development and as a functional attempt to meet his emotional needs by getting attention and nurture.

Intervention: Once this was formulated, a training session was delivered to the staff supporting Mike that helped them develop a more empathic understanding of him and his level of emotional development. Time was also spent drawing up a personalized assault cycle so that staff members were aware of the triggers for his behaviour, the signs of escalation and appropriate and safe methods of de-escalation. A core staff team was set up comprising those who felt most confident and able to support him. On every shift, he was informed who would be available for him if he needed anything. This named worker did not necessarily spend the whole shift with Mike, but rather let him know where they were if he needed them. They did, however, spend blocks of 'quality time' with him on each shift, which involved doing activities with him, appropriate for his level of emotional development. For Mike, who was moving into the early rapprochement stage of emotional development (see Chapter 7), this involved activities that helped him to develop his relationships, learning about turn-taking, negotiation and give and take. Playing football or tag games with him in the garden, colouring together, simple games such as snap and picture dominoes and doing household tasks together helped him to experience and learn about basic relational skills. A simple pictorial timetable was drawn up each morning with the day's activities on it, and community activities were modified to be appropriate for his abilities and interests – these took place at quiet times that were not over-stimulating. The blocks of one-to-one time with a named worker were always included on the timetable after trips out on community activities.

Outcome: Improvements in Mike's behaviours were seen almost immediately. His outbursts of difficult behaviour decreased and the episodes of him lying down and refusing to come home became very rare, only occurring when over-stimulated, such as when he was in a gift shop at a tourist attraction he had visited. Mike began to tolerate time alone and would take himself off to his room to watch DVDs on his own. His progress has continued, but he had two changes of provider and residence due to service restructuring, both of which resulted in deteriorations in his behaviour until new staff had been trained and worked with him appropriately.

This approach has been used with Mike for the last five years, with only very occasional monitoring and refresher training needed. He now lives in his own supported tenancy with one-to-one support during the day. In recent years he has, to everyone's surprise, coped with losing night-time support and is now on his own every night with assistive technology monitoring him. He has coped with the death and funeral of someone important to him. He is able to socialize with his neighbours and has also coped with staff changes. There are very occasional aggressive incidents, but it is easy for staff supporting him to see the triggers. He still rocks and flaps but this is usually due to high emotional arousal. Meeting Mike's need for emotional attachment and safety has not only reduced his difficult behaviours but also appears to have helped him grow and develop emotionally. He is able to tolerate being on his own as well as developing the robustness needed to cope with some difficult life events.

SHARING IDEAS AND FORMULATIONS WITH STAFF TEAMS

When introducing this way of working into a service organization (see Table 9.1), it is likely to be the first time they have come across such an approach. As there has been little consideration of the emotional lives and inner worlds of people with ID to date, services tend to expect behavioural or medical approaches and it is important to get a sense of whether this more 'emotionally aware' way of working is acceptable and feasible in a service. It is also important to note any service issues such as high staff turnover or lack of support for staff, which may preclude the use of this approach. If the initial formulation feedback is accepted and it appears the organization is willing to work in this way, the next step is to negotiate training with all staff working with the individual. In this training, staff members are made aware of the process of attachment and emotional development and its vulnerability to disruption in people with ID. This can be followed by more specific information about how the person they support has been affected in their emotional development. This entails a careful clinical judgement about what personal historical information may need to be shared with the staff team to increase their understanding and empathy. The amount of information shared needs to be balanced carefully against the need for privacy and confidentiality. Agencies supporting individuals will need to abide by data protection legislation and guidance, therefore there should be organizational policies in

Table 9.1 Summary of elements of 'good enough' emotionally nurturing care

Core staff group	• Made up of 6–7 staff members
	• Enables client to develop trust, emotional safety and attachments in a safe, contained way
	• Group size ensures the client is always supported by someone they are 'attached to' despite staff absence
Attuned care	• Staff are aware of the individual's intellectual and comprehension issues and modify their support style appropriately
	• Staff are aware of the individual's emotional arousal cycle and strategies that help the person feel calmer
	• Staff are aware of significant anniversaries for the person that may impact on their mood and are prepared to respond accordingly
Consistency	• Staff are all following the same procedures and routines around tasks necessary in support
Reliable	• Minimal changes to the staff rota
	• Any staff changes and breaks are explained and planned for
	• Staff do not make promises or arrangements without ensuring they can be followed through
Demonstrating nurture	• Through warm, interpersonal style with the person, use of considered touch, as appropriate
	• Doing things now and then for the person to 'treat' them, make them feel special
Boundaries	• Keeping contact to shifts, not sharing phone numbers or social media contacts. This can be explained as 'the rules from the boss' so as not to be felt personally rejecting.

place regarding staff's need to keep confidential any information known about those they support.

Consent should be sought, where possible, from the client about what may be shared. If the person does not have the capacity to make a decision about giving consent, views should be sought from family and/or other involved professionals to make a decision in the person's best interests, as described in the Mental Capacity Act (2005). In deciding what to share, other factors may be considered, such as what historical information staff members already have access to in the form of physical records, the significance of which may not be understood properly by them, and also what myths and rumours there may be about the person they are supporting.

Staff members who are helped to 'know' and understand the person they support are more likely to be able to be thoughtful in their work, leading not only to an enhanced and attuned care experience for the individual, but also, in the author's experience from staff feedback, a more enriched and satisfying work experience for staff.

Such training can be emotionally intense for staff, as they are being given a different perspective on their client. There may be relief in actually understanding why the person is the way they are, coupled with upset regarding understanding what has happened to the person. There may be guilt and sadness at the service provision that has been delivered previously which hasn't met the individual's needs. The subject matter may lead staff to think of their own and their children's early emotional experiences. They may have family members or friends who have ID and relate the information to them. Efforts need to be made to 'contain' the session emotionally for the staff. Warning them that the material may be difficult, that it's okay to leave the room for a few minutes and also the offer of being available to discuss any personal issues at a later date are ways of offering this. Noone and Hastings' (2010) work in developing mindfulness offers additional ways of helping staff to manage these difficult emotions. In the author's experience, it is important that key figures in the organization, such as team leaders and managers, are present to ensure that everyone has the same information simultaneously. Non-attendance of these people can make implementation of new strategies difficult, leading to staff frustration.

Follow-up sessions should be arranged with the team and these should be monthly in the first instance. The purpose of the sessions is to give staff the chance to discuss any practical issues arising and consolidate the understanding gained at the training session. In addition, as emotional functioning has been acknowledged explicitly with the team, difficult feelings around the person they support may surface and need to be normalized for staff so that they can be expressed and discussed, rather than being 'acted out' in their work.

WORKING THROUGH THERAPY

In Disability Psychotherapy, individual therapy is appropriate to help a person not only process difficult or traumatic experiences, but also to experience some of the emotional elements that may have been missed out on earlier in life. This approach can be useful when other clinical ways of working have failed to bring about lasting changes in the person's difficult or challenging behaviours. Evidence of early life disruptions which may have impacted on attachments and emotional development are also a good indicator for attempting to use such an approach. Some level of verbal ability in the individual is useful, although not essential, as, by drawing from art or play therapy approaches, adaptations can be made (Baikie, 2004; Upton, 2009). In using this approach, the relationship between client and therapist is the therapeutic tool. There are no goals or agendas set for the session, as what the person talks and communicates about is the material of the session. The therapist consciously gives the client a relationship experience where the missed elements of early care are made concretely and overtly available to them.

This section is not an account of how to undertake psychotherapy with this client group. For this, the reader is directed to Beail and Newman (2005), Sinason (2010) and Hodges (2003). Instead, this section will draw upon this approach to raise awareness of how a person can be given the experience of a relationship that includes consistent, reliable, predictable, nurturing, contained and attuned care (see Table 9.2).

Table 9.2 Summary of elements in an emotionally nurturing therapeutic relationship

Establishing the therapeutic space	• Ensuring the same comfortable, private room is available to see the client each week at the same time • Ensuring the room looks the same each week before the client enters • Bookings of room and therapist time may need to be made well ahead
Contract setting and adherence to boundaries	• Stick to session times even if the client arrives very early or late • If the client leaves early, assure them that the therapist will stay in the room, as it is 'their time' • Give plenty of notice of planned breaks with reassurance of return
Concrete communications of nurturing	• Examples might include: checking the person is comfortable in the room, letting them choose their seat where possible, taking their coat, providing refreshments, as appropriate

(Continued)

Table 9.2 (*Continued*)

Early sessions	• May use 'getting to know you' practical activities or assessments to give the client a focus
	• Reassure clients in early sessions that they can decide not to come and there will be no consequences
Therapeutic elements	• The relationship is the therapeutic tool – there is no session agenda
	• Use active listening and reflection to let the person know they are being attended to
	• Be aware of cognitive issues and adapt approach as necessary
	• Use and understanding of unconscious communications comes via supervision, further training and clinical experience
	• Be aware of the need for emotional regulation in session, especially towards the end
	• Educate the person that they may feel tired after the session, encourage self-care and nurture
Process notes	• Write a narrative of the session as soon as possible afterwards to process what has happened
	• Reviewing in monthly batches reveals patterns not possible to see week to week
Liaison with support staff	• Some monitoring to check how the client is coping with the emotional material of sessions
	• Especially needed at the beginning and end of work and at times of significant disclosures and insights
Supervision/ support	• Needed by the therapist to process session material as well as containment and self-care

Establishing a Therapeutic Safe Base

Before therapy starts, it is important to attend to dynamic administration (Barnes, Ernst and Hyde, 1999) in establishing boundaries to the work by ensuring that a suitable room is available to see the person at the same day and time each week. Sessions are usually up to 50 minutes long, and the room should be comfortable and sited where there will be no interruptions and minimal distractions from outside. Prior to the first session, the clinician should explain to both the person and their supporters that the sessions will be at the same time each week. Other elements of the therapeutic contract, such as confidentiality and intention to give warnings of any planned breaks or changes, are also explained. Sometimes at the start of the therapy, people will attend sessions extremely early or late or try to stay past the ending time, but the agreed times should be adhered to. The therapist should take advantage of any naturally arising opportunities to reinforce the idea of the sessions being protected, for example at the beginning of the session saying to the client, 'let's make sure the sign is on the door so no one comes into our room'. These elements give the client a sense that the sessions, or the 'therapeutic space', have clear boundaries and are containing; they also indicate that the therapist is reliable and predictable.

Starting the Work and Informed Consent

Gestures on the part of the therapist, such as offering the client a drink, taking their coat, ensuring they are comfortable and that the room feels okay for them, communicate a sense of warmth and nurture. Initially in the work, the therapist looks for opportunities to demonstrate nurturing, understanding and attunement through active listening, reflection and 'mirroring' of the client's emotions. If the person finds it difficult to talk initially, the use of more concrete 'getting to know you' work can be useful in giving a structure and an opportunity for the therapist and client to become more at ease with each other. This might include activities such as writing or drawing, for example, lists of the person's likes, dislikes, people in their lives, family tree, hopes for the future and what makes them feel basic emotions. The therapist also needs to think creatively about adapting their approach to 'fit' the idiosyncratic cognitive needs of each individual who is worked with. Beail (2013) gives an account of adaptations that need to be made regarding cognitive issues when working with people with ID. He describes how clients may struggle verbally to express experiences they are thinking about; they may not have the mentalization abilities to understand that others have thoughts and feelings different to their own; chronologies may be difficult if they struggle with sequences and there may be real difficulties in language comprehension and information processing. All of these factors need to be considered by the therapist in adapting their approach when working with people with ID.

Client consent is an issue that needs consideration, as the person may not feel they have a choice in attending and may acquiesce accordingly. At the beginning of the work, a general explanation should be given, that they have been asked to come because they have been feeling upset or sad or angry and the therapist will be here each week at this time to talk about whatever is important to them, to try and help them be less upset about things. The person is told each week that it is up to them if they want to come back next week and that if they do the therapist will be there, but if they don't, that is okay. A review of the sessions may be arranged with the client in the early months of the work, to see whether they wish to continue. In this way, the client is given a real experience over time of what it is they are agreeing to and the therapist can determine whether acquiescence is an issue and/or if the client is trying to please them. It is useful to be aware that clients in supported services may not be given a choice each week by staff about whether they want to attend, as they are often just told they have an appointment. As well as being explicit with the client, as outlined above, it is also useful to monitor things such as the client telling staff they are unwell or wanting to go and do other activities instead of coming to the session, as this may be occurring because the person does not feel able specifically to say they do not want to come.

As the person engages in the process and they begin to experience the therapist as reliable and predictable, therapy becomes a 'secure base' where the client feels contained and understood. They may then be able to 'explore' and process previous life experiences and relationships. The timescale of this varies widely, with some clients being able to start this almost immediately and others taking longer.

Understanding Meanings

The person may communicate by the usual means such as words, tone of voice and body language. However, some clients may not have the emotional vocabulary or mentalization abilities to talk about their emotions or experiences, or their ID may impair their ability to remember or narrate their experiences. Here, emotions and experience may be communicated unconsciously by the client to the therapist through mechanisms such as projections or projective identification (see Hodges, 2003 for more detail). Awareness of transference, that is how the client relates to the therapist based on their internal representations of previous relationship experiences, and countertransference, that is the feelings the therapist has towards the client and what the therapist experiences emotionally in the sessions, enables the therapist to be aware of and monitor these unconscious emotional communications.

Process notes, or narrative records of what occurred and what was felt in the sessions, help the therapist to think through and work out the meaning of what has happened and been communicated in the room. Occasionally reviewing these notes, several months at a time, identifies themes that are not possible to notice week to week. Similarly, regular clinical supervision with an experienced psychodynamically-orientated supervisor is essential to aid this process of understanding the client's emotional communications.

Emotional Regulation

Helping the client to regulate their emotional state is an important part of therapy. If they become upset or cry, passing the tissues and reassuring the person with a soothing voice and body language that it is acceptable and appropriate to be upset gives them a sense that their emotions are 'containable' and can be tolerated by another. This is often a new experience for a person, who in the past may not have been able to find the words to be understood or may have expressed their emotions in inappropriate ways, leading to aversive reactions. Similarly, the client may become angry in the session or shout. As long as it is safe to do so, the experience of this being tolerated and contained by the therapist, rather than reacted to, is often novel for the client. It is important to remain aware of timing in the session so the person does not leave in a distressed state. Talking about neutral topics towards the session end helps the person to be calm before they leave, but with reassurance that the upsetting subjects can be talked about again in the future. The emotional work in therapy can be exhausting, and clients should be encouraged and, if necessary, supported to relax or do something pleasant or nurturing for themselves later in the day.

When a person is embedded within a care system, permission may need to be sought to speak to carers about how they are coping in between sessions. Without breaking therapeutic confidentiality, checks can be made regarding whether there have been changes in functioning or behaviour, nightmares or repetitively talking about topics, which might indicate that the therapeutic work has been 'too much' for the person. Thought can then be given to how to manage the sessions better so that the material is not overwhelming. Additionally, some work may need to be undertaken with carers to support them in how to react if the person is talking about distressing topics. Advice to carers may include not asking searching questions regarding what the person is saying, but rather listening sympathetically and reassuring the person as much as possible that their situation is different now and that they are safe, and so on. Once the person has felt 'heard', reminding them that they are going to therapy to discuss these issues before then trying to redirect onto something distracting and preferably nurturing is also important in helping them contain their feelings.

As the work progresses, opportunities arise to help the person's emotional understanding by labelling feelings, normalizing them and gently helping the person to understand them. The person's emotional defences, or strategies they have used to avoid feeling emotional pain, can be gently challenged within this holding, containing environment. Eventually, the person may be able to consider the consequences and impacts of their emotions and the way they were previously expressed. Over time, the person can begin to feel and process their emotions, rather than act them out through difficult behaviours.

Therapeutic Ruptures and Endings

Therapist holidays, absences, changed sessions or other difficulties within the relationship can lead to 'therapeutic ruptures' or deteriorations in the therapy relationship. The client may become angry or upset or they may miss the next session. However, such events can provide opportunities for the person to have an experience of 'relationship repair' wherein the difficulty is acknowledged and thought about together with the therapist. This helps the person develop emotional robustness and learn that difficulties can be faced and overcome, leaving both partners in the relationship able to move forward. The experience of being apologized to can be a rare and powerful one for clients, especially for those who have come from emotionally barren and disrupted backgrounds and subsequently developed difficult and challenging behaviours.

It is essential that endings are thought about early on in therapy, especially if the work has been long term or open-ended, as many clients with ID have experienced abandonments or losses earlier in their lives. An ending period of between six weeks and three months allows the person to process their feelings of sadness, anger and regret about the therapy stopping. There may be increases in distressed behaviours during this period and feelings from previous losses may also re-emerge. It is important that the person has enough opportunities for these to be acknowledged, discussed and thought about.

Having an ending date early in the therapy enables this issue to be kept 'live' all the way through the work.

It can be seen that the therapeutic relationship has a two-fold purpose. First, the individual is able to experience the early emotional ingredients for development within a secure attachment relationship that they may have missed out on earlier in life, as well as being able to 'work through' other difficult life experiences. Distressed emotions are able to be understood, processed and faced rather than being emotionally overwhelming and leading to uncontrollable distressed or challenging behaviours.

To illustrate the above issues, the following is an account of the first 18 months of therapeutic work with 'Matt', who gave permission for this to be shared as he wanted to help others to get similar therapeutic help. He chose his own pseudonym, which is of someone who is a hero to him.

Case Example: Matt

Initial assessment information: Matt is a 30-year-old, well-built, strapping 'lad' who initially appeared to have a very mild or borderline ID. He experienced extreme deprivation and lack of protection as a child. As a teenager and then a young adult, the police were regularly involved with Matt regarding sexually inappropriate behaviour, physical aggression, property damage and drunk and disorderly behaviour.

Matt has been in supported living with a provider that has expertise in forensic issues for the last ten years. The provider gave the kind of emotionally nurturing support outlined earlier, which has given Matt a level of emotional security and helped him to build a full, active and enjoyable life. There has been a substantial reduction in challenging behaviours during this time, with a complete cessation of any sexual offending, although there are still occasional threats of physical aggression and episodes of drunk and disorderly behaviour. At the time therapy commenced, he was struggling to cope with any changes in his life and had experienced several bereavements in recent years. In the six months prior to therapy, he had become much more challenging to support. He appeared to be in a highly agitated state much of the time and was often verbally aggressive and threatening. He was ringing the staff office multiple times a day with varying demands about things he wanted attending to in his life or home, or staff that he wanted on shift with him, but then was very rejecting and often abusive to staff when they tried to address these requests.

Therapy intervention: In the early stages of therapy, Matt was fidgety and would get up and wander around the room. He was only able to stay in the sessions for about 20 minutes and would often leave to investigate any noises he heard outside. He usually spoke monotonously about his latest passion, such as fishing. At this stage he was not able to tolerate any reflections, typically responding with an aggressive 'that's what I said isn't it?' He was unable to say how or why he was upset, often responding with 'I'm fine'.

During this early stage of therapy, efforts were made concretely to demonstrate therapist availability and the therapeutic elements of consistency, reliability and predictability. This was done by staying in the room for the available 50 minutes, even if Matt left early, when he would be told 'I will be here, this is your time'. If Matt wandered in and out of the room, the door was propped open to show that the therapist was still there. The therapist was conscious of using body language and vocalization to demonstrate active listening and did not respond to or challenge any aggressive verbalizations from Matt, except to apologize if something had been done to upset him. The first few months of work with Matt were very much a process of 'pre-therapy', with the purpose of showing Matt, as concretely as possible, that the therapist was available, consistent, reliable, boundaried and listening to him. Matt was always asked if he wanted to come back next week. Sometimes he said no and was told that the therapist would be here in the room anyway, as this was his time. Matt consistently attended.

Over the next couple of months, the same fidgetiness and leaving sessions continued, but Matt began to accept reflections of his emotions as well as very gentle interpretations of his behaviours such as 'changes make you feel very upset'. It seemed that Matt had begun to understand that he was being listened to and over the next four months Matt talked about some of his early traumatic experiences. He talked about the same incidents repeatedly, each time giving more detail. Sessions became increasingly longer than the initial 20 minutes.

During this period, the therapist was able to 'bear witness' to Matt's experiences, giving him the message that his emotional pain was containable. The therapist's tone of voice and body language were able to soothe and helped to provide regulation of his emotional state. Matt began to cry during this period, which continued throughout the work. There also began the process of 'mind-mindedness' (see Chapter 2) with opportunities arising naturally to inform Matt about emotions, giving words to them and normalizing them as well as helping him to understand that what had happened to him was wrong and had not been his fault.

About nine months into the work, it became apparent that Matt was very competent at masking his cognitive difficulties. Undertaking a cognitive assessment was discussed and thought about together over the next few weeks. When completed, it showed that Matt's IQ score was in the moderate range, much lower than the impression he gave. It was found he had specific difficulties regarding processing information and verbal comprehension. Staff training, undertaken with his permission, resulted in Matt noticing that staff were talking to him differently. Matt was able to experience being 'attuned to' by both staff and the therapist. On being given simplified feedback of the assessment findings, Matt responded 'I've had it all my life you know…' as well as '…it takes me ages to get the words out.'

This additional understanding of Matt resulted in him being able to express how he felt when people did not take his difficulties into account. He began to verbalize his frustration and anger if either the therapist or staff overwhelmed him or spoke in a way he did not understand. This gave multiple opportunities for relationship 'ruptures' to be 'repaired' through talking about and acknowledging the issue and then the therapist apologizing and making changes as appropriate.

For the next few months, interpersonal issues were the key themes that Matt brought to the therapy sessions. Rather than becoming agitated, he was able to talk and cry about missing people in his life and began to be able to show empathy and concern regarding people he knew who were ill. During this time, it was discovered that Matt had been spending large amounts of money phoning sexually explicit chat lines. This was very expensive as he was staying on the line for a long time, primarily for someone to talk to. He initially became agitated and aggressive with staff when this was discovered, but then became tearful and remorseful. After a few weeks, Matt was able to talk about this and his feelings of loneliness and the service could then work with him about how to help. Matt began to show remorse regarding other outbursts as well. He also began to say how he was feeling about other issues in the expectation that something would be done by the service to help. The work to this point had been about a year and a half of weekly meetings.

Therapy outcomes: Matt made very significant progress due to being able to experience a secure, reliable attachment relationship that could contain him and his experiences. Within this, he had been able to develop the ability to think about and verbalize his emotions and reflect on the impact of his previous modes of expression. At this point, incidents of agitation and verbal aggression were still occurring, but were much less frequent and less severe than previously.

SAFE EMOTIONAL WORKING

The emotional work outlined in this chapter can be intense for those providing it. Working with people who show distressed or challenging behaviours means that carers may find themselves in anxiety-provoking situations with clients. They may have memories triggered of traumatic personal experiences or they may have very difficult feelings about the clients they are supporting. Schuengel et al. (2010) discuss how caring situations can activate carers' own attachment experiences. If these issues are left unresolved, they can add to the emotional stress of the carer and impact on their ability to be empathic and attuned to the needs of those they are supporting. Therefore, it is important that staff themselves are emotionally supported in being able to carry out this work.

Staff need regular meetings together, not only for necessary update information, but also to be able to share experiences and be reminded of why the person is the way they are and why management strategies are in place. Regular individual supervision should be an opportunity to reinforce this, as well as a confidential place to share feelings and emotions that may have been aroused through work. Additional support mechanisms such as extra support or counselling may be needed by staff. It is important that services acknowledge the potential emotional impact of this work and encourage staff to be open about this rather than fear being seen as 'weak', which may then adversely affect their ability to care or lead them to 'act out' these difficult feelings towards clients.

Those providing therapy also need to ensure they are supported in this work by receiving regular clinical supervision to ensure that they have space to process the emotional load of the work they are undertaking. Psychodynamic supervision will assist with the technical aspects such as understanding the unconscious aspects of the work. Additionally, such therapeutic work, often long term in nature, needs to be understood and supported by management so that therapists are able to carry out the work whilst being contained themselves.

HELPING SERVICE SYSTEMS TO UNDERSTAND THE WORK

The ways of working that have been described may be perceived as a novel way of thinking about the difficulties of people who have distressed or challenging behaviours. Getting this way of thinking accepted within a service system is important not only in encouraging service providers to think about staffing and reduce staff movement, but also for longer-term therapeutic work to be supported, as it is often contrary to service expectations.

There is growing research evidence in support of this way of working (Frankish, 1989, 1992; Jackson and Beail, 2013), but this is dependent on the relatively small number of active practitioners using this approach. Individual pieces of clinical work showing the benefits of the approach can often act as 'proof of principle' within a care system, for example working with people described as 'revolving door' clients, who have not responded to or engaged with other approaches and who are the cause of anxiety to staff and management.

In the author's experience, when the proof of principle has been established, interest in the approach grows across the service. In one service, awareness training was requested and set up with both direct support staff and other professionals. This then led to an increase in requests for this way of working and also greater acceptance of attachment and emotion-centred formulation and intervention plans when delivered. Other multi-disciplinary professionals, including those working primarily in behavioural ways, have subsequently sought supervision regarding incorporating the approach into their own practice.

CONCLUSION

This chapter has outlined an approach to working with people with ID who are in distress which attempts to address some of the unmet attachment and emotional development needs of the individual. Clinical experience has shown that giving the person support that is attuned and allows them to experience what they have missed in early life can result in powerful and enduring change, going beyond the resolution of the presenting difficulties as individuals emotionally develop and grow. Case work has demonstrated that those who are able to experience this support via both staff and therapy simultaneously have made the most rapid and sustained improvements, although further research is needed to support this.

Colleagues in other disciplines using different theoretical approaches have been able to understand and incorporate these principles in their own work and practices, as have direct care staff and their managers. It is hoped that the insights shared in this chapter will enable the reader to think about using these ideas in their own work, whatever theoretical approach is being used.

This chapter has outlined an approach, drawn from Disability Psychotherapy, which not only acknowledges the extraordinary levels of emotional distress that an individual may have experienced, often with uncompleted emotional development and lack of support, but also emphasizes their humanness. It addresses the most fundamental human needs of having emotional attachments and being emotionally cared for and looked after. These are the elements of care that sometimes feel lost in the midst of services juggling the multiple demands of provision, budgets, commissioners and involved professionals, but which are crucial to remember and keep in mind.

REFERENCES

Baikie, A. (2004) The creative use of limited language in psychotherapy by an adolescent with a severe learning disability. In D. Simpson and L. Miller (eds) *Unexpected Gains: Psychotherapy with People with Learning Disabilities*. London: Karnac Books.

Barnes, B., Ernst, S. and Hyde, K. (1999) *An Introduction to Groupwork: A Group-Analytic Perspective*. London: Palgrave Macmillan.

Beail, N. (2013) The role of cognitive factors in psychodynamic psychotherapy with people who have intellectual disabilities. *The Psychotherapist*, 53: 8–10.

Beail, N. and Newman, D. (2005) Psychodynamic counselling and psychotherapy for mood disorders. In P. Sturmey (ed.) *Mood Disorders in People with Mental Retardation*. Kingston, New York: NADD Press.

Bishop, D. (2003) *Test for Reception of Grammar – 2*. London: Pearson.

Bowlby, J. (1979) *The Making and Breaking of Affectional Bonds*. London: Tavistock Publications.

Bowlby, J. (1988) *A Secure Base: Parent–child attachment and healthy human development*. London: Routledge.

Breakwell, G. (1997) *Coping with Aggressive Behaviour*. Leicester, UK: British Psychological Society.

Emerson, E. and Gone, R. (2012) Social Context. In E. Emerson, C. Hatton, K. Dickson, R. Gone, A. Caine and J. Bromley (eds) *Clinical Psychology and People with Intellectual Disabilities* (2nd edition, Chapter 3). Oxford: Wiley-Blackwell.

Frankish, P. (1989) Meeting the emotional needs of handicapped people: A psychodynamic approach. *Journal of Mental Deficiency Research*, 33: 407–414.

Frankish, P. (1992) A psychodynamic approach to emotional difficulties within a social framework. *Journal of Intellectual Disability Research*, 36: 559–563.

Frankish, P. (2013a) Facing emotional pain – a model for working with people with intellectual disabilities and trauma. *Attachment: New Directions in Psychotherapy and Relational Psychoanalysis*, 7: 276–282.

Frankish, P. (2013b) Measuring the emotional development of adults with Intellectual Disabilities. *Advances in Mental Health and Intellectual Disabilities*, 7: 272–276.

Gerhardt, S. (2004) *Why Love Matters*. Hove, UK: Brunner-Routledge.

Hodges, S. (2003) *Counselling Adults with Learning Disabilities*. London: Palgrave Macmillan.

Jackson, T. and Beail, N. (2013) The practice of individual psychodynamic psychotherapy with people who have intellectual disabilities. *Psychoanalytic Psychotherapy*, 27: 108–123.

Mahler, M., Pine, F. and Bergman, A. (1975) *The Psychological Birth of the Human Infant*. New York: Basic Books.

Mattison, V. and Pistrang, N. (2004) The endings of relationships between people with learning disabilities and their keyworkers. In D. Simpson and L. Miller (eds) *Unexpected Gains: Psychotherapy with People with Learning Disabilities*. London: Karnac Books.

McCarthy, J. (2001) Post-traumatic stress disorder in people with learning disability. *Advances in Psychiatric Treatment*, 17: 163–169.

Mental Capacity Act (2005) *Code of Practice*. London: TSO.

Noone, S.J. and Hastings, R.P. (2010) Using acceptance and mindfulness-based workshops with support staff caring for adults with intellectual disabilities. *Mindfulness*, 1: 67–73.

Quarmby, K. (2011) *Scapegoat. Why We Are Failing Disabled People*. London: Portobello Books.

Schuengel, C., Kef, S., Damen, S. and Worm, M. (2010) People who need people: Attachment and professional caregiving. *Journal of Intellectual Disability Research*, 54: 38–47.

Seager, M. (2014) Using attachment theory to inform psychologically minded care services, systems and environments. In A. Danquah and K. Berry (eds) *Attachment Theory in Adult Mental Health: A guide to clinical practice*. Oxon: Routledge.

Sinason, V. (2010) *Mental Handicap and the Human Condition*. London: Free Association Books.

Upton, J. (2009) When words are not enough: Creative therapeutic approaches. In T. Cottis (ed.) *Intellectual Disability, Trauma and Psychotherapy*. London: Routledge.

Wechsler, D. (2008) *Wechsler Adult Intelligence Scale*: Fourth edition. London: Pearson.

Winnicott, D.W. (1964) *The Child, the Family and the Outside World*. Harmondsworth: Penguin Books.

Chapter 10

ATTACHMENT TRAUMA AND PATHOLOGICAL MOURNING IN ADULTS WITH INTELLECTUAL DISABILITIES

Deanna J. Gallichan[1] and Carol George[2]

[1]*Community Learning Disabilities Team, Plymouth Community Healthcare CIC, Plymouth, UK*
[2]*Department of Psychology, Mills College, Oakland, California, USA*

Clinicians know from experience that adults with intellectual disabilities (ID) are at risk for sub-optimal parental attachments and maltreatment from within and outside of the family. Until now, thinking about attachment in this population has been broad brush and has lacked a coherent conceptual framework to understand the role attachment plays in clinical problems. This has been largely due to a lack of reliable and valid attachment assessments for this population.

In this chapter, we address these issues using the first direct developmental adult attachment assessment that has demonstrated face and conceptual validity for this population: the Adult Attachment Projective Picture System (AAP; George and West, 1999; 2012). This developmental attachment approach, which follows the founding tenets of attachment theory (Bowlby, 1969/1982; 1973; 1980), is concerned with the ways in which childhood experience in attachment relationships is consolidated in adulthood into a representation (i.e., a mental 'blueprint' or internal working model) of behaviour, evaluations of relationships and of the self as deserving of protection and care (see Main, Kaplan and Cassidy, 1985). Unlike attachment measures used in infancy and

---

Attachment in Intellectual and Developmental Disability: A Clinician's Guide to Practice and Research, First Edition. Edited by Helen K. Fletcher, Andrea Flood and Dougal Julian Hare.
© 2016 John Wiley & Sons, Ltd. Published 2016 by John Wiley & Sons, Ltd.

childhood, one does not need directly to observe attachment behaviour in typically developing adults in order to assess it. Rather, it is possible to assess the person's attachment representation by asking them to think about attachment situations and analyzing the content and form of the resulting narrative (George and West, 2012). Research has demonstrated that individuals' 'stories' about attachment situations are closely linked to their actual attachment experiences. This linkage has not been established for paper and pencil questionnaires assessing attachment 'style'. There is robust evidence that these self-report measures assess a different construct to narrative measures derived from the developmental tradition (see Roisman *et al.*, 2007 and Crowell *et al.*, 2008 for more detail). The implication here is that if we are interested in how adults with ID think and feel about their childhood attachment experiences, we need to use a measure derived from the developmental tradition.

In Gallichan and George (2014), we established initial face validity for using the AAP narrative assessment with adults with ID by comparing AAP outcomes against biographical and clinical case records. We focused on adults with mild ID because the narrative approach requires a minimal level of verbal ability. In this chapter, we follow up on a striking observation from our initial study: the AAP narratives of adults with ID frequently included themes of danger, maltreatment and being terrorized by bullies. Here, we examine this response pattern more closely through the lens of attachment trauma. We first outline some basic tenets of attachment theory as it pertains to trauma, including how trauma is related to mourning.

WHAT IS ATTACHMENT TRAUMA?

The *Oxford English Dictionary* defines psychological trauma as the 'emotional shock following a stressful event; a distressing or emotionally disturbing experience.' In the field of mental health, trauma is characterized by persistent and extreme levels of anxiety and fear. Attachment research has shown that attachment trauma is not isomorphic with the broad list of events conceived as trauma in the post-traumatic stress literature (Moss, Cyr and Dubois-Comtois, 2004). It is also not confined to loss and physical or sexual abuse, which is the typical lens on trauma used in the field of attachment (Liotti, 2004; Hesse, 2008). Solomon and George (2011a) argued that ideas about what constitutes attachment trauma must extend to all experiences that are 'assaults to attachment,' not just loss and abuse. Assaults might also include: unpredictable parental rage; unexplained lengthy separations; chronic parent hospitalization or life-threatening disease (e.g., cancer). What is central to the attachment theory perspective of trauma is the combination of frightening experiences with parents' inaccessibility and failure to provide protection at exactly those times when children need their parents the most (Bowlby, 1969, 1973, 1980; Main and Solomon, 1990; George and Solomon, 2008; Solomon and George, 2011b). The result is children who feel helpless, isolated, abandoned and vulnerable (George and Solomon, 2008; Solomon and George, 2011b).

Our assessment approach to adults with ID relies on representational assessment; that is, assessing the person's state of mind with respect to attachment, not their actual experiences. According to attachment theory, individuals attempt to manage parental disappointments and failures by using defensive processes to edit, sort and exclude the memories and affects that are most difficult and threatening (Bowlby, 1980). Defensive processes create representational models of the self as functional, and attachment figures as caring, excluding difficulties from consciousness (Bowlby, 1980; George and West, 2012). It is difficult to maintain these defensive processes and representational patterns when experiences are characterized by persistent attachment assaults and parental failed protection. The emotional intensity of these experiences becomes potentially devastating (Bowlby, 1980; George and West, 2012). Experience and affect become traumatic, and defensive processing risks taking a pathological form, with the goal now to block, not just edit, traumatizing attachment experience and parental failures.

Bowlby called this form of defensive processing 'segregated systems' (conceived as an updated form of psychoanalytic repression). He viewed segregated defences as brittle, unreliable and prone to breaking down during times of stress, subsequently unleashing full-blown traumatic responses. When segregated system defences break down, individuals risk becoming emotionally flooded and dysregulated; they are unable to maintain coherent or productive coping strategies to manage their distress, including seeking care from others (George and Solomon, 2008; Solomon and George, 2011b).

Bowlby's (1980) discussion centred on defensive responses to loss through death. He proposed that the only way to restore equilibrium was through the process of mourning the person who had died. George and West (2012) expanded on Bowlby's view to explain how mourning is also required to restore mental and behavioural equilibrium in response to all attachment trauma, not just bereavement. Mourning requires the person to consciously acknowledge traumatic events and the feelings associated with failed protection by attachment figures. When mourning is complete, internal working models of self and reality are rebalanced and individuals no longer need to live in a state of chronic fear (Bowlby, 1980). Individuals are then able to reach out to attachment figures and other people for care and develop their own resources for handling threatening stress (Bowlby, 1980; George and West, 2012).

The cost of not mourning trauma is to live with a state of mind that blocks the capacity for updating models of self and attachment experience that match reality. Bowlby (1980) conceived of this representational state as 'pathological mourning.' Pathological mourning risks current events triggering a major breakdown during which individuals become flooded and overwhelmed with grief, rage and pain. Bowlby described clinical cases in which this breakdown was accompanied by emotional dysregulation, including severe psychiatric symptoms (e.g., fugue states, dissociation). In short, pathological mourning has the potential to derail normal behavioural and psychological wellbeing.

Following Bowlby (1980), George and West (2012) defined three different forms of pathological mourning for attachment trauma, all of which have been shown to be risk factors for psychological and behavioural distress in community and clinical populations (Buchheim and George, 2011; Delvecchio et al., 2014; George, Petrowski and West, 2014). The etiology and signs of these forms are qualitatively distinct. One form is *failed mourning*, which describes a persistent state of being unable to initiate the mourning process. Defences create a sense of emotional numbness, effectively neutralizing and distancing the self from memories of attachment trauma. Representations of self compensate for trauma by portraying a unitary sense of self as strong, capable and emotionally impervious to distress, but current events can trigger a major grief reaction (Bowlby, 1980; George and West, 2012).

Two other forms of pathological mourning are characterized by becoming consumed with attachment trauma. These are *unresolved chronic mourning* and *preoccupation with personal suffering*. *Unresolved chronic mourning* describes a representational self that can become unpredictably flooded and overwhelmed by trauma. When triggered, individuals risk being consumed by feelings of depression, helplessness and debilitating mental and behavioural lapses, such as dissociative states (see also Liotti, 2004 and Hesse, 2008). *Preoccupation with personal suffering* describes a representation of self that lives in a state of being consumed with the details of sorrow, pain and grief; 'living in the war zone' of threat and fear (George and West, 2012).

Our work to date suggests that pathological mourning may play a unique role in case formulation and intervention with individuals with ID. We now turn to review evidence of attachment trauma in adults with ID.

ATTACHMENT TRAUMA AND INTELLECTUAL DISABILITIES

People with ID have been shown to be particularly vulnerable to all forms of maltreatment, as compared to individuals without disabilities (Cousins, 2006; Murphy, 2007; Murray and Osborne, 2009), and to individuals with other types of disabilities (Horner-Johnson and Drum, 2006). This vulnerability is thought to be due to multiple factors: their reliance on others; difficulty in placing individuals in protective environments; the difficulty that people with ID have in recognizing or articulating that they are being abused; and underreporting, which makes it hard to obtain accurate rates of abuse (Murphy, 2007; Murray and Osborne, 2009). This vulnerability is reflected in safeguarding policies and practice guidelines for vulnerable adults ('No Secrets', Department of Health, 2000; Mandelstam, 2011).

Another severe maltreatment risk documented for people with ID is bullying. Bullying involves actions or coercion intended to abuse, intimidate, persecute or aggressively impose domination over others, typically those who are smaller or weaker than the bully (O'Connell, Pepler and Craig, 1999; Stevens, Van Oost and De Bourdeaudhuij, 2000). Bullying is now understood as a severe problem with far-reaching consequences, including worsened social, economic and health outcomes in adulthood, and psychological distress and psychiatric symptoms (Takizawa, Maughan and Arseneault, 2014). Mencap's (2007) survey highlighted the scale of the problem for people with ID; of 900 people they questioned, 88% had experienced bullying and victimization. Sadly, this survey also showed that many people with ID found it hard to report bullying, regarding it as a normal part of everyday life. Others found it hard to give a full account of the treatment they experienced and/or were are afraid to 'speak up' for fear of retaliation or disbelief. Even when reported, bullying does not necessarily stop because anti-bullying strategies are not sufficiently incorporated into services for people with ID (Sheard *et al.*, 2001). This means that for adults with ID, bullying is likely to be a pervasive problem with devastating psychological consequences.

People with ID are also prone to other traumatic threats, including severe chronic health conditions such as epilepsy (MacLeod and Austin, 2003; McGrother *et al.*, 2006). Moreover, the stigma of having an intellectual disability itself can provoke feelings of shame and loss, and this knowledge has been considered as a form of trauma for some individuals that undermines self-esteem and mental health (Sinason, 1992; Szivos and Griffiths, 1992; Dagnan and Sandu, 1999; Dagnan and Waring, 2004; Jahoda *et al.*, 2010).

It is attachment figures' responses that influence whether or not these events become traumatizing (Bowlby, 1980; George and Solomon, 2008). If caregivers are consistently helpless to provide comfort and protection in such circumstances, this can compound the trauma in those moments when there is the greatest need for care (George and Solomon, 2008). Research has shown that children's disabilities can overwhelm parents, rendering them helpless and limiting their capacity for the sensitive parent–child interaction and communication required to support attachment security (Pianta *et al.*, 1996; Barnett *et al.*, 1999). Pianta *et al.* (1996) suggested that receiving the child's disability diagnosis signified the 'loss' of a normal child, an experience from which some parents are never able to grieve and recover (see Chapter 3 for further discussion). Unresolved parents (i.e., parents in chronic mourning about the diagnosis) reported significantly higher parenting stress and poorer social support than parents who were able to grieve, and their children were at the highest risk for insecure attachment (Marvin and Pianta, 1996; Pianta *et al.*, 1996; Sheeran, Marvin and Pianta, 1997; Oppenheim *et al.*, 2007).

Parents can also be rendered helpless by professionals or a system of care that separates children and their attachment figures for long periods of time (Solomon and George, 1999). These kinds of separations were heavily criticized following the inquiry into the Winterbourne View scandal in the UK (Department of Health, 2012). According to attachment theory, these separations only serve to threaten attachment-caregiving relationships and heighten feelings of helplessness, isolation and vulnerability (Bowlby, 1973; Solomon and George, 1999).

Given evidence of vulnerability to multiple forms of attachment trauma, we now consider the extent to which adults with ID are vulnerable to pathological mourning. Research and clinical files help us estimate attachment trauma risk, however, addressing this precise question requires detailed assessment. In our first small study, we found evidence of attachment trauma in all five cases (Gallichan and George, 2014). We explore here patterns of pathological mourning in a larger sample of adults with ID.

USING THE ADULT ATTACHMENT PROJECTIVE PICTURE SYSTEM TO ASSESS PATHOLOGICAL MOURNING

The Adult Attachment Projective Picture System (AAP; George, West and Pettem, 1999; George and West, 2012) is a developmental measure of attachment status, with demonstrated potential for adults with ID (Gallichan and George, 2014). The AAP is a free response measure comprised of eight line drawings, one of which is a neutral warm-up and seven of which depict attachment situations. The attachment scenes are: *Window* – a child looks out of a window; *Departure* – an adult man and woman stand facing each other with suitcases positioned nearby; *Bench* – a youth sits alone on a bench (see Figure 10.1); *Bed* – a child and a woman sit at opposite ends of the child's bed; *Ambulance* – a woman and a child watch as a stretcher is loaded into an ambulance; *Cemetery* – a man stands by a gravestone; *Corner* – a child stands in a corner, head turned and hands raised (see Figure 10.2).

Figure 10.1 The *Bench* attachment scene from the Adult Attachment Projective Picture System.

Figure 10.2 The *Corner* attachment scene from the Adult Attachment Projective Picture System.

Participants are instructed to tell a story about each stimulus, guided by probes: *What is happening in this picture? What happened before? What are the characters/people thinking or feeling? What might happen next?* Three administration modifications for adults with ID were made: (i) slight alterations to the standard wording of the probes; (ii) extra neutral scenes at the beginning of the procedure to allow more time for individuals to get used to the story-telling task; (iii) permission to include some positive feedback during the neutral scenes to encourage task confidence (see Gallichan and George, 2014). There was no evidence that language capacity or disability severity in this sample interfered with responding to the AAP stimuli.

Responses are audio recorded and coded by a certified reliable judge[1] from verbatim transcripts. Cases are first evaluated for classification group designation, differentiating among the four traditional groups used in the field: secure, dismissing, preoccupied and unresolved. Discussion of the AAP coding for classification group designation is beyond the scope of this chapter. The reader is referred to George and West (2012) for complete details. In summary, secure individuals are able to think about their attachment past without extensive reliance on defences. Attachment relationships are portrayed as important, even though they are not necessarily 100% satisfactory. Dismissing individuals use defensive processing to distance themselves from attachment distress, often deflecting needs for care and the desire for attachment figures' comfort to other activities (e.g., achievements in work or school) or people (e.g., peers and sexual partners). Preoccupied individuals appear confused about attachment. Their responses are vague about the people or events associated with story themes, and their responses vacillate among different and sometimes opposing ideas. Attachment representations in all three of these groups demonstrate individuals' capacities to contain any fears or threats that emerge and the characters in their stories 'go forward' with life. This containment ranges from: thoughtful consideration of the problem, or seeking comfort from others (secure); taking practical but not thoughtful action (dismissing); others helping out or vague confidence that situations will work out in the end (preoccupied). In contrast, unresolved individuals are derailed by attachment fears and show no evidence of the ability to contain or 'resolve' these threats in their narratives. In short, they remain emotionally flooded and overwhelmed.

The AAP coding and classification system is completely derived from and validated on attachment theory, a point that is especially important to our identification and interpretation of attachment trauma. The coding system evaluates mental representation of attachment, which reflects individuals' current evaluation of past experience. Although the AAP never asks a person to describe his or her experiences, there is a strong correspondence between the AAP narratives and real experience, as determined from biographical information (George and West, 2012).

The AAP has demonstrated concurrent and predictive validity. Concurrent validity analyses demonstrate a significant correspondence between attachment groups classified using the AAP and other validated developmental attachment measures (Buchheim, George and West,

2003; Buchheim *et al.*, 2006; George and West, 2012). Research has demonstrated significant predictive validity for the AAP, including research examining the correlates of the unresolved classification and traumatization (Subic-Wrana *et al.*, 2007; Aikins, Howes and Hamilton, 2009; Béliveau and Moss, 2009; Benoit *et al.*, 2010; Joubert, Webster and Hackett, 2012; von Wietersheim *et al.*, 2014). It has been used in a range of attachment studies investigating neurophysiology, biochemical processes and emotion expression (Buchheim and Benecke, 2007; Buchheim *et al.*, 2009). The AAP has also been used to understand clinical cases (Isaacs *et al.*, 2009; Finn, 2011; Lis *et al.*, 2011; George and Buchheim, 2014).

The work presented in this chapter centres on understanding attachment representations as related to attachment trauma, and on the qualities of self and attachment relationships that determine if individuals are, or are not, in states of persistent mourning. Attachment trauma is evaluated from two kinds of story material. The first involves indications of segregated systems, the pathological form of defensive exclusion described by Bowlby (1980), discussed above. Segregated systems indicators (called markers) are identified by words and themes that depict danger and failed protection, as defined by attachment theory (e.g., death, being frightened or out of control). Once identified, segregated systems markers are evaluated as either normative or traumatic. Segregated systems markers are coded as normative if they are commonly pulled for by the stimulus (e.g., a death in *Ambulance*, being scared of taking a new job in *Departure*). Traumatic segregated systems markers designate severe threat or risk (e.g., isolation, abandonment, abuse, war) and are also evidenced by representational freezing, called constriction, which represents a desperate attempt to regulate overwhelming emotions (e.g., *I can't think; I can't do this one; Nothing happens, Take it away!*). (Note that constriction is not related to verbal ability or uncooperativeness). The second is indications of derealization, defined as material that depicts an out-of-body experience, such as situations or people that are evil or grotesque; sexualization; surreal and dream-like experiences (e.g., the girl is *floating above the bench*). These markers were first identified in the AAP cases of severe physical or sexual maltreatment (Buchheim and George, 2011). In psychiatry, derealization is associated with dissociation symptoms and extreme stress reactions to trauma (i.e., post-traumatic stress; Weiner and Mckay, 2013) and has been linked to experiences of complex or multiple attachment traumas, complicated grief and pathological mourning (Bowlby, 1980; Parkes, 2006; Buchheim and George, 2011; Solomon and George, 2011a).

Pathological mourning status is determined by evaluating the total number of traumatic segregated systems and derealization markers in relation to the attachment classification group. This total is termed 'attachment trauma markers.' Discriminant analyses of the original AAP validity sample show that six or more markers in a transcript place the individual at risk for pathological mourning. *Failed mourning* is a pathological form of dismissing attachment, *preoccupied with personal suffering* is a pathological form of preoccupied attachment, and *chronic unresolved mourning* is a pathological form of unresolved attachment. There are no established cut-offs for adults with ID and, in efforts to be conservative without prior research in this population, we used the established rubric.

Demonstrated validity for the AAP trauma coding system shows that traumatic content differentiates among psychiatric patients with borderline and anxiety diagnoses and community controls. Moreover, it correlates positively with other assessments of unresolved loss and abuse, and differentiates pathological from normative grief (Buchheim and George, 2011; Delvechhio *et al.*, 2014; George, Petrowski and West, 2014).

THE CURRENT STUDY: ATTACHMENT TRAUMA AND PATHOLOGICAL MOURNING IN ADULTS WITH INTELLECTUAL DISABILITIES

The participants in the current study were 12 men and 8 women between 18 and 55 years of age. All participants had received information about this study from their local Community Learning Disabilities Team in the UK (the work base of the first author). Individuals who met the study inclusion criteria were invited to participate. Inclusion criteria included:

1) A documented intellectual disability (e.g., assessed using the Wechsler Adult Intelligence Scale; Wechsler, 2008);
2) The absence of a degenerative neurological condition (e.g., dementia);
3) An ability to see the AAP stimuli;
4) The use of speech to communicate;
5) The capacity to provide informed consent for participation.[2]

Consent procedures were completed by the first author prior to AAP administration. All cases were blinded and made anonymous. The AAP transcripts were coded by the authors. The second author was blind to all information about the participants, except for the fact that participants had an intellectual disability. Both authors evaluated cases for classification group placement and presence of trauma markers.

This study extends our previous research in seeking to document the prominence of attachment trauma and pathological mourning in these new cases. We were especially interested in themes of bullying, as they might appear in people's minds as a form of attachment trauma. Bullying AAP themes are not unusual in adolescents, but even then themes are typically normative (e.g., the bully steals a child's lunch money) and not necessarily threatening. Bullying is uncommon in the AAPs of typically developing adults and our previous work suggested that mental representations in this population were indeed traumatic (e.g. the case study 'Sue' in Gallichan and George, 2014).

Our analyses showed that attachment trauma was evident in the narratives of 90% of the participants (18/20 cases). Trauma markers were most frequently coded in the *Corner* and *Bench* responses. This pattern is similar to that observed in typically developing adults, in part because these two stimuli pull for narratives about especially distressing situations when alone. The trauma themes in our sample were similar to those coded for typically developing adults, including maltreatment (physical, neglect, molestation), escape from danger (e.g., flee the house), abandonment and characters portrayed as helpless or out of control (e.g., trapped, drunk, enraged, having flashbacks). The mean number of segregated systems trauma makers per transcript was 5.75, ranging from 3–21 markers. Only three cases included derealization markers (e.g., surreal themes). In sum, the vast majority of transcripts contained evidence of trauma but traumatic derealization was rare.

Twelve out of twenty (60%) of our participants described bullying in response to at least one AAP stimulus, most typically in *Bench* (50%, 6/12 cases). Several individuals described bullying in response to both *Bench* and *Corner* (42%, 5/12 cases). The majority of stories for which bullying was coded contained traumatic themes (83%, 10/12 cases) marked by helplessness, terror or derealization. As we noted above, this content is unusual when bullying appears in typical adolescent or adult samples.

Our analysis of pathological mourning showed that the majority of participants were assigned to this group (65%, 13/20), the majority of which was *chronic unresolved mourning*, (85%, 11/13). One case (8%) was judged *preoccupation with person suffering* and one case (8%) was judged *failed mourning*.

We now provide two case examples that exemplify the most common form of pathological mourning in our sample: *unresolved chronic mourning*. We include biographical descriptions and attachment representation punctuated by AAP responses to some of the stimuli. The administrator prompts are standardized to the AAP procedure and are omitted here. AAP attachment trauma markers (traumatic segregated systems and derealization) are shown in bold font.

Case Example: June – Unresolved Chronic Mourning for Loss and Abuse

Background: June was in her 50s and lived in a group residential home. She had mild to moderate ID and a genetic wasting condition. June was raised in extremely poor and neglectful conditions. She had several siblings, including a sister who also had ID and the same condition as June. June's father had a history of severe drinking problems, and the children spent time in care due to parental neglect. June was reportedly sexually assaulted in her teens, and again later during an inpatient admission at a hospital for people with ID.

June's middle age years were characterized by loss and separation. Her mother died and her father's declining health prompted a move to residential care. Here, June made several allegations of assault against men with whom she was romantically involved. There was a period of quite intensive involvement from the multi-disciplinary team, including some extensive psychological therapy to help her to process these issues. Her father then died, followed a few years later by her disabled sister.

AAP content and trauma coding: June's AAP narrative revealed two self systems. June was able to maintain an organized state of mind in response to several AAP stimuli by telling stories with themes of personal agency and functional relationships. For example, finding her parents not at home, the girl in *Window* searched inside and out of the house determined to find them (agency). She described a theme of disability in *Bed* (something wrong with the child's leg), with a mother who was simultaneously present yet cross with the boy (i.e., functional synchrony).

The segregated traumatized self was unleashed in response to *Cemetery* and *Corner*. There were twelve trauma markers in June's transcript, seven in response to *Cemetery* and five in response to *Corner*. June's stories described violence and helplessness. In contrast to the other responses, she had no representation of self as having agency, being saved or even coming through these events, and attachment figures were described as threatening and failing to protect, giving some clues as to the etiology of her chronic mourning. June was not able to contain her fear, and her representation of attachment remained dysregulated to the level that characterized unresolved chronic trauma.

Cemetery:

> ...That man's looking down on that grave there. It must be his wife or one of his family there ...somebody done something to his family, or they were in, may, somebody reported a **shot** and that and **killed them** and then he got buried ... they've brought the police and they've brought the ambulance ... yeah, but the man was dead already so the man who is there in the picture might go to his grave, ... it must be his friend or something to do with his family, I think he's going to do something wrong ... yeah, so he knows the man who got **killed** but he knows the people who done it. Yeah, so I think he will go and, go and do something wrong ... yeah ... well either **he'll get killed or someone else will get killed**. Well there's a lot of graves there, there's one, two, three, four, five, six, seven of them so another would be eight **if he gets killed**.

The *Cemetery* scene is thought to elicit thinking and memories of the self as confronting the past. June told a disturbing story about multiple violent deaths, which started to make sense when considering that many of June's family members were dead, including her abusive father and her sister. This response suggested that loss was associated with danger and destruction for June, perhaps reflecting abusive experiences, and fears of her own death. It is also possible that the theme of loss was traumatic not just because of loss of people, but loss of the self through disability.

Corner:

> Oooh, somebody, somebody **hit him** on the neck there, the boy's going like that, somebody's **hitting him.** He may have said something to somebody and **clouted him one.** Feeling sad, his face is sad. Yeah, but they shouldn't do that. Instead of hitting somebody they hit across like that, or hit them, **hit somebody somewhere where you can't, er, see it,** but you can see that, yeah, that's not right. It must be his father doing it, or someone else doing it to him. **He just standing there letting them do it,** but it's not right to stand there and let them do it, he should try to get away from them but he's not moving, **he's standing still and letting them do it.** I feel sorry for that boy.

The *Corner* story depicted the child as helpless in the face of severe abuse, possibly perpetrated by an attachment figure ('it must be his father'). What is perhaps most disturbing is June's personal viewpoint, expressed in the middle segment, that it would be best to hit the child where others couldn't see what was happening. Her representation of maltreatment suggested that abuse was wrong only if it was detected. It is difficult to know exactly from the available details of June's background the experiential source of her *Corner* response. Previous work with the AAP has demonstrated that the narratives have clear autobiographical sources. June's theme of abuse could reflect experiences in her family of origin, though she had never explicitly disclosed any abuse at the hands of her parents. Another possibility could be that this story may also reflect her experiences of sexual abuse and of living in institutional care. Sexual abuse is a crime notable for its lack of witnesses, and the ability to be perpetrated without detection. Moreover, given what we now understand about the practices in old institutions for people with ID, it is not unreasonable to suspect that June may have experienced abuse there that went undetected.

Clinical presentation and support needs: June's presentation fit the notion that she was governed by two selves, patterns that fit Bowlby's (1980) conceptualization of segregated representational selves. One was a presentation of self as organized, stable and capable. She was described as being generally on an emotional 'even keel'. She appeared to be concerned with being in control, and with status and hierarchies, and was described as being 'bossy'. She was attuned to health care and was keen to attend medical appointments, seemingly enjoying interaction with healthcare professionals. Nevertheless, there appeared to be another self, characterized by periods of depression and lack of engagement with staff. She was reportedly in one of these periods not long before she participated in the AAP research, and this was interpreted by some as related to grieving for her recently deceased sister.

June rarely spoke of her childhood experiences, except for an occasional remark that her father was frequently 'drunk' and 'angry'. She distanced herself from her feelings with fiction, regularly copying out sections of children's novels, usually with themes of abuse and parental loss. Indeed, the staff found these written pieces were one of the only ways to discuss difficult feelings with her (albeit indirectly). This interest hints at a representational self from which all of June's sadness and failed protection from loss and abuse was segregated from consciousness.

June's residential placement had been fairly stable over 20 or so years, and she had known many long-standing and consistent staff members during this time. It was therefore interesting that the intense psychological distress that characterized her first few years in care, eventually seemed to calm as she aged, although she was still prone to depressive episodes. Although June remained in a state of chronic mourning, as revealed by the AAP, we might hypothesize that the long-standing consistency of her care staff allowed her to form some trusting relationships for the first time in her life, and that perhaps these allowed her a greater degree of emotional stability than she had previously experienced.

Case Example: Terry – Unresolved Chronic Mourning with Bullying

Background: Terry's case demonstrates how bullying may be experienced as a form of attachment trauma in adults with ID. Terry was middle aged, and had experiences both of being bullied and being the bully. Terry experienced violence and neglect from his parents. He was repeatedly removed from the family and taken into care during childhood, with multiple care breakdowns and experiences of sexual abuse. He was therefore deprived of consistent childhood caregiving, with repeated experiences of abuse and loss.

In adulthood, Terry began sleeping rough, prostituting himself and getting involved with gangs. He committed several offences involving criminal damage, and was given a prison sentence for one offence. Terry committed this offence as part of a gang, but the gang members also bullied Terry; he reported that he was frightened of them, and particularly afraid that they would sexually assault him. The gang took advantage of Terry's vulnerability by running away from the scene of the fire and leaving Terry to be arrested by himself. Terry served his prison term in a secure unit, during which time he was described as both a bully ('he ran the ward') and a victim ('vulnerable').

AAP content and trauma coding: Terry was able to maintain an organized and regulated state of mind throughout most of the AAP. Characters in the 'alone' and 'dyadic' pictures showed agency and basic functional care. Although the mother in *Bed* would not respond to her son's bid for her to hug him, he accepted the mother's distance as the result of the boy's misbehaviour and was not dysregulated by this. When attachment figures were not available, Terry described how other adults could provide functional care (e.g., a nurse in *Ambulance*). Terry's regulating capacity began to falter in response to *Cemetery*. Recall that we do not interpret responses to the *Cemetery* stimulus as only related to death, but rather as representations of confrontation with the past. Terry began the *Cemetery* response by stating that this was his favourite picture, which in itself is an unusual response. He immediately digressed into a surreal description of vampires (coded as derealization). In spite of the stress evidenced by derealization,

Terry told a constructive story about a father's visit to a family member's grave. He became completely unravelled, however, by the frightened, bullied representation of self triggered by the *Corner* stimulus.

Corner:

Got his, got his um, what's it called, he got his hands up and, and he got his face, what's it called, look, looking down on the… um…on the floor and err…I don't know, err he's not err, not look, not looking at people and err, I think it's um, what's it called, I think it's something happened or something and err, he, he don't want to talk to anyone about it. I think he, um, someone might have been um, what's it called, um, horrible to him, what's it called, um, taking advantage or someone might have been picking on him, or being what's it called, um, being err, a bully and err, why, why this um, what's it called, why they looking down on him for, I think, I think he's um what's it called, scared, scared, and what's it called worried and um yeah that it. He's got his hands up and yeah, that it.

Terry's depiction of bullying described the fear associated with meanness (picking on) and power assertion (they are looking down on him). The character is helpless, nobody steps forward to protect and help him, and he is left with 'his hands up',[3] strongly reminiscent of Terry's arrest after his gang abandoned him. The AAP suggests that these experiences were associated with traumatic dysregulation for Terry: this was the point in his AAP when he failed to contain frightening material. Remember that Terry's context of early abuse, parental failed protection and caregiver helplessness was key here: it is the combination of the bullying experiences with the failure of attachment figures to protect and comfort the person that elevates the experience to attachment trauma. It is possible to formulate Terry's inpatient experiences of being a bully and a victim as a reflection of this state of chronic mourning. When Terry took on a bully persona, he may have been attempting to protect himself from his peers in view of his earlier traumatic experiences, but this solution only perpetuated the problem, by creating another bully and more victims.

Clinical presentation and support needs: Terry's unresolved chronic mourning status suggested that he would be vulnerable to repeated episodes of intense psychological distress, possibly

> accompanied by mental health breakdown and chaotic behaviour. Clinical records show this to be the case; in the first few years following Terry's release from the secure unit, he was highly anxious, frequently absconded or went on drinking binges. He would put pressure on himself to cope, then break down and become enraged by the institutional mechanisms designed to keep him safe. Recently, Terry seems to have stabilized; he has found employment and lives in his own flat (so no longer has a residential 'institution' to rage against). Since Terry's release, he has been consistently and intensively supported by a specialist provider skilled in the psychological care of traumatized individuals with ID. Although Terry has needed little in terms of physical care, his relationship with his support providers has allowed him to form trusting relationships with people who have been available, responsive, sensitive and actively sought to repair the relationship when it has been ruptured (e.g. by Terry absconding). We hypothesize that this support, plus regular multi-disciplinary input and monitoring from the Community Learning Disabilities Team have been key factors in Terry's increasing stability over time. Terry's case demonstrates the resources and skill required to achieve greater stability for traumatized individuals in a state of chronic mourning.

CONCLUSIONS

As with our earlier study (Gallichan and George, 2014), we found that the AAP analysis demonstrated good face validity with the case histories of the individuals in our sample and offered useful clinical insights. We successfully identified cases that fit pathological mourning patterns using the same AAP standards established in the typically developing adult population.

Half of our participants represented bullying as traumatizing and a severe threat to self in their AAP stories. Some of these individuals have received clinical input since their participation in this study, which has allowed further exploration of their real life experiences. This process has uncovered descriptions of severe and prolonged bullying, including daily assaults such as being spat at and urinated on. The AAP implicates caregiver helplessness and failed protection in these experiences (Solomon and George, 2011b), so it has been crucial to understand the ways in which attachment figures have been unavailable or unable to keep the person safe. It is currently unclear whether our results tell us something unique about the bullying experiences of people with ID, or whether they shed light on how bullying may be experienced as attachment trauma for adults more generally. It may be that people with ID could help us understand the typically developing population; this would be a departure from the usual order of discovery.

In summary, the use of the AAP attachment trauma risk system allows us to build a more sophisticated theoretical understanding of the ways in which abuse dysregulates the attachment system for people with ID. It allows us to understand the significance of caregiver helplessness and failed protection in the development of attachment trauma and pathological mourning. In particular, it allows us to differentiate among pathological mourning groups. We have focused on *unresolved chronic mourning* here. *Failed mourning* and *preoccupation with personal suffering* are extreme forms of what is considered overall organized internal working models of attachment ('dismissing' and 'preoccupied' classifications, respectively). As has been shown with typically developing adolescents and adults, we have other cases in our adult intellectual disability samples that demonstrate how these forms of pathological mourning also pose considerable risk for psychological distress. We conclude, in concert with our earlier proposal in Gallichan and George (2014), that the AAP is a clinically useful measure for this population.

IMPLICATIONS FOR RESEARCH AND PRACTICE

Our research participants were drawn from a clinical sample, so one avenue for future research is to compare attachment trauma in referred and non-referred adults with ID. This presents a challenge given the high percentage of adults with ID referred to specialist services, and we may instead need to focus on individuals who present with lower levels of psychological distress or challenge. It may also be possible to compare adults with ID to clinical samples drawn from the typically developing population (e.g. working-age adult mental health services), to try to further our understanding of the impact of disability status in attachment trauma, particularly our findings in relation to bullying.

A limitation of our work is that, at present, we have only assessed people with mild, or mild to moderate, levels of intellectual disability because the AAP requires some verbal ability. We suspect that the concept of attachment trauma may be relevant to individuals with more severe levels of ID, who tend to be understood in terms of behavioural challenge rather than mental health risk, but this requires further study and the development of other forms of assessment (see Chapter 4 for further discussion of assessing individuals with moderate to severe ID).

RECOMMENDATIONS FOR CLINICAL PRACTICE

Clinical work should pay attention to the extent to which people with ID have felt their primary attachment figures to be available and responsive, particularly in cases where the person has experienced trauma and abuse. The attachment model designates that the feeling of being alone, without comfort or protection, is essentially what frightens and derails people; these feelings of aloneness represent risks of separation and ultimately, in some instances, loss. Clinicians should also listen out closely for experiences of bullying, and consider these within an abuse and trauma framework. In addition to the traumatic events themselves, therapeutic attention should also attend to separation, loss and mourning processes, which attachment theory has stressed are crucial processes even for situations where attachment figures are still alive and involved with the person (Bowlby, 1973; 1980). These situations in the present can compound dysregulation risk that has its origins in childhood experience (Solomon and George, 2011b).

According to attachment theory, mourning is only possible when individuals are supported in close relationships. Clinicians working in this area are well aware that relationships are often impoverished for people with ID, and frequently consist only of people who are paid to be there (a fact that many people with ID seem, in the first author's experience, to be acutely aware of). Clinicians should consider the extent to which a person's environment and network of relationships supports the mourning of loss, or perpetuates pathological mourning (e.g. by consisting only of support staff who can deal with functional tasks, but who are ill-equipped to offer emotional support and by frequent changes of staff team that prevent the person from building up long-standing relationships where they may begin to experience trust). Where attachment figures are present and involved with the person, clinicians must take care not to take a blaming stance, and to consider ways in which family relationships could be maintained and enhanced. Sensitive exploration of caregiver helplessness and mourning of loss could be facilitated, where appropriate, by systemic family therapy.

The extent to which these practice recommendations may link to pathological mourning status is an area of future exploration and research.

NOTES

1. Information about AAP training is available at www.attachmentprojective.com/training/
2. Consent included consent for the research, including the AAP stories, to be written up in an academic journal or academic book format, as long as their real name was not used.
3. Terry uses the phrase 'his hands up' at the beginning of the response. Typically, we would view this as a description of the stimulus, but Terry repeats this phrase at the end, suggesting that it may have more significance for him. The case history implies that this element of the stimulus triggered the memory of a traumatic experience for Terry.

REFERENCES

Aikins, J.W., Howes, C. and Hamilton, C. (2009) Attachment stability and the emergence of unresolved representations during adolescence. *Attachment and Human Development*, 11: 491–512.

Barnett, D., Hill Hunt, K., Butler, C.M., McCaskill IV, J.W., Kaplan-Estrin, M. and Pipp-Siegel, S. (1999) Indices of Attachment Disorganzation among toddlers with neurological and non-neurological problems. In J. Solomon and C. George (eds) *Attachment Disorganization* (pp. 189–212). New York: The Guilford Press.

Béliveau, M.J. and Moss, E. (2009) Le rôle joué par les événements stressants sur la transmission intergénérationnelle de l'attachement. (The role of stressful life events on the intergenerational transmission of attachment.) *European Review of Applied Psychology/Revue Européenne de Psychologie Appliquée*, 59: 47–58.

Benoit, M., Bouthillier, D., Moss, E., Rousseau, C. and Brunet, A. (2010) Emotion regulation strategies as mediators of the association between level of attachment security and PTSD symptoms following trauma in adulthood. *Anxiety, Stress and Coping*, 23: 101–118.

Bowlby, J. (1969/1982) *Attachment and Loss. Vol. 1: Attachment*. New York: Basic Books.

Bowlby, J. (1973) *Attachment and Loss. Vol. 2: Separation: Anxiety and Anger*. London: Pimlico.

Bowlby, J. (1980) *Attachment and Loss. Vol. 3: Loss: Sadness and Depression.* London: Pimlico.
Buchheim, A. and Benecke, C. (2007) Affective facial behavior of patients with anxiety disorders during the adult attachment interview: A pilot study. *Psychotherapie Psychosomatik Medizinische Psychologie (Psychotherapy Psychosomatics Medical Psychology)*, 57(8): 343–347. DOI: 10.1055/s-2006-952030.
Buchheim, A., Erk, S., George, C., Kächele, H., Ruchsow, M., Spitzer, M., Kircher, T. and Walter, H. (2006) Measuring attachment representation in an fMRI environment: A pilot study. *Psychopathology*, 39: 144–152.
Buchheim, A. and George, C. (2011) The representational, neurobiological, and emotional foundation of attachment disorganization in borderline personality disorder and anxiety disorder. In J. Solomon and C. George (eds) *Disorganized Attachment and Caregiving* (pp. 343–382). New York: The Guilford Press.
Buchheim, A., George, C. and West, M. (2003) The Adult Attachment Projective (AAP) – Psychometric properties and new research. *Psychotherapie Psychosomatik Medizinische Psychologie (Psychotherapy Psychosomatics Medical Psychology)*, 53: 419–427.
Buchheim, A., Heinrichs, M., George. C., Pokorny, D., Koops, E., Henningsen, P., O'Connor, M-F. and Gündel, H. (2009) Oxytocin enhances the experience of attachment security. *Psychoneuroendocrinology*, 34(9): 1417–1422.
Cousins, J. (2006) *Every Child is Special: Placing disabled children for permanence.* British Association for Adoption and Fostering, London, UK.
Crowell, J., Fraley, R.C. and Shaver, P.R. (2008) Measurement of individual differences in adolescent and adult attachment. In J. Cassidy and P.R. Shaver (eds) *Handbook of Attachment: Theory, Research and Clinical Applications* (2nd edition, pp. 599–634). New York: The Guilford Press.
Dagnan, D. and Sandu, S. (1999) Social comparison, self-esteem and depression in people with intellectual disability. *Journal of Intellectual Disability Research*, 43(4): 372–379.
Dagnan, D. and Waring, M. (2004) Linking stigma to psychological distress: Testing a social–cognitive model of the experience of people with intellectual disabilities. *Clinical Psychology and Psychotherapy*, 11(4): 247–254.
Delvecchio, E., Di Riso, D., Salcuni, S., Lis, A. and George, C. (2014) Anorexia and attachment: Dysregulated defense and pathological mourning. *Frontiers in Psychology*, 5: 1218. DOI:10.3389/fpsyg.2014.01218.
Department of Health (2000) *No Secrets: Guidance on developing and implementing multi-agency policies and procedures to protect vulnerable adults from abuse.* London, UK.
Department of Health (2012) *Department of Health Review: Winterbourne Hospital, Interim Report.* London, UK.
Finn, S. (2011) Use of the Adult Attachment Projective System (AAP) in the middle of long-term psychotherapy. *Journal of Personality Assessment*, 93: 427–433.
Gallichan, D.J. and George, C. (2014) Assessing attachment status in adults with intellectual disabilities: The potential of the Adult Attachment Projective Picture System. *Advances in Mental Health and Intellectual Disabilities*, 8(2): 103–119.

George, C. and Buchheim, A. (2014) Use of the Adult Attachment Projective Picture System with a severely traumatized patient: A psychodynamic perspective. *Frontiers in Psychology*, 5. DOI: 10.3389/fpsyg.2014.00865.

George, C., Petrowski, K. and West, M. (2014) *Pathological mourning and psychiatric risk: Mental distress correlates of failed mourning, preoccupation with personal suffering, and unresolved chronic attachment.* Unpublished manuscript.

George, C. and Solomon, J. (2008) The Caregiving System: A Behavioural Systems Approach to Parenting. In J. Cassidy and P. Shaver (eds) *Handbook of Attachment: Theory, Research and Clinical Applications* (2nd edition, pp. 833–856). London: The Guilford Press.

George, C. and West, M. (1999) Developmental vs. social personality models of adult attachment and mental ill health. *British Journal of Medical Psychology*, 72: 285–303.

George, C. and West, M. (2012) *The Adult Attachment Projective Picture System.* New York: The Guilford Press.

George, C., West, M. and Pettem, O. (1999) The Adult Attachment Projective: Disorganization at the level of representation. In J. Solomon and C. George (eds) *Attachment Disorganization* (pp. 462–507). New York: The Guilford Press.

Hesse, E. (2008) The Adult Attachment Interview: Protocol, methods of analysis, and empirical studies. In J. Cassidy and P.R. Shaver (eds) *Handbook of Attachment: Theory, Research and Clinical Applications* (2nd edition, pp. 552–598). New York: The Guilford Press.

Horner-Johnson, W. and Drum, C.E. (2006) Prevalences of maltreatment of people with intellectual disabilities: A review of recently published research. *Mental Retardation and Developmental Disabilities Research Reviews*, 12(1): 57–69.

Isaacs, M., George, C. and Marvin, R.S. (2009) Utilizing attachment measures in custody evaluations: Incremental validity. *Journal of Child Custody*, 6: 139–162.

Jahoda, A., Wilson, A., Stalker, K. and Cairney, A. (2010) Living with stigma and the self perceptions of people with mild intellectual disabilities. *Journal of Social Issues*, 66(3): 521–534.

Joubert, D., Webster, L. and Hackett, R.K. (2012) Unresolved attachment status and trauma-related symptomatology in maltreated adolescents: An examination of cognitive mediators. *Child Psychiatry and Human Development*, 43: 471–483.

Liotti, G. (2004) Trauma, Dissociation and Disorganized Attachment: Three Strands of a Single Braid. *Psychotherapy: Theory, Research, Practice, Training*, 41: 472–486.

Lis, A., Mazzeschi, C., Di Riso, D. and Salcuni, S. (2011) Attachment, assessment, and psychological intervention: A case study of anorexia. *Journal of Personality Assessment*, 93: 434–444.

MacLeod, J.S. and Austin, J.K. (2003) Stigma in the lives of adolescents with epilepsy: A review of the literature. *Epilepsy and Behaviour*, 4(2): 112–117.

Main, M., Kaplan, K. and Cassidy, J. (1985) Security in infancy, childhood and adulthood: A move to the level of representation. In I. Bretherton and

E. Waters (eds) *Growing points of attachment theory and research. Monographs of the Society for Research in Child Development*, 50 (1–2, Serial No. 209): 66–104.

Main, M. and Solomon, J. (1990) Procedures for identifying infants as disorganized/disoriented during the Ainsworth Strange Situation. In M.T. Greenberg, D. Cicchetti and E.M. Cummings (eds) *Attachment in the Preschool Years* (pp. 121–160). Chicago: University of Chicago Press.

Mandelstam, M. (2011) *Safeguarding Adults at Risk of Harm: A legal guide for practitioners*. Social Care Institute for Excellence, London. Retrieved 31.07.15 from http://www.scie.org.uk/publications/reports/report50.asp

Marvin, R.S. and Pianta, R.C. (1996) Mothers' reactions to their child's diagnosis: Relations with security of attachment. *Journal of Clinical Child Psychology*, 25(4): 436–445.

McGrother, C.W., Bhaumik, S., Thorp, C.F., Hauck, A., Branford, D. and Watson, J.M. (2006) Epilepsy in adults with intellectual disabilities: Prevalence, associations and service implications. *European Journal of Epilepsy*, 15(6): 376–386.

Mencap (2007) *Bullying Wrecks Lives: The experiences of children and young people with a learning disability*. London: Mencap.

Moss, E., Cyr, C. and Dubois-Comtois, K. (2004) Attachment at early school age and developmental risk: Examining family context and behavior problems in controlling-caregiving, controlling -punitive, and behaviorally disorganized children. *Developmental Psychology*, 40: 519–542.

Murphy, G. (2007) Intellectual disability, sexual abuse and sexual offending. In A. Carr, G. O'Reilly, P. Noonan-Walsh and J. McEvoy (eds) *The Handbook of Intellectual Disability and Clinical Psychology Practice* (pp. 831–866). London: Routledge.

Murray, M. and Osborne, C. (2009) *Safeguarding Disabled Children: Practice guidance*. Department for Children, Schools and Families, Nottingham, UK.

O'Connell, P., Pepler, D. and Craig, W. (1999) Peer involvement in bullying: Insights and challenges for intervention. *Journal of Adolescence*, 22(4): 437–452.

Oppenheim, D., Dolev, S., Koren-Karie, N., Sher-Censor, E., Yirmiya, N. and Salomon, S. (2007) Parental resolution of the child's diagnosis and the parent–child relationship. In D. Oppenheim and D.F. Goldsmith (eds) *Attachment Theory in Clinical Work with Children: Insights from the reaction to diagnosis interview* (pp. 109–137). New York: The Guilford Press.

Parkes, C.M. (2006) *Love and Loss: The roots of grief and its complications*. New York: Routledge.

Pianta, R.C., Marvin, R.S., Britner, P.A. and Borowitz, K.C. (1996) Mothers' resolution of their child's diagnosis: Organised patterns of caregiving representations. *Infant Mental Health Journal*, 17(3): 239–256.

Roisman, G.I., Holland, A., Fortuna, K., Fraley, R.C., Clausell, E. and Clarke, A. (2007) The Adult Attachment Interview and self-reports of attachment style: An empirical rapprochement. *Journal of Personality and Social Psychology*, 92: 678–697.

Sheard, C., Clegg, J., Standen, P. and Cromby, J. (2001) Bullying and people with severe intellectual disability. *Journal of Intellectual Disability Research*, 45(5): 407–415.

Sheeran, T., Marvin, R.S. and Pianta, R.C. (1997) Mothers' Resolution of Their Child's Diagnosis and Self-Reported Measures of Parenting Stress, Marital Relations, and Social Support. *Journal of Paediatric Psychology*, 22(2): 197–212. DOI: 10.1093/jpepsy/22.2.197.

Sinason, V. (1992) *Mental Handicap and the Human Condition*. London: Free Association Books.

Solomon, J. and George, C. (1999) The development of attachment in separated and divorced families. *Attachment and Human Development*, 1: 2–33.

Solomon, J. and George, C. (2011a) The disorganized attachment-caregiving system: Dysregulation of adaptive processes at multiple levels. In J. Solomon and C. George (eds) *Disorganized Attachment and Caregiving* (pp. 3–24). New York: The Guilford Press.

Solomon, J. and George, C. (2011b) Dysregulated caregiving across two generations. In J. Solomon and C. George (eds) *Disorganized Attachment and Caregiving* (pp. 25–51). New York: The Guilford Press.

Stevens, V., Van Oost, P. and De Bourdeaudhuij, I. (2000) The effects of an anti-bullying intervention on peers' attitudes and behaviour. *Journal of Adolescence*, 23(1): 21–34.

Subic-Wrana, C., Beetz, A., Langenbach, M., Paulussen, M. and Beutel, M. (2007) Connections between unresolved attachment trauma and retrospectively remembered childhood traumatisation in psychosomatic inpatients. *Journal of Psychosomatic Research*, 61: 399–410.

Szivos, S. and Griffiths, E. (1992) Coming to terms with learning difficulties: The effects of group work and group processes on stigmatising identity. In A. Waitman and S. Conboy-Hill (eds) *Psychotherapy and Mental Handicap* (pp. 59–80). London: Sage.

Takizawa, R., Maughan, B. and Arseneault, L. (2014) Adult Health Outcomes of Childhood Bullying Victimization: Evidence From a Five-Decade Longitudinal British Birth Cohort. *The American Journal of Psychiatry*, 171(7): 777–784.

von Wietersheim, P.J., Holzinger, K., Zhou, X. and Pokorny, D. (2014) Attachment in AAP episodes and family relationships in CCRT-LU narratives of patients with bulimia nervosa and healthy controls. *Journal of Psychosomatic Research*, 76: 519.

Wechsler, D. (2008) *Wechsler Adult Intelligence Scale*, fourth edition (WAIS-IV). San Antonio, TX: NCS Pearson.

Weiner, E. and Mckay, D. (2013) A preliminary evaluation of repeated exposure for depersonalization and derealization. *Behavior Modification*, 37: 226–242.

Chapter 11

ATTACHMENT, PERSONALITY DISORDER AND OFFENDING: CLINICAL IMPLICATIONS

Lesley Steptoe[1], William R. Lindsay[2,3,4], Caroline Finlay[2] and Sandra Miller[2]

[1] Psychology Department, NHS Tayside, Dundee, Scotland, UK
[2] Danshell Healthcare, York, UK
[3] Abertay University, Dundee, Scotland, UK
[4] Deakin University, Melbourne, Australia

> **Case Example: Billy**
>
> Similar to many people with an intellectual and developmental disability (IDD), Billy had a disrupted upbringing. His father had lived with his mother for some years but they broke up and lost contact before Billy was born. His mother was a binge drinker and has continued to drink in a similar pattern to the present day. Billy's mother did not have IDD and when she was not drinking, her children were looked after quite capably. They were well-dressed, attended primary school and the house was kept clean and organized. However, her drinking binges were regular and could last up to three or four days. During these times, she did not attend to any of her childcare or domestic responsibilities and was aggressive towards her children. As Billy grew up, he did not attend school during periods when his mother was drinking and

---

Attachment in Intellectual and Developmental Disability: A Clinician's Guide to Practice and Research, First Edition. Edited by Helen K. Fletcher, Andrea Flood and Dougal Julian Hare.
© 2016 John Wiley & Sons, Ltd. Published 2016 by John Wiley & Sons, Ltd.

> he was eventually fostered for short periods of time because of occasional neglect. It was always noted that he had a very good relationship with his mother but that these periods of neglect and separation made him anxious for her welfare. As he grew older, in his late teens, he began to give his mother money when she asked. She would always spend this money on drinking binges and these binges would, in turn, increase his anxiety to panic levels. His mother became increasingly dependent on the money that he gave her and he started to steal in order to get money to give to his mother. Giving her money had the effect of reducing his anxiety and panic in the short term but increasing it in the medium and long term by perpetuating her days of binge drinking and her dependence on him. There was always a paradox in his relationship with his mother, in that he felt very close to her and wanted to be with her to the extent that he was quite happy to give her this money. However, she was extremely unreliable and would often fail to attend when he arranged to meet her; she would occasionally only see him if he had money and visits would eventually increase his anxiety because she spent his money on alcohol.
>
> During adolescence Billy began to develop behavioural characteristics and routines consistent with a borderline personality disorder. He developed significant mood swings, appeared to have a greater and greater need to maintain close relationships and began a pattern of frequent self-harm. He first came into contact with services in his teens after he had been apprehended by the police for stealing a box of batteries. This was not the first theft he had been involved with, but previous incidents had not been pursued. On this occasion, he attacked the police who then brought charges of theft and assault. Subsequently, over the next ten years, he periodically became involved with the police for a number of reasons including theft, violence and absconding. He continued with occasional self-harm.

Billy's case illustrates the way in which attachment in childhood has been linked to personality disorder and emotional problems through many years of clinical and research work. This chapter begins by reviewing some of the main pieces of research relating attachment to personality disorder and emotional problems before describing how the evidence base can inform work with people with intellectual and developmental disabilities (IDD).

ATTACHMENT AND PERSONALITY DISORDER

The complex patterns of social interactions, emotional regulation and cognitive processes that form within insecure attachment relationships become self-perpetuating throughout adulthood (Feeney and Noller, 1996; Bartholomew, Kwong and Hart, 2001). Behavioural correlates of attachment difficulties encountered in childhood are undoubtedly related to problems in adulthood. These behavioural correlates include difficulties such as distressed child–parent interactions, increasing oppositional behaviour by the child, withdrawal by the child, difficulties at school and/or emotional problems in the child. Some of the most persuasive evidence emerges from studies on mentally disordered offenders, in which clinical problems have been related to interpersonal difficulties with parents and authority figures in childhood. In a large and lengthy follow-up study of over 1000 patients with mental disorders (the MacArthur study), Monahan *et al.* (2001) found strong relationships between child abuse and violence in adulthood. If child abuse is considered to be a behavioural correlate of attachment problems and developmental adversity in childhood, then these kinds of studies are extremely important. Monahan *et al.* (2001) found that 36% of patients who experienced serious physical abuse in childhood committed a violent incident in the year following discharge from hospital compared to 17% of those who did not report experiencing violence in childhood. Interestingly, in this study the experience of sexual abuse in childhood did not affect whether or not the individual committed a violent act during the follow-up period. Witnessing parental violence and disputes was related to an increase in violence during the follow-up period. In this study, those who had lived with both parents until the age of 15 were less likely to be violent in adulthood. The MacArthur study has been very influential in understanding violence in adulthood and strongly indicates the relationship between problematic interpersonal relationships between the child and their parents and subsequent violence in adulthood.

A similar piece of work investigating the relationship between developmental variables and violence was conducted by Harris, Rice and Quinsey (1993) on a large sample of mentally disordered men in an institution. They similarly found a strong predictive relationship between living with only one parent prior to the age of 15 and violence in adulthood. Although this may seem an almost peremptory way of viewing the person's developmental history, having a single parent before the age of 15 is probably a marker for a whole range of attachment difficulties that can occur in such families. Indeed, studies like these have led to such attachment problems becoming a known risk factor contributing towards the prediction of violence in individuals. Therefore, attachment problems are extremely important when considering variables related to violence.

One of the most potent risk factors for future violence is receiving a diagnosis of a personality disorder. In a meta-analysis of studies relating personality disorder to crime, Fazel and Danesh (2002) reviewed studies covering a total of 20,000 prisoners and found that antisocial personality disorder was a reasonable predictor of future aggression and significantly more prevalent among inmates in correctional settings than among the general population.

West and Sheldon-Keller (1994) suggest that having a maladaptive interpersonal style is a key tenet of most personality disorders. Extreme attachment insecurity may relate to the development of personality disorder in two ways. First, insecure attachment indicates a relatively fixed response to stressful interpersonal situations. This response is generally unhelpful in mediating stress and anxiety and in attaining positive interpersonal relationships and emotional wellbeing. In contrast, secure attachment is associated with a more flexible approach within interpersonal relationships and with flexibility in responding to stress. Secure individuals can expect both to rely on others within close relationships at times of stress and to have the internal resources to modulate the negative effects (Bartholomew, 1997).

In a study of 1407 adolescents and young adults, Brennan and Shaver (1998) found a significant overlap between attachment style and personality disorder, although there were no specific relationships between types of attachment and categories of personality disorder. There was, however, strong concordance between insecure attachment and general personality pathology. The authors hypothesized that early attachment to caregivers and early attachment experiences accounted for much of the variance in both adult attachment style and personality disorder. In a large and well-organized study of 639 adolescents and their mothers, Johnson *et al.* (1999) investigated the relationship between abuse in childhood and diagnosis of personality disorder in adulthood. They found that those with documented childhood abuse or neglect were four times more likely than those without to be diagnosed with personality disorder, supporting the hypothesis of Brennan and Shaver (1998).

It is common for attachment patterns to be discussed as categorical concepts (Bartholomew, Kwong and Hart, 2001). However, such classification systems lose much of the underlying variance between individuals who fall within one category. Capturing the complexity and variation of attachment requires a more dimensional approach to measurement. Dimensional models permit differentiation amongst individuals with the same attachment style on the basis of extremity or severity. Dimensional measurement takes into account that many individuals do not have basic, pure attachment patterns and that the boundaries between attachment patterns are not always distinct or rigid (Bartholomew, Kwong and Hart, 2001). Similarly, categorical measurement of personality disorder has been developed to facilitate communication and treatment decisions in clinical settings. Two personality disorders, borderline personality disorder and antisocial personality disorder, have been strongly implicated in the development of problems in adulthood; the former is associated with emotional and psychiatric difficulties while the latter is associated with violence and criminality.

ATTACHMENT AND BORDERLINE PERSONALITY DISORDER

Borderline personality disorder (BPD) has received considerable attention from attachment theorists and researchers. Two key features of BPD are traits of unstable and intense interpersonal relationships and frantic efforts to avoid real or imagined abandonment. The affective instability component is manifested by a failure to regulate attachment anxiety appropriately. There is a tendency for the person to show extreme anger and recurrent suicidal threats and gestures that reflect a desperation underlying the individual's attempts to have their attachment needs met. For example, Barone (2003) assessed the internal working models of participants with and without BPD using the Adult Attachment Interview (AAI; George, Kaplan and Main, 1985). The findings supported the hypothesis that some developmental relationship experiences seem to constitute pivotal risk factors underlying BPD. A study by Choi-Kain *et al.* (2009) lent further support to the evidence for a relationship between attachment style and the development of BPD. Further studies (Dutton *et al.*, 1994; Sack *et al.*, 1996; Brennan and Shaver, 1998) suggest that attachment anxiety is a defining feature of BPD. There is also evidence that individuals experiencing symptoms of BPD may show high approach behaviour (e.g. seeking care or excessive closeness) and avoidant behaviours (angry withdrawal, devaluation of relationship partners) (Sack *et al.*, 1996).

ATTACHMENT AND ANTISOCIAL PERSONALITY DISORDER

The fact that researchers have found a relationship between attachment and antisocial personality disorder (ASPD) is not surprising. Childhood insecurity and parental maltreatment provide a context for the development of inappropriate socialization strategies, heightening the child's risk or susceptibility to negative social influences outside the family. For example, Patterson and colleagues (Patterson, 1986; Patterson, Reid and Dishion, 1992; Granic and Patterson, 2006) found distinct patterns of family interaction that have significant consequences for the child over their lifetime. From as early as 18 months, some families may promote a child's coercive behaviour such as temper tantrums and hitting because those behaviours have functional value in terminating conflict within the family. In non-distressed families, in which prosocial behaviours are reinforced, the child learns that interactions such as talking and negotiating are followed by a termination of conflict. In distressed families, not only are coercive behaviours promoted but prosocial behaviours may not be particularly effective in terminating family conflict (Granic and Patterson, 2006). As these children develop, they fail to learn prosocial behaviours, problem-solving and language skills but become highly skilled in antisocial behaviours. There is a body of established empirical evidence linking distressed family interactions to antisocial behaviour in later life. Researchers note that participants with ASPD show the full range of insecure attachment patterns, but report that there is no evidence for an orderly relationship between attachment and personality disorder (Hart, Dutton and Newlove, 1993; Allen, Hauser and Borman-Spurrell, 1996; Van IJzendoorn and Bakermans-Kranenburg, 1996).

ATTACHMENT AND EMOTIONAL REGULATION

Evidence has been developed over the last four decades establishing that the foundation for good mental health is built from repeated experiences of loving, caring, sensitive and secure attachments. In contrast, attachment insecurities, negative models of self and others and both internal and interpersonal deficits in emotional regulation are associated with inconsistent, rejecting or neglectful attachment experiences. The latter place the individual at risk for psychological and emotional disorders (Barone, 2003; Wei *et al.*, 2004; Critchfield *et al.*, 2008; Choi-Kain *et al.*, 2009; Cole, Llera and Pemberton, 2009). These studies reflect the ways in which different forms of insecurity of attachment prejudice emotional regulation, social adjustment and mental health. Secure attachment has generally been associated with positive affect and good emotional regulation (Consedine and Magai, 2003). Mikulincer and Shaver (2007) reviewed a large amount of information in relation to adult attachment. They concluded that when a securely attached individual encounters internal or external events that might provoke negative emotions, they can engage in problem solving, planning and cognitive appraisal. They are also able to place the negative events in perspective and utilize support from people with positive resources for solving problems, thus reducing stressful effects. The securely attached individual is also more likely to have developed self-regulating skills and can focus on constructive solutions rather than ruminating or catastrophizing. This is certainly consistent with the empirical research developed by Patterson and associates described previously.

Insecure attachment is generally associated with negative affect (Consedine and Magai, 2003). For example, dismissing, avoidant attachment has been associated with an emotional regulatory style characterized by affect minimization (Cassidy, 1994). Young adults who have a dismissing avoidant attachment style are rated as more hostile and defensive (Mikulincer, 1998). Armsden *et al.* (1990) and Mikulincer (1998) found that securely attached adolescents reported significantly higher self-esteem and significantly lower emotional dysregulation and depression symptoms than those with insecure attachment. In a series of studies on college students, Roberts, Gotlib and Kassel (1996) found that insecure attachment was related to depressive symptoms mediated by feelings of low self-worth and poor self-esteem. Therefore, there has been a wealth of research and theoretical writing suggesting a strong relationship between insecure attachment and emotional problems. On the other hand, secure attachment appears to provide a buffer against the psychological distress typically associated with major life stresses (Mikulincer, 1998).

DEVELOPMENTAL ADVERSITY LEADING TO ATTACHMENT PROBLEMS FOR PEOPLE WITH IDD

The presence of IDD itself can be considered a developmental risk factor. Communication difficulties associated with a diagnosis of IDD may impede the development of attachment or significantly alter the nature of the attachment, resulting in consequences for emotional wellbeing and personality (Clements, 2000). As previously mentioned, developmental adversity and abuse in childhood have been considered a proxy variable for later attachment problems in adulthood. Research on developmental risk factors for people with IDD has found similar trends to those found in mainstream research. For example, Novaco and Taylor (2008) investigated whether exposure to parental anger and aggression was related to assault and violence in male forensic patients with IDD and found that, as per non-IDD studies, witnessing parental violence in childhood was significantly related to anger and aggression in adulthood. In a clinical study of cases presenting with inappropriate sexual behaviour, Beail and Warden (1995) found that all the men presenting at their clinic had a history of sexual abuse in childhood or adolescence. In another study investigating the experience of abuse in childhood, Lindsay, Steptoe and Haut (2012) found that around twice as many violent offenders had experienced physical abuse in childhood compared to sex offenders. Interestingly, the opposite was true for sexual abuse in childhood, with almost twice as many sex offenders having been sexually abused in childhood than violent offenders; however, a reported history of abuse was not present for the majority of offenders in either group.

In a major study of 477 people with IDD referred to offender services, O'Brien *et al.* (2010) found that in relation to developmental adversity, 24% had suffered from some type of severe deprivation in childhood and 55% had documented histories of child abuse and neglect including non-accidental injury (12%), sexual abuse (11%) and neglect (5%). Interestingly, in this large sample of offenders with IDD, socio-economic deprivation was the single most common type of childhood adversity. What this study suggests is that developmental adversity, an important correlate of attachment difficulties, is a leading factor in the trajectory for criminality in adulthood for offenders with IDD, similar to mainstream populations (Monahan *et al.*, 2001). However, the study does not investigate the differences between those with recorded adversity and those without, and there remains a significant need for such work in this population.

Case Example: Rusty

Rusty is a 28-year-old woman with a mild IDD (measured IQ 68). Her adaptive behaviour is relatively good and she is able to shop, cook and clean her flat unsupported. In all of these personal aspects, she has no need for the intervention of services. Rusty was brought up with her mother and her mother's partner who had a history of alcohol abuse. Once she contacted services (through violence at college) she disclosed extensive sexual abuse during her childhood by her mother's partner. She also recounted frequent violent exchanges between the two. When we reported these disclosures to the police, it was impossible to charge him because of the inconsistent nature of Rusty's evidence and because her mother denied any occurrence of sexual abuse.

Rusty had difficulties at school with non-compliance and oppositional behaviour, but her problems came to a head at college when she began to 'test' staff that she seemed closest to with episodes of aggression and false allegations of inappropriate sexual behaviour. She was first charged by police for destroying property at college and at that point came into contact with the forensic IDD services. She also began to engage in frequent cannabis use and developed serious psychotic symptoms. Contact with police and the psychotic symptoms led to her first hospital admission. At first, she said that she settled in hospital, but after some weeks she began testing staff attachments with a familiar pattern of absconding, aggression and allegations of inappropriate sexual behaviour. She also demonstrated significant mood swings and had periods when she was seriously depressed alternating with periods when she was very active and engaged (but not to the extent of being manic). During the times when she was very engaged, she was extremely sociable and staff enjoyed her company. She was also thoughtful with other patients. The consistent approach employed by staff led to the formation of good

> working therapeutic attachment bonds and Rusty said, 'they don't tell me to go away no matter what I do.'
>
> Rusty was eventually discharged into a supported community placement. Assessment of her attachment style found that she featured on both 'anxious' and 'fearful' attachment, resulting in disorganized relationships with the staff team in the new community placement. By this time, her continued offending had lessened hugely in frequency and the main difficulties were related to absconding and engaging with individuals who were antisocial influences in that they were the source of drugs. She also placed herself in financially and sexually vulnerable situations.

MEASUREMENT OF ATTACHMENT IN PEOPLE WITH IDD

Measurement of attachment has been covered comprehensively elsewhere in this book (see Chapter 4). Specifically in relation to offenders with IDD, Keeling, Rose and Beech (2007) adapted the Relationship Scales Questionnaire (RSQ; Griffin and Bartholomew, 1994) for use with offenders who have lower levels of intellectual functioning and/or literacy deficits. Each scale was adapted in an effort to simplify content and language and to improve readability. Their findings suggested that one subscale of the RSQ had fair reliability and validity, while the remaining subscales had varied psychometric properties that were less than optimal. The findings suggested that the RSQ was not a suitable scale for use with people with mild intellectual disability.

Given the problems reported by Keeling, Rose and Beech (2007) on the use of the RSQ, Steptoe, Lindsay and Carson (2015a) constructed an adaptation of the Relationships Questionnaire (RQ) for use with people with IDD. They adapted the RQ by simplifying the language and syntax so that the revised RQ had acceptable Flesch Kincaid reading grades. A standardization study indicated that the adapted version performed in a way very similar to the original. In a factor analysis, the emerging factors were anxious avoidant attachment style, dismissing/independent attachment style and secure attachment style. Therefore, they concluded that the adapted RQ could be used reliably for people with IDD. This was the measure used for the assessment of attachment style with Rusty and we were able to adjust her treatment and management as described as a result of the understanding of her attachments.

ATTACHMENT AND EMOTION FOR PEOPLE WITH IDD

Larson, Alim and Tsakanikos (2011) found no consistent relationship between attachment style and mental health or emotional problems in people with IDD. In a study that built upon the development of the adapted RQ for people with IDD reported above (Steptoe, Lindsay and Carson, 2015a), the same authors (Steptoe, Lindsay and Carson, 2015b) used the adapted RQ to investigate the relationship between attachment style and emotional problems. They compared male offenders with IDD and a control group with IDD and no offending history, referred for problems with placement breakdown, mental health difficulties and emotional problems. In terms of attachment style, 48% of the offender group and 35% of the control group reported secure attachment on the adapted RQ. This compares to 59% of people in the general public reporting secure attachment (Ainsworth *et al.*, 1978). None of the offender group and 16% of the control group fell into the anxious attachment category, while 39% of the offender group and 36% of the control group fell into the category of avoidant attachment. The remainder of the participants were classified in the disorganized attachment category (13% of offenders and 16% of controls). Since there were no consistent and significant differences between groups, participants were combined to look at the relationship between attachment style and emotional problems. Across this study, there were significant consistent relationships with negative correlations between secure attachment and aggression/hostility and positive correlations between anxious attachment and aggression/hostility. It is important to note that attachment was a self-report rather than a report by caregivers. In other studies (e.g. Larson, Alim and Tsakanikos, 2011), attachment style and behavioural or emotional difficulties were reported by carers and it is a procedural problem that both reports may be contaminated by the same behavioural presentation of the individual being rated. This was not a concern in this study because the attachment measure was one of self-report.

These empirical relationships are manifest in practical terms and can be seen with the case illustrations. The case that introduced this chapter was Billy, who had spent short periods of time in foster care as a child because of his mother's drinking binges and periods of neglect.

Case Example continued: Billy

In his early 20s, Billy gained his own tenancy with 2–4 hours of support a day. The relatively low level of support was provided because Billy's adaptive behaviour skills were so good. In fact, he was able to look after himself extremely well in terms of his everyday needs. However, he became increasingly depressed and anxious because he felt vulnerable without access to caregivers 24 hours a day. This was a direct expression of his difficulties with attachments, in that he felt extremely unsafe when left to rely on his own resources. He began to steal items which had no value to him and came into increasingly frequent contact with the police. He then began to have more frequent thoughts of self-harm and, over a period of three months, reported that he had made 45 'suicide attempts'. These were all relatively minor overdoses of over-the-counter medication or stepping out in front of slow-moving vehicles. There were around 40 incidents of him presenting at the hospital Accident and Emergency department over this period of time.

Billy was taken into hospital because he had become unmanageable in his tenancy as a result of the thefts and self-harm. Following his admission, he settled down almost completely with one incident of self-harm over the four months of his hospital admission. He himself stated that he felt safe in hospital and expressed a clear wish to be placed in an establishment where there was 24-hour staffing available. He said that he did not want to stay in a single tenancy but would rather be placed in a residential home. This was an unusual request that was in opposition to the prevailing culture of the social work department that strived to place individuals with Billy's level of ability in their own tenancy. In this case, our assessment of his attachment difficulties and current emotional presentation was crucial in the determination of his placement. There was no doubt that his own assessment of his needs was consistent with our understanding of his difficulties with attachments. These difficulties could be traced clearly to his developmental experiences. Despite the prevailing ethos, it was agreed that Billy could be placed in a residential home with 24-hour staffing. Even this proved difficult because it was not a hospital and Billy would have preferred staying in hospital. However, following his move we began weekly sessions aimed at helping him to understand the relationship

> between his attachment difficulties, his well-developed adaptive behaviour and the constant availability of support staff. As a result of these sessions, he had only three incidents of self-harm in the subsequent four months and settled over a period of two years.
>
> Perhaps one of the most important things was that he continued to have a close relationship with his mother. We set up weekly meetings that incorporated an outing to the shops in addition to meeting his mother in a cafe. The importance of the regularity of the meeting was that Billy's mother was very unreliable and so if she failed to attend, then there would be other enjoyable activities that could be incorporated. We were careful to explain the reason for the meeting and Billy understood that his mother was unreliable and was prepared on every occasion that she might not turn up. He became quite sanguine about the possibility that she would not attend, knowing that another meeting had already been arranged for the following week. This was the most successful and settled period of his life and illustrates the way in which an understanding of insecure attachment leading to emotional difficulties can make a significant impact in individual cases.

PERSONALITY DISORDER, EMOTION AND ATTACHMENT IN PEOPLE WITH IDD

Over the last two decades, there has been a steady clinical and research interest in the relationship between the assessment of psychiatric disorders in clinical settings, the assessment of personality disorders and their relationship to normal personality dimensions (Reynolds and Clark, 2001; Quirk et al., 2003; Caperton, Eden and Johnson, 2004; Edens, 2009). High levels of neuroticism and low levels of extroversion feature strongly in a variety of psychiatric populations (Zuckerman, 1999). As an example, Quirk et al., (2003) examined the relationship between assessed psychiatric problems, personality features and PD in 1342 inpatients. Neuroticism scores were strongly related to anxiety disorders and BPD, while introversion was related to Post Traumatic Stress Disorder and BPD. The strongest relationships to emerge in this field are between coercive personality characteristics and acting out PDs (antisocial, narcissistic, aggressive) (Morey et al., 2003; Edens, 2009); neurotic personality characteristics and several psychiatric disorders such as depression, paranoia, social introversion, anger, obsessiveness and schizophrenia (Reynolds and Clark, 2001; Morey et al., 2003; Caperton, Eden and Johnson, 2004); externalizing psychopathology and antisocial and paranoid traits; and finally internalizing psychopathology and BPD traits (Morey et al., 2003; Edens, 2009).

Lindsay et al. (2010) studied these relationships using a forensic sample of 212 male participants with IDD. They previously established the validity of two circumplex assessments of normal personality (Lindsay et al., 2009) and used these to study the relationship between personality, PD and risk, using validated risk assessments. The findings suggested an orderly convergence of emotional problems, personality and risk. Externalizing emotional problems such as aggression and impulsiveness had a significant relationship with antisocial PD and narcissistic PD, while internalizing emotional problems such as depression and anxiety correlated significantly with avoidant PD. There were similar strong relationships between externalizing emotional problems and dominant personality characteristics, and significant negative correlations between externalizing emotional problems and nurturant personality dimensions. There was a strong relationship between narcissistic PD and dominant personality characteristics, and further negative statistical relationships between avoidant PD and dominant personality characteristics, and negative correlations between antisocial PD and nurturant personality characteristics.

Steptoe (2011) extended this research into the area of attachment style. She recruited 38 male offenders with IDD and administered the adapted RQ together with measures of personality disorder and personality. The measures of PD were previously established as reliable and valid assessments based on formal diagnostic categories (Lindsay et al., 2006). There were significant positive correlations between secure attachment style and submissive and compliant personality features. More importantly, there was a significant positive correlation between avoidant attachment style and coercive personality features, and significant negative correlations between avoidant attachment and compliant and submissive personality features. All the statistical relationships that did occur were orderly, with secure attachment style correlating positively with warmth/nurturant personality and negatively with dominance/hostile personality but most of the relationships were non-significant with small effect sizes.

She then reviewed the relationship between attachment style and the two most common categories of personality disorder among the participants, which were borderline personality disorder and antisocial personality disorder. There were no significant relationships between attachment style and BPD. When it came to ASPD, the relationships were as expected, with a significant positive correlation between anxious/avoidant attachment style and ASPD, a significant positive correlation between dismissive/avoidant attachment and ASPD and a significant negative correlation between secure attachment style and ASPD. These results reinforced the existing research on the importance of early experiences in the development of antisocial tendencies that has been found in mainstream research. In this small sample of participants with IDD, there was a link between insecure attachment and ASPD, while secure attachment appeared to be protective in relation to antisocial tendencies.

CLINICAL IMPLICATIONS

The case of Rusty demonstrates the way in which issues of attachment are linked to personality disorder, which, in turn, is related to practical difficulties in working clinically with individual cases.

Case Example continued: Rusty

Rusty settled initially when admitted to hospital but soon started to destroy property and make allegations of inappropriate sexual behaviour against staff. We quickly realized that her increasing difficulties were related to the instigation of an 'Independence programme' whereby she planned to go to the local shops, more distant shops and eventually go out for days to the local college and occupation centre on her own. We then adjusted all of the treatment and management programmes to increase the support available when she was outside the unit, slowed down the pace of the Independence programme so that she could accommodate developments more easily and altered her psychological treatment programmes to emphasize consistency and continued support.

The psychological treatment addressed the attachment issues somewhat indirectly. Rusty attended 'social problem solving treatment' and 'anger treatment', both of which were based on cognitive behavioural therapy principles and had been evaluated systematically. The difficulty for Rusty was consistent attendance and we decided at an early stage that we would provide treatment over a long period of time whether or not she attended. Because of her fearful/anxious attachment style, we predicted that she would confront the limits of our patience with non-attendance and non-compliance, and this was, in fact, what happened. She attended the first few sessions of the social problem-solving group and then started to miss sessions. We made it clear that she was expected to attend and that when she did, we would be pleased to see her. Following her absence from a few sessions, she attended and was a willing participant. However, as the work of psychological therapy became more personal, confronting idiosyncratic issues, she began to pretend that she was asleep and complained of boredom. Again, we accepted this and simply told her that it was good that she attended and that she might enjoy future sessions. In fact, Rusty has now been in group and individual treatment for two years and her improvement has been significant. However, she continually returns to 'testing' our willingness to maintain her in the therapeutic relationship. Our position is always the same – that we are happy to see her and happy when she makes progress. The results of treatment have been universally positive, with reductions in measured anger, anxiety, depression and social insecurity. On measures of social problem solving, she has shown increases in positive orientation and decreases in impulsive style, suggesting good progress in social problem-solving situations. These are reflected in her criminal behaviour, with significant reductions in police contact for crime.

The Independence programme was also successful, with several setbacks over the course. Although Rusty has the adaptive skills to manage shops, leisure facilities and other community facilities quite capably, her emotional difficulties and attachment needs meant that the whole programme had to be conducted in a more measured fashion than would be indicated by her personal skills. She was shadowed for some time and then went independently to the local shops. Following these outings, she had short individual sessions to review her progress and any difficulties she had felt. We always emphasized that any developments would be made in agreement with her. The setbacks included emotional outbursts, refusal to go out and occasional absconding, but eventually the difficulties were overcome and she became reassured that as she became increasingly independent, she would always be supported by the service.

CONCLUSION

In this chapter, we have reviewed mainstream research that identified the relationship between correlates of attachment difficulties and problems in adulthood such as criminality and severe emotional difficulties. These correlates of attachment problems are generally developmental adversity and abuse in childhood. We have then identified research linking attachment style to personality disorders. There are undoubtedly links between personality disorders and criminality, and personality disorders and severe emotional difficulties. The two primary personality disorders indicated in this research are borderline personality disorder and antisocial personality disorder.

The relationships that have been found have not been specific. In one of the principal studies, Brennan and Shaver (1998) found a significant overlap between attachment style and personality disorder, in that insecure attachment had a strong significant association with personality pathology. However, there were no specific relationships between types of insecure attachment and categories of personality disorder. We have also reviewed research on the way in which repeated interactions in families during childhood can lead to antisocial tendencies in adolescents and adulthood.

The small amount of research on people with IDD suggests that attachment style can be reliably assessed and that similar processes occur in this population. Behavioural correlates of attachment difficulties, for example witnessing family violence, were significantly associated with violence in adulthood for offenders with IDD. Steptoe and colleagues (Steptoe, 2011; Steptoe, Lindsay and Carson, 2015a, 2015b) have found expected relationships between attachment style, emotional difficulties and personality disorder. Secure attachment has been associated with low levels of emotional difficulty and positive personality features such as warmth and nurturance, while insecure attachment has been associated with higher levels of emotional difficulties such as hostility and personality features of coercion and dominance. Therefore, the existing research would suggest that developmental experiences and attachment style are at least as important in people with IDD as they have been found to be in the general population. We have illustrated the practical application of this knowledge with individual cases where attachment difficulties have been a significant aspect in relation to the development of problems. Addressing these attachment difficulties has been an essential aspect of ongoing treatment and management.

REFERENCES

Ainsworth, M.D.S., Blehar, M.C., Waters, E. and Wall, S. (1978) *Patterns of Attachment: A Psychological Study of the Strange Situation*. Hillsdale, N.J: Erlbaum.

Allen, J.P., Hauser, S.T. and Borman-Spurrell, E. (1996) Attachment theory as a framework for understanding sequelae of severe adolescent psychopathology: An 11-year follow-up study. *Journal of Consulting and Clinical Psychology*, 64: 254–263.

Armsden, G.C., McCauley, E., Greenberg, M.T., Burke, P.M. and Mitchell, J.R. (1990) Parent and peer attachment in early adolescent depression. *Journal of Abnormal Child Clinical Psychology*, 18: 683–697.

Barone, L. (2003) Developmental protective and risk factors in borderline personality disorder: A study using the Adult Attachment Interview. *Attachment and Human Development*, 5: 64–77.

Bartholomew, K. (1997) Adult attachment processes: Individual and couple perspectives. *British Journal of Medical Psychology*, 70: 249–263.

Bartholomew, K., Kwong, M.J. and Hart, S.D. (2001) Attachment. In W.J. Livesley (ed.) *Handbook of Personality Disorders: Theory, Research, and Treatment*. London: The Guilford Press.

Beail, N. and Warden, S. (1995) Sexual abuse of adults with learning disabilities. *Intellectual Disability Research*, 39: 382–387.

Brennan, K.A. and Shaver, P.R. (1998) Attachment styles and personality disorders: Their connections to each other and to parental divorce, parental death, and perceptions of parental caregiving. *Journal of Personality*, 66: 835–878.

Caperton, J.D., Eden, J.F. and Johnson, J.K. (2004) Predicting Sex Offender Institutional Adjustment and Treatment Compliance Using the Personality Assessment Inventory. *Psychological Assessment*, 16(2): 187–191.

Cassidy, J. (1994) Emotion regulation: Influences of attachment relationships. *Monographs of the Society for Research in Child Development*, 59: 228–249.

Choi-Kain, L.W., Fitzmaurice, G.M., Zanarini, M.C., Laverdiere, O. and Gunderson, J.G. (2009) The relationship between self reported attachment styles, interpersonal dysfunction, and borderline personality disorder. *Journal of Nervous and Mental Disease*, 197(11): 816–821.

Clements, J. (2000) Development, Cognition and Performance. In E. Emerson, C. Hatton, J. Bromley and A. Caine (eds) *Clinical Psychology and People with Intellectual Disabilities* (pp. 39–53). John Wiley & Sons, Ltd: Chichester.

Cole, P.M., Llera, S.J. and Pemberton, C.K. (2009) Emotional instability, poor emotional awareness, and the development of borderline personality. *Development and Psychopathology*, 21(4): 1293–1310.

Consedine, N.S. and Magai, C. (2003) Attachment and emotion experience in later life: The view from emotions theory. *Attachment and Human Development*, 5(2): 165–187.

Critchfield, K.L., Levy, K.N., Clarkin, J.F. and Kernberg, O.F. (2008) The relational context of aggression in Borderline Personality Disorder: Using adult attachment style to predict forms of hostility. *Journal of Clinical Psychology*, 64(1): 67–82.

Dutton, D., Saunders, K., Starzomski, A. and Bartholomew, K. (1994) Intimacy-anger and insecure attachment as precursors of abuse in intimate relationships. *Journal of Applied Social Psychology*, 24(15): 1367–1386.

Edens, D.F. (2009). Interpersonal characteristics of male criminal offenders: Personality, psychopathological, and behavioural correlates. *Psychological Assessments*, 21: 89–98.

Fazel, S. and Danesh, J. (2002) Serious mental disorder in 23,000 prisoners: A systematic review of 62 surveys. *Lancet*, 359(9306): 545–550.

Feeney, J.A. and Noller, P. (1996) *Adult Attachment*. Thousand Oaks, CA: Sage.

George, C., Kaplan, N. and Main, M. (1985) *The Adult Attachment Interview*. Unpublished manuscript. University of California, Berkeley.

Granic, I. and Patterson, G.R. (2006) Toward a comprehensive model of antisocial development. A dynamic systems approach. *Psychological Review*, 113: 101–131.

Griffin, D. and Bartholomew, K. (1994) The metaphysics of measurement: The case of adult attachment. *Advances in Personal Relationships*, 5: 17–52.

Harris, G.T., Rice, M.E. and Quinsey, V.L. (1993) Violent recidivism of mentally disordered offenders: The development of a statistical prediction instrument. *Criminal Justice and Behaviour*, 20: 315–335.

Hart, S., Dutton, D.G. and Newlove, T. (1993) The prevalence of personality disorder among wife assaulters. *Journal of Personality Disorders*, 7(4): 329–341.

Johnson, J.G., Cohen, P., Brown, J., Smailes, E.M. and Bernstein, D.P. (1999) Childhood maltreatment increases risk for personality disorders during early adulthood. *Archives of General Psychiatry*, 56(7): 600–606.

Keeling, J.A., Rose, J.L. and Beech, A.R. (2007) A preliminary evaluation of the adaptation of four assessments for offenders with special needs. *Journal of Intellectual and Developmental Disability*, 32(2): 62–73.

Larson, F., Alim, N. and Tsakanikos, E. (2011) Attachment style and mental health in adults with intellectual disability: Self-reports and reports by carers. *Advances in Mental Health and Intellectual Disabilities*, 5: 15–23.

Lindsay, W.R., Hogue, T., Taylor, J.T., Steptoe, L., Mooney, P., Johnston, S. and Smith, A.H.W. (2006) Two studies on the prevalence and validity of personality disorder in three forensic learning disability samples. *Journal of Forensic Psychiatry and Psychology*, 17: 485–506.

Lindsay, W.R., Holland, A.J., Taylor, J.L., Michie, A.M., Bambrick, M.B., O'Brien, G. and Wheeler, J. (2009) Diagnostic Information and Adversity in Childhood for Offenders with Learning Disability Referred to and Accepted into Forensic Services. *Advances in Mental Health and Learning Disabilities*, 3: 19–24.

Lindsay, W.R., Steptoe, L. and Haut, F. (2012) The sexual and physical abuse histories of offenders with intellectual disability. *Journal of Intellectual Disability Research*, 56: 326–331.

Lindsay, W.R., Taylor, J.L., Hogue, T.E., Mooney, P., Steptoe L. and Morrissey, C. (2010) Relationship between assessed emotion, personality, personality disorder and risk in offenders with intellectual disability. *Psychiatry, Psychology and Law*, 17(3): 385–397.

Mikulincer, M. (1998) Adult attachment style and individual differences in functional as well as dysfunctional experiences of anger. *Journal of Personality and Social Psychology*, 74: 513–524.

Mikulincer, M. and Shaver, P.R. (2007) *Attachment in Adulthood: Structure, dynamics and change*. New York: The Guilford Press.

Monahan, J., Steadman, H.J, Silver, E., Appelbaum, P., Robbins, P., Mulvey, E.P. and Banks, S. (2001) *Rethinking Risk Assessment: The MacArthur study of mental disorder and violence*. New York: Oxford University Press.

Morey, L.C., Warner, M.B., Shea, M.T., Gunderson, J.G., Sanislow, C.A., Grilo, C. and McGlashan, T.H. (2003) The representation of four personality disorders for non-adaptive and adaptive personality dimensional model of personality. *Psychological Assessment*, 15: 326–332.

Novaco, R.W. and Taylor, J.L. (2008) Anger and assaultiveness of male forensic patients with developmental disabilities: Links to volatile parents. *Aggressive Behavior*, 34: 380–393.

O'Brien, G., Taylor, J.L., Lindsay, W.R., Holland, A., Carson, D., Steptoe, L. and Wheeler, J. (2010) Multicentre study of adults with learning disabilities referred to services for antisocial offending behaviour: Demographic, individual, offending and service characteristics. *Journal of Learning Disabilities and Offending Behaviour*, 1(2): 5–15.

Patterson, G.R. (1986) Performance models for antisocial boys. *American Psychologist*, 41: 432–444.

Patterson, G.R., Reid, J.B. and Dishion, T.J. (1992) *Anti-social Boys: A social interactional approach*, volume 4. Eugene, OR: Castalia.

Quirk, S.W., Christiansen, N.D., Wagner, S.H. and McNulty, J.L. (2003) On the Usefulness of Measures of Normal Personality for Clinical Assessment: Evidence of the Incremental Validity of the Revised NEO Personality Inventory. *Psychological Assessment*, 15(3): 311–325.

Reynolds, S.K. and Clark, L.A. (2001) Predicting Dimensions of Personality Disorder from Domains and Facets of the Five Factor Model. *Journal of Personality*, 69: 199–222.

Roberts, J.E., Gotlib, I.H. and Kassel, J.D. (1996) Adult attachment security and symptoms of depression: The mediating roles of dysfunctional attitudes and low self-esteem. *Journal of Personality and Social Psychology*, 70: 310–320.

Sack, A., Sperling, M.B., Fagen, G. and Foelsch, P. (1996) Attachment style, history and behavioural contrasts for a borderline and normal sample. *Journal of Personality Disorders*, 10: 88–102.

Steptoe, L. (2011) *Attachment, childhood adversity, emotional problems and personality disorder in offenders with mild intellectual disability.* Doctoral thesis, Abertay University, Dundee, Scotland. Retrieved 08 04 2015 from: http://hdl.handle.net/10373/1943

Steptoe, L., Lindsay, W. and Carson, D. (2015a) *The assessment of attachment in people with intellectual disabilities.* Manuscript submitted for publication.

Steptoe, L., Lindsay, W. and Carson, D. (2015b) *Attachment, anger and psychological symptoms in offenders and controls with intellectual disability.* Manuscript submitted for publication.

van IJzendoorn, M.H. and Bakermans-Kranenburg, M.J. (1996) Attachment representations in mothers, fathers, adolescents and clinical groups: A meta analytic search for normative data. *Journal of Consulting and Clinical Psychology,* 64: 8–21.

Wei, M., Mallinckrodt, B., Russell, D.W. and Abraham, W.T. (2004) Maladaptive perfectionism as a mediator and moderator between adult attachment and depressive mood. *Journal of Counselling Psychology,* 51(2): 201–212.

West, M.L. and Sheldon-Keller, A. (1994) *Patterns of Relating: An adult attachment perspective.* New York: The Guilford Press.

Zuckerman, M. (1999) *The Vulnerability to Psychopathology: A biosocial model.* Washington, DC: American Psychological Association.

Chapter 12

GETTING INTIMATE: USING ATTACHMENT THEORY TO UNDERSTAND INTIMATE RELATIONSHIPS IN OUR WORK WITH PEOPLE WITH INTELLECTUAL DISABILITIES

Nancy Sheppard and Myooran Canagaratnam
The Tavistock Clinic, London, UK

INTRODUCTION

Attachment theory emphasizes the influence of early experiences of caregiving on the quality of later relationships, mediated by psychological constructs termed 'internal working models' (Bowlby, 1969/1982; 1973; 1980). Infants with experience of consistent, sensitive caregiving develop secure attachment patterns and internal working models which entail positive expectations of relationships with others. This results in an inclination to be closely involved with others. There are demonstrable links between measures of secure attachment in infancy and general measures of social competence in middle childhood and adolescence (Sroufe, 2005).

The experience of close relationships is as important to people with an intellectual disability (ID) as it is to those without a disability (Mason *et al.*, 2013). However, people with ID often experience difficulties in establishing and maintaining these relationships for a number of reasons (e.g. poor social skills and increased social isolation, lack of

Attachment in Intellectual and Developmental Disability: A Clinician's Guide to Practice and Research, First Edition. Edited by Helen K. Fletcher, Andrea Flood and Dougal Julian Hare.
© 2016 John Wiley & Sons, Ltd. Published 2016 by John Wiley & Sons, Ltd.

opportunities to meet people due to dependence on others and low socio-economic status; Department of Health, 2001). Social isolation has been linked to poorer mental health in this population (Deb, Thomas and Bright, 2001). Despite these barriers, many individuals with ID are able to develop a range of intimate relationships including friendship (Mason *et al.*, 2013), romantic (Rushbrooke, Murray and Townsend, 2014) and parenting relationships (Willems *et al.*, 2007).

This chapter will consider the intimate relationships of individuals with ID, through the lens of attachment theory, and with reference to empirical research and our own clinical experience working in the Learning and Complex Disabilities Service at The Tavistock Clinic, London. We will describe how attachment theory has been helpful in understanding some of the difficulties our service users experience in their close and intimate relationships, in the context of other barriers which people with ID face in this area. We will also discuss how secure attachment promotes positive relationships, through which people with ID can live positive and fulfilling lives.

DEVELOPMENT OF INTIMATE RELATIONSHIPS

Initially, an infant's main relationships are with the primary caregiver and other significant carers who might include grandparents, other members of the extended family or professional child carers. Middle childhood is marked by the increasing importance of friends and peers, and the development of relationships with other adults such as teachers and mentors. During adolescence, close relationships with particular individuals may develop. In adulthood, intimate relationships may exist with friends, colleagues and romantic partners/spouses, and may also encompass parenting relationships with an adult's own children and grandchildren.

How might the development of this array of intimate relationships be understood with respect to attachment theory? Whilst Bowlby claimed that attachment behaviour plays a key role throughout the life cycle, his description of the attachment behavioural system mainly focuses on infancy and the preschool years (Bowlby 1969/1982; 1973; 1980). Several subsequent authors have picked up the baton and explored attachment in middle childhood, adolescence and adulthood. Mayseless (2005) explores a number of developmental processes which characterize the changes in the attachment behavioural system in middle childhood from an evolutionary perspective. In particular, she draws attention to the decrease in the intensity of attachment behaviour in the context of the relationship with primary caregivers, theorizing that this partial withdrawal (both emotionally and behaviourally) from investment in close relationships with parents or primary caregivers allows greater investment in exploration and learning. The stage is thereby set for achievement of key developmental tasks: learning to be self-sustaining and autonomous, learning to live in a group and finding a mate that doesn't share the same gene pool. The primary caregiver has a key role in supporting this process. In addition to providing a safe haven to a relationship partner in distress, the caregiver provides a secure base by responding in a manner that encourages exploration of the world, safe in the knowledge that he or she can return for comfort, reassurance or assistance if needed. This exploration may involve playing, working, learning, discovering and, crucially, forging new relationships.

However, the presence of an intellectual disability, with associated mismatch between an individual's physical and cognitive maturation, can complicate the developmental processes described above. For caregivers, there may be a risk of encouraging over-dependency and obedience (Clegg and Lansdall-Welfare, 1995). This inhibits exploration and can potentially impact on the formation of intimate relationships. The story of Aamina, a young woman with learning disability who was seen in our service, illustrates how well-meaning and thoughtful parents can inadvertently foster over-dependency.

Case Example: Aamina

Aamina's parents had struggled to come to terms with Aamina's difficulties and together the family carefully constructed a complex and intricate web of support involving family members, professional carers and therapists. The overt aim was to scaffold Aamina's learning and support her development. Unconsciously, this network may have served to protect both the family and Aamina from the painful reality of her disabilities. Nonetheless, this safety net served Aamina well through childhood. However, as she developed into a young woman, this web took on a gradual metamorphosis until it was more of a 'cocoon', restricting Aamina's capacity to express independent wishes and develop her own relationships.

Aamina was referred to our service for Psychotherapy assessment following an acute episode of bizarre behavioural symptoms. There had been a number of recent stressors including Aamina's grandparents emigrating back to their home country, Aamina's father losing his job and Aamina leaving school and starting college, which were thought to have precipitated the episode.

When she attended the clinic, Aamina appeared withdrawn and was extremely anxious when away from one of her parents or another close family member. She was also reluctant to go back to college. Her parents described her as shy and lacking in confidence to a high degree, so much so that she would be reluctant to try anything new. Her parents were concerned that her passivity and her reluctance to explore the world around her were seriously restricting her capacity to develop independence.

Whilst Aamina had developed friendships with one or two children at school, she was not a girl with lots of friends. She described strong feelings about one particular girl, Maya, whom she had known for a number of years. It seemed that Maya had been emotionally bullying Aamina and yet she felt drawn to her and expressed a wish to be friends with her.

Aamina attended for individual psychotherapy sessions, and her parents attended for parallel support sessions. In time, it emerged that Aamina's conflicted feelings about Maya were mirrored in her feelings about her parents, whom she loved intensely and needed to protect and support her, but also felt angry at for making decisions about her with which she didn't agree. One decision was ending her time at her special school and moving her to a new environment (mainstream college) where she felt different and anxious. Through the individual sessions Aamina was able to become more assertive about her own needs, protesting when she did not want to go on a holiday with her parents because it would mean missing a valued class. Aamina was more able to value herself and express her needs and wishes. Her parents, too, moved in their position from thinking of Aamina as needing to be protected and 'guarded' to being a young woman who might forge her own direction and be helped to take risks with new relationships. The family gained confidence in working together to take steps towards Aamina being more independent.

> The therapeutic support offered an opportunity for Aamina, her parents and other family members to reflect on and build resilience to the pain of their experiences of Aamina's disability. With the confidence they built together, they were more able to support and empower Aamina to make new relationships and imagine a future with small steps towards greater independence. The family was able to see the possibility of a young woman growing into an adult and developing romantic and intimate relationships.

ATTACHMENT AND ROMANTIC RELATIONSHIPS

There has been particular interest in the influence of attachment on romantic relationships in adolescence and adulthood. Weiss (1982) highlighted the attachment features of committed adult romantic relationships, in that a person derives comfort and security from a partner, wants to be with the partner (especially at times of stress) and protests when the partner threatens to become unavailable. Hazan and Shaver (1987) conducted empirical studies of adult attachment using self-report measures of experiences and attitudes to relationships. The studies demonstrated how the three main attachment styles observed in infants manifest as 'secure', 'avoidant' and 'anxious ambivalent' styles within the context of adult romantic relationships. These three styles differed in participants' reports of early family relationships, working models of attachment and love experiences, supporting the link between infant and adult attachment.

Bartholomew (1990) and Bartholomew and Horowitz (1991) subsequently proposed an expanded model of four adult attachment styles, based on Bowlby's proposal that individuals develop internal working models of self and others. Bartholomew argued that the working model of self might be positive or negative (e.g. the self is seen as worthy of love and attention or as unworthy). Similarly, the working model of others might be positive or negative (others may be caring and trustworthy or unreliable and rejecting). As a result, four attachment styles of 'Secure', 'Preoccupied', 'Dismissing' and 'Fearful' could be defined. 'Secure' individuals have a model of self and others which is positive, and are comfortable with intimacy and autonomy within relationships. The 'Preoccupied' style corresponds to Hazan and Shaver's (1987) anxious-ambivalent style, and entails a model of self which is negative (unworthy) and a model of others which is positive. These individuals tend to be overly dependent within relationships. Bartholomew (1990) proposed that there are two different types of what Hazan and Shaver termed 'avoidant' attachment style. In the Dismissing-avoidant style, there is a positive model of self and a negative model of others. Individuals with this style emphasize achievement and self-reliance and avoid intimacy. In the Fearful-avoidant style, there is a negative model of both self and others. Fearful individuals seek intimacy but distrust others and so tend to avoid close relationships due to the risk of loss and rejection.

Research evidence in the non-ID population supports the link between romantic attachment security and the quality of couple relationships (Mikulincer and Shaver, 2007) as measured in terms of indices such as trust, commitment and self-reported relationship satisfaction. An important mediating factor is thought to be communication pattern, with secure individuals exhibiting a more open and positive interpersonal style, resulting in more positive relationship outcomes. There are few studies on the influence of attachment styles in adults with ID, not least because of issues in assessing attachment in the population of adults with ID (e.g. Larson, Alim and Tsakanikos, 2011; Weiss *et al.*, 2011; Schuengel *et al.*, 2013; as discussed in Chapter 4). Whilst we do not routinely use measures of adult attachment in our work, we have been able to use knowledge of adult attachment to understand the relationship issues experienced by our service users, and to guide therapeutic interventions.

Case Example: Patrick

Patrick presented with a preoccupied style of attachment in the context of romantic relationships, which contributed to his vulnerability to the social stressors he experienced. He came to see us as he wanted help with social skills. He had mild ID and talked about how he had always been very shy and not very good at making friends. In the assessment, Patrick talked about how he had always felt that he was not good enough both at home and at school. He had found himself surviving by blending into the background, until he met Marta with whom he had started a relationship and who had encouraged him to move away from his home town. Patrick and Marta's relationship had ended soon after and Patrick talked of feeling petrified and alone, a feeling that was familiar to him from his childhood. Feeling desperate, Patrick found his way to a homeless hostel where his ID was identified and he received some help to find accommodation and to claim some benefits.

Patrick had since commenced a relationship with a new partner; however, he said that he was scared that he would lose the relationship. He spoke about the extreme feelings of jealousy he experienced whenever his partner went out. He had tried to address his fears with his partner but had been met with aggressive outbursts which left him feeling stupid and paranoid. Patrick recognized he had fallen into a tricky bind with his new partner, his jealousy and fear of losing the relationship were keeping him in a relationship where he didn't feel valued. By helping Patrick to recognize and understand patterns in his close relationships, we were able to support him to feel a little more confident in his current relationship. He was subsequently able to find a voice to express how he felt about intimacy with his partner.

In contrast, our work with Pauline illustrates how a more secure attachment style can be a key protective factor in terms of mental health.

Case Example: Pauline

Pauline and George met and 'fell in love' at their day centre and remained in a relationship for 25 years until George died, leaving Pauline a widow. Pauline was referred for bereavement counselling and spoke of the 'ups and downs' of her time with George. Pauline felt they had a good relationship, they were good friends and supported one another through difficult times (for instance, having to move house because their landlord had sold the property they lived in, and George's protracted illness) and through good times (when Pauline passed her college course and when planning each other's birthday parties). Pauline also talked of having 'blazing rows' with George, which she was insightfully able to compare to the rows she had engaged in as a

> teenager with her mum and dad. The key in the therapy seemed to be that Pauline had developed a strong bond and a secure attachment with her mother, which allowed them to forgive one another, to make up and carry on living together. Pauline spoke fondly of how George would 'drive her mad' at times but that she worked hard to make sure they made up and also had some fun together.

It has been proposed that prototypical romantic love consists of the integration of three components: attachment, caregiving and sexuality (Shaver, Hazan and Bradshaw, 1988).The following sections consider how attachment relates to each of these additional components within the context of romantic relationships in people with ID.

Attachment and Caregiving within Romantic Relationships

Bowlby (1969/1982) described how the caregiving system acts to provide protection or support to individuals in need. It therefore acts in a complementary manner to the attachment system of the relationship partner. Two caregiving processes have been distinguished: 'Safe haven' caregiving, in which the individual responds to reduce the relationship partner's distress, and 'secure base' caregiving, in which the individual supports their relationship partner's exploration and personal growth (Feeney and Collins, 2004).

There is evidence that attachment exerts a significant influence on quality of caregiving (Feeney, 2008). Studies using self-report measures assessing the quality of caregiving have found that secure individuals are more sensitive to romantic partners' needs and describe themselves as more likely to provide emotional support to their distressed partners (Kunce and Shaver, 1994). These self-reports are corroborated by partners' reports. Authors such as Gillath, Shaver and Mikulincer (2005) argue that attachment insecurity interferes with the altruistic tendency to attend empathically to others' distress, the key mechanism by which sensitive caregiving takes place. In our work with Dana and Zoltan it was helpful to use this premise as a basis in understanding difficulties they presented as a couple.

Case Example: Dana and Zoltan

We were asked to see Dana for some sessions of bereavement work following the death of her mother. In the referral letter to our team, Dana was described as having mild ID and significant physical disabilities. Dana lived with her partner, Zoltan, and was thought by support staff to be functioning in the borderline ID range. Zoltan was Dana's main carer but she also had regular support from a physiotherapist and an occupational therapy assistant who visited regularly. In addition, the couple had daily support with Dana's personal care, budgeting and household chores from a support worker provided by a local voluntary agency. Dana had talked to the OT assistant and said she was worried that Zoltan was getting very angry with her when she was upset about her mother's death and was becoming frustrated and impatient with her when she struggled to get out of her chair.

Dana was invited to an assessment and brought Zoltan with her. Following the initial assessment, the therapists talked to the team about the information Dana and Zoltan had given. Dana had spoken sensitively of Zoltan's early experience; he had been brought up from birth by extended family (a maternal aunt) as his mother had two very disabled older children who needed constant care. Zoltan reluctantly talked of an impoverished, inconsistent relationship with his aunt and older cousins and it was suspected that Zoltan's aunt may have suffered from undiagnosed but severe mental health issues. Zoltan recalled long periods alone in his room, hearing his aunt and cousins shouting and developing watchful wariness in trying to read his aunt's mood from an early age. Zoltan was no longer in contact with his aunt, but remained in close contact with his birth mother into adulthood. In the assessment, it was hypothesized that he had developed insecure attachments to his main caregiver.

In addition, Zoltan's intellectual difficulties had gone unrecognized until he and Dana came to the United Kingdom to find work. They had been in the UK for 15 years and, over this time, Dana's physical health had deteriorated requiring additional care and adaptations in the home. The team drew on elements of attachment theory and psychodynamic theory to help make

> sense of Zoltan's reported frustration. It was helpful to think about Zoltan's changed behaviour towards Dana from the perspective of his insecure attachment to his own caregivers, coupled with a projected anger at Dana's deteriorating physical state and his need to care for her. Dana and Zoltan agreed to some joint sessions and, among other issues, were able to explore their relationship in the context of the formulation, and Dana reported some positive developments in Zoltan's caring role.

Attachment and Sexuality

Evidence indicates that attachment style influences patterns of sexual attitudes, experiences and behaviour within romantic relationships. A study of adolescents demonstrated that securely attached adolescents engaged in sex primarily to show love for their partner, and they experienced fewer negative emotions and more positive and passionate emotions during sexual activity than their insecurely attached peers (Tracy et al., 2003). Feeney and Noller (1990) conducted a study of the sexual attitudes of university students. The study found that individuals classified as avoidant tended to endorse multiple relationships, and sexual activity involving limited commitment and emotional depth (e.g. one-night stands). Conversely, anxious preoccupied individuals reported frequent and intense 'love' experiences with rapid physical and emotional involvement (Feeney and Noller, 1990). Feeney (2008) reviews further studies on attachment pattern and sexuality which provide evidence that anxious (preoccupied) attachment in women has been linked to measures of sexual promiscuity. It has been postulated that these high rates of sexual activity may reflect the women's desire for intense closeness, and anxiety about rejection from partners if they do not oblige their requests (Schachner and Shaver, 2004).

Eagles (2007) explains these observed patterns by conceptualizing attachment and sexuality as separate and partially antagonistic systems. This, he claims, explains the commonly observed split between love and desire. Eagles views integration of attachment and sexuality as a developmental task, and states that attachment security is a key influence on an individual's success at achieving this. He hypothesizes that the more unresolved (insecure) an individual's early attachment relationship, the greater difficulty the individual will have in shifting from early parental caregiver to current partner as the primary attachment figure. The result is that the avoidant or preoccupied individual will unconsciously equate their current partner and early parental figure, which dampens sexual desire due to the incest taboo.

Regardless of their attachment pattern, people with ID often face issues in the expression of their sexuality in terms of the anxiety it raises in their caregivers. It is not unusual for staff support networks to seek advice or call a care planning meeting to undertake a risk assessment of a developing intimate relationship. Matters of informed consent and understanding of equal and loving sexual relationships are scrutinized and a wide number of professionals may be consulted before an individual might be encouraged or supported to go on a date, let alone start a sexual relationship. Sinason (1992) provides an understanding of the unconscious fears which may be operating within a support network over the expression of sexuality. This can ultimately result in denial of sexuality and infantilization of people with ID. Our work with Gunel illustrates some of the struggles that people with ID might face in exploring their sexuality, which relate both to early attachment and to the issues those around them face in balancing a wish to promote autonomy with the need to protect vulnerable individuals.

Case Example: Gunel

Gunel, a young woman with moderate ID, struggled for the right to make choices regarding her sexuality and to take risks in pursuit of romantic relationships. At the time of referral, Gunel lived with her older sister. Gunel's mum had died when she was young and both girls had lived with their dad into their early adulthood. Then their dad had met another partner, re-married and moved back to his home country, leaving them in the family home. Their relationship with their father remained positive but they rarely visited or saw him after the move. Gunel came to our service complaining that she and her sister were constantly arguing, that she wanted to move out into a supported living scheme but her sister was over-protective and whenever a facility was suggested, she would dismiss it as not good enough or unable to meet Gunel's needs.

Gunel had two support workers who assisted her to attend college and go out at weekends. It was at the college where she met up with an old school friend, Uzge. Gunel and her friend started to go out together in the evening and Uzge introduced Gunel to other friends of hers. In her counselling sessions, Gunel described an evening where she had met and made friends with another woman, Martha. Over time, Gunel talked more and more of Martha and then said she thought she had fallen in love with her. Gunel reported that her support workers and her sister were struggling to accept her feelings for another woman and wouldn't let her contact Martha or meet up with her. Gunel felt frustrated and was determined to pursue her feelings for Martha. She requested support from her counsellor to talk to her sister and the support staff and a meeting was arranged to bring everyone together to explore the difficulties each faced.

In the meeting we were able to explore the different perspectives in the network. Gunel's sister reported a difficult time for both of them around their mother's death where Gunel's behaviour had become particularly challenging at school. Gunel's two support workers were thoughtful and psychologically minded and were of the view that Gunel was searching for a replacement mother figure in her pursuit of a relationship with Martha. Gunel's sister was worried that if she was encouraged to pursue a relationship with Martha she would be terribly hurt and this would trigger the desperate feelings they had both experienced around their mother's death and their father's decision to move abroad. It was clear from the meeting that there was an overwhelming need in the network to protect Gunel, but, as a result, her feelings were being dismissed as a whim. As professionals we were able to support the network to move gradually towards both understanding Gunel's feelings from an attachment perspective whilst retaining respect for her autonomy and her choice to take a risk. With Gunel's agreement, the network was offered some consultation sessions in order to build confidence in the workers so that they may, in turn, support Gunel with her relationships.

Gunel was very well supported and was secure enough in her attachments with her caregivers that she could consider her vulnerabilities in relation to risk. Gunel was also emotionally intelligent and, with the counsellor's support, was able to demonstrate to her caregivers that she was prepared to take the risk of pursuing her romantic feelings and accept the consequences. She did write to Martha, who sensitively wrote back to let her know that there was no possibility in her mind of a romantic relationship. This was, of course, extremely painful for Gunel, but she did manage the rejection with the support of a network of carers around her.

Working with carers can offer an important function in helping professionals and family members to free themselves up from their caregiving roles and transition to a more adult-to-adult type relationship with the individual with ID, rather than an adult-to-child relationship. At the same time, those supporting people with ID do need to be mindful of the potential risks. For some people with ID, patterns of sexual behaviour associated with insecure attachment can leave them particularly vulnerable to exploitation. A number of authors have aimed to highlight the vulnerability of people with ID to sexual exploitation, and statistics suggest that as many as 1 in 2 women with ID have experienced an abusive sexual relationship (Brown and Craft, 1989; Turk and Brown, 1993; Burns, 2000; McCarthy, 2001). McCarthy (2000) found that women tolerated being mistreated by splitting off their relationships into two and trying to think of the sex as less important than the companionship and status that they achieved. McCarthy (2000) reported that women with ID may be motivated to sell sex through the desire to experience themselves as having intrinsic value, status and identity as a woman. Others have noted the wish for people with ID to be in a relationship over and above any difficulties that the partnership might evoke (Brownridge, 2006; Jeffreys, 2008).

Case Example: Shanice

Shanice was referred by her team of support staff who were extremely anxious for her safety. In consultation with the staff group it was a regular task to support the network to make risk assessments and plans to ensure against Shanice facing harm from other people. Staff reported that Shanice would be very keen to go out and spend time in social activities typical of a young woman of her age (22 years), for instance going to pubs, clubs and the cinema. Shanice was highly resistant to being with staff members but struggled with the concept of keeping herself safe, and when out and about, she would talk indiscriminately to strangers, giving intimate details and her name and address. When staff tried to work with her on keeping safe, it became apparent that Shanice was looking for an intimate relationship and had a very limited understanding of the reciprocal nature of such a relationship.

Shanice idealized romantic love; she often talked of meeting 'Mr Right', about weddings and marriage and spent much of her time at home watching romantic films. However, staff felt that in her search for romance, Shanice had confused love with sexual contact and were concerned that she would be vulnerable to abuse as a result. On several occasions, staff had had to put in measures to prevent unknown men coming to Shanice's flat claiming to be her friend. The staff group and the supported living organization had helped Shanice to engage in work around keeping safe and understanding relationships, which had helped a little but they were left with the constant anxiety that she remained extremely vulnerable to exploitation. They felt torn between Shanice's safety and restricting her right to adult relationships.

The support from our service helped the staff understand Shanice's vulnerability in the context of her attachment relationships and to navigate the precarious path between risk, choice and human rights to intimate relationships. Staff reported feeling less concerned when, one year on, Shanice had started saying she didn't think the 'guys' she was meeting were 'any good' and wanted to go about finding 'Mr Right' through a dating agency. They encouraged her to enrol in a local agency for people with ID and, although they remained anxious about risk, felt more confident in their capacity as a team to safely support Shanice in her search for love.

ATTACHMENT AND THE PARENTING RELATIONSHIP

In their review article, Aunos and Feldman (2002) calculated that between 60 and 90% of people with mild ID want to marry and raise a child. However, in the most reliable survey of adults with ID in the UK, only around 7% have children and, of this group, about 40% of parents do not live with their children (Emerson *et al.*, 2005).

The International Association for the Scientific Study of ID Special Interest Research Group on Parents and Parenting with ID (IASSID SIRG, 2008) has highlighted the significant barriers to parenting faced by this population. These include opposition from others to their childbearing, ongoing scrutiny once the child is born and poverty, ill health and lack of access to resources such as appropriate housing and practical support. At the same time, the IASSID SIRG reported that many people with ID succeed at parenting, and there is no evidence for a systematic correlation between IQ and parenting capacity above an IQ of 60. In spite of this, parents with ID are more likely to have their children removed by child welfare authorities and placed in care away from the home (Booth, Booth and McConnell., 2005).

For people with ID, as for those without ID, the impact of having a child removed from their care can be devastating and long lasting, as illustrated by our work with Grace, a 50-year-old woman referred to our team by her General Practitioner (GP).

Case Example: Grace

Grace was a frequent attender at her GP surgery, complaining of severe back pain with no explainable cause. Although she had a good relationship with the surgery staff, they were becoming increasingly concerned that her pain had an underlying emotional aetiology.

Grace was sceptical about the usefulness of talking therapy but, after an uncertain start, she did begin to attend regularly. In the sessions it transpired that Grace had an extremely difficult start in life. She had been born in prison and removed into care at a very early age. However, when her mother was released, she was returned to her parents' care only to be removed again one year later after her father lost his temper with her and tried to strangle her. Grace lived in a number of children's homes until she was 18 years old. She had been diagnosed with ID when she was a baby and had some physical difficulties related to cerebral palsy. In her therapy sessions, Grace talked about how she didn't blame her mother because she herself had a 'terrible time' when she was a girl. Over time, Grace opened up more about herself; she had hinted that she had a secret which she movingly revealed just before a Christmas break. Grace talked of how she, too, was a mother and that her son had been removed from her care when only a few weeks old. Slowly, Grace was able to draw together links between her unerring physical pain and discordant feelings of anxiety that she could not fathom. With careful exploration and support, Grace was able to realize that her feelings were interconnected with the notion of her son reaching his 18th year and a smouldering but unbearable glimmer of hope that he may try to find her.

Grace used her sessions to make sense of her own past and her experience in care. It was striking that she could talk with relative ease about her own traumatic childhood with a catalogue of neglect and abusive experiences before going into care so young herself, but Grace could hardly bring herself to talk of the experience of losing her son. In discussion with the team it was possible to explore how we could understand a familial pattern in the painful experiences of bearing and losing a child. In this context, we saw the trace of the parental bond that Grace had developed within the few weeks that she had had with her baby after his birth. We felt that because of this glimmer, she found the strength to talk about and bear her own pain but not the imagined pain that her son might experience from being separated from her. Over the period of the therapy, Grace's back pain eased but she remained distressed and anxious in her relationships with others. At the end of the work with Grace, The Tavistock Centre team formulated that although Grace had been able to realize her pain as being displaced emotional pain, it would be almost impossible for this pain to be relieved fully, as it represented the traumatic lesion caused by the repeated breaking of parental bonds.

As discussed in Chapter 2, Ainsworth's pioneering work provided evidence for a relationship between parental sensitivity and children's attachment security (Ainsworth, Bell and Stayton, 1974). Subsequent evidence supported trans-generational transmission of attachment patterns, in that parents with secure, autonomous mental representations tend to have children with secure attachment, whereas insecurely attached parents usually have insecure children (Main, Kaplan and Cassidy, 1985; Van IJzendoorn, 1995). Attachment theory is not only helpful in understanding a parent's capacity to respond sensitively to a child's needs, but also to request and receive the support that they might need to provide optimal parenting. The latter can be particularly important in people with ID, as illustrated by Sally and Tyrone's story.

> ### Case Example: Sally and Tyrone
>
> Sally and Tyrone were a couple with ID who were referred for therapy by the social worker of their son, Madison. They had been in a long-term relationship and Madison had been a planned baby. Sally and Tyrone had lived together for a few years, but Tyrone had struggled to care for himself and Sally had essentially been caring for Tyrone. Once Madison was born, Tyrone started to look very unkempt and had got into debt as he had been unable to manage his money. It was clear that the social worker saw a strong bond between the pair but was concerned as Sally was not coping well with caring for both Madison and Tyrone.
>
> Sally's own early history was unclear; she had been in and out of foster care, but early on had developed a good relationship with one foster carer with whom she still kept in touch and who was helping out with the baby. Tyrone was still in touch with his father but had had a troubled childhood and talked of how he had experienced physical abuse from both parents. His mother left him with his father when he was two years old and he had no further contact with her. In our team meeting we explored how the couple's different attachment styles were manifesting in their care of Madison. We felt that, despite her unclear history, Sally had developed a secure attachment with her foster carer which had served her well in her capacity to care for others. Tyrone was clearly more needy and insecure in the relationship and had struggled to share Sally when Madison came along.
>
> Sally and Tyrone's relationship had reached a crisis when Sally found out about the debts, and she had asked Tyrone to leave the flat. He had been living on the streets before services took him in and he was offered a place in a supported living project. Sally was worried about Tyrone being in supported living and thought he would lose touch with Madison. In the therapy sessions, she spoke of how she was determined not to allow Madison to experience the upbringing that she had and she sought help from Madison's social worker who responded in a supportive way. The staff at

> Tyrone's housing project encouraged Tyrone to keep in touch with Sally, and the social worker had asked them to come along to think about how they could parent Madison together successfully.
>
> The therapy was hard for both Sally and Tyrone. After they separated, Tyrone struggled to attend, although Sally did continue and was able to engage with help. In exploring her feelings about bonding with Madison, Sally was able to link her impoverished early experience with her fear about Madison experiencing difficulties. Sally talked tentatively about her early memories, but it was clear that a warm and loving foster carer had afforded her an attachment experience that she was able to draw on in her capacity to engage with help. Despite her fears of not coping, the social worker was always impressed that Sally asked for help if she felt she needed it and would seek out support in the form of parents' groups and play groups for Madison. Sally was able to use her counselling sessions to gain some insight into her difficulty in sustaining relationships and also reported a more balanced view of the challenges that parenting might offer her as Madison grew older. It was the confidence in her capacity to accept help and to make good use of a therapeutic relationship that allowed us to close the case when Madison started school, as we too felt a degree of confidence that Sally would continue to ask for help appropriately.

CONCLUSION

Individuals presenting to mental health services frequently report having difficulties in their relationships. We have found it useful in our clinical work to use attachment theory to help us understand these issues. At the same time, the concept of secure attachment is useful in terms of identifying factors promoting resilience and recovery in people with ID. Research into the nature of close relationships in people with ID, and specifically into the role attachment plays in this population, is at a very early stage. This chapter has therefore drawn largely from theory and research around the non-ID population in conjunction with our own clinical experience of working with people with ID.

People with ID desire the same range of close relationships as those without ID, but face many barriers to achieving these. When considering issues in relationships, attachment perspectives should be placed in the context of these barriers, which include practical issues around opportunities, the need to balance risk against autonomy in vulnerable individuals and, more generally, the attitudes of family, caregivers, professionals and wider society towards the forming and maintaining of relationships in people with ID.

REFERENCES

Ainsworth, M.D.S., Bell, S.M. and Stayton, D.J. (1974) Infant–mother attachment and social development: 'Socialisation' as a product of reciprocal responsiveness to signals. In M.J.M. Richards (ed.) *The Integration of a Child into a Social World.* (pp. 99–135). London: Cambridge University Press.

Aunos, M. and Feldman, M.A. (2002) Attitudes towards Sexuality, Sterilization and Parenting Rights of Persons with Intellectual Disabilities. *Journal of Applied Research in Intellectual Disabilities*, 15: 285–296.

Bartholomew, K. (1990) Avoidance of intimacy: An attachment perspective. *Journal of Social and Personal Relationships*, 7: 147–178.

Bartholomew, K. and Horowitz, L.M. (1991) Attachment styles among young adults: A test of a four-category model. *Journal of Personality and Social Psychology*, 61(2): 226–244.

Booth, T., Booth, W. and McConnell, D. (2005) The prevalence and outcomes of care proceedings involving parents with learning difficulties in the family courts. *Journal of Intellectual Disability Research*, 18: 7–17.

Bowlby, J. (1969) *Attachment and Loss. Volume 1: Attachment.* London: Hogarth Press and the Institute of Psychoanalysis.

Bowlby, J. (1973) *Attachment and Loss. Volume 2: Separation: Anxiety and Anger.* London: Hogarth Press and the Institute of Psychoanalysis.

Bowlby, J. (1980) *Attachment and Loss. Volume 3: Loss: Sadness and Depression.* London: Hogarth Press and the Institute of Psychoanalysis.

Bowlby, J. (1982) *Attachment and Loss. Volume 1: Attachment*, 2nd edition. London: Pimlico.

Brown, H. and Craft, A. (1989) *Thinking the Unthinkable: Papers on Sexual Abuse and People with Learning Difficulties.* London: FPA Education Unit.

Brownridge, D.A. (2006) Partner violence against women with disabilities. *Violence against Women*, 8: 805–822.

Burns, J. (2000) Waiting to be Asked: Women with Learning Disabilities. *Clinical Psychology Forum.* January.

Clegg, J.A. and Lansdall-Welfare, R. (1995) Attachment and Learning Disability: A theoretical review informing three clinical interventions. *Journal of Intellectual Disability Research*, 39(4): 295–305.

Deb, S., Thomas, M. and Bright, C. (2001) Mental disorder in adults with intellectual disability. 1: Prevalence of functional psychiatric illness among a community-based population aged between 16 and 64 years. *Journal of Intellectual Disability Research*, 45(6): 495–505.

Department of Health (2001) *Valuing People: A New Strategy for Learning Disability for the 21st Century*. London: The Stationery Office.

Eagles, M. (2007) Attachment and Sexuality. In D. Diamond, S.J. Blatt and J.D. Lichtenberg (eds) *Attachment & Sexuality*. New York: Analytic Press.

Emerson, E., Malam, S., Davies, I. and Spencer, K. (2005) *Adults with Learning Disabilities in England 2003/4*. London: Health and Social Care Information Centre.

Feeney, B.C. and Collins, N.L. (2004) Interpersonal safe haven and secure base caregiving processes in adulthood. In W.S. Rholes and J.A. Simpson (eds) *Adult Attachment: Theory, Research, and Clinical Implications* (pp. 300–338). New York: The Guilford Press.

Feeney, J.A. (2008) Adult romantic attachment: Developments in the study of couple relationships. In J. Cassidy and P. Shaver (eds) *Handbook of Attachment: Theory, Research, and Clinical Applications* (pp. 456–481). London: The Guilford Press.

Feeney, J.A. and Noller, P. (1990) Attachment style as a predictor of adult romantic relationships. *Journal of Personality and Social Psychology*, 58: 281–291.

Gillath, O., Shaver, P.R. and Mikulincer, M. (2005) An attachment theoretical approach to compassion and altruism. In P. Gilbert (ed.) *Compassion: Its nature and use in psychotherapy* (pp. 121–147). London: Brunner-Routledge.

Hazan, C. and Shaver. P. (1987) Romantic love conceptualized as an attachment process. *Journal of Personality and Social Psychology*, 52(3): 511–524.

International Association for the Scientific Study of Intellectual Disabilities Special Interest Research Group on Parents and Parenting with Intellectual Disabilities (2008) Parents Labelled with Intellectual Disability: Position of the IASSID SIRG on Parents and Parenting with Intellectual Disabilities. *Journal of Applied Research in Intellectual Disabilities*, 21: 296–307.

Jeffreys, S. (2008) Disability and the male sex right. *Women's Studies International Forum*, 31: 327–335.

Kunce, L.J. and Shaver, P.R. (1994) An attachment-theoretical approach to caregiving in romantic relationships. In K. Bartholomew and D. Perlman (eds) *Advances in Personal Relationships* (pp. 205–237). London: Jessica Kingsley Publishers.

Larson, F., Alim, N. and Tsakanikos, E. (2011) Attachment style and mental health in adults with intellectual disability: Self-reports and reports by carers. *Advances in Mental Health and Intellectual Disabilities*, 5: 15–23.

Main, M., Kaplan, N. and Cassidy, J. (1985) Security in infancy, childhood, and adulthood: A move to the level of representation. In I. Bretherton and E. Waters (eds) *Growing Points of Attachment Theory and Research* (pp. 66–104). Washington, DC: Society for Research in Child Development.

Mason, P., Timms, K., Hayburn, T. and Watters, C. (2013) How do people described as having a learning disability make sense of friendship? *Journal of Applied Research in Intellectual Disability*, 26(2): 108–118.

Mayseless, O. (2005) Ontogeny of Attachment in Middle Childhood: Conceptualisation of Normative Changes. In K.A. Kerns and R.A Richardson (eds) *Attachment in Middle Childhood*. New York: The Guilford Press.

McCarthy, M. (2000) Consent, abuse and choices: Women with intellectual disabilities and sexuality. In R. Traustadottir and K. Johnson (eds) *Women with Intellectual Disabilities: Finding a place in the world* (pp. 132–159). London: Jessica Kingsley Publishers.

McCarthy, M. (2001) Women with Learning Disabilities – Experiencing their Sexuality in a Healthy Way. *Tizard Learning Disability Review*, 6(1): 16–21.

Mikulincer, M. and Shaver, P.R. (2007) *Attachment in Adulthood: Structure, dynamics, and change*. New York: The Guilford Press.

Rushbrooke, E., Murray, C. and Townsend, S. (2014) The Experiences of Relationships by People with Intellectual Disabilities: A Qualitative Study. *Journal of Applied Research in Intellectual Disability*, 27(6): 531–541.

Schachner, D.A. and Shaver, P.R. (2004) Attachment dimensions and sexual motives. *Personal Relationships*, 11: 179–195.

Schuengel, C., Clasien de Schipper, J., Sterkenburg, P.S. and Kef, S. (2013) Attachment, intellectual disabilities and mental health: Research, assessment and intervention. *Journal of Applied Research in Intellectual Disability*, 26(1): 34–46.

Shaver, P.R., Hazan, C. and Bradshaw, D. (1988) Love as attachment: The integration of three behavioral systems. In R.J. Sternberg and M. Barnes (eds) *The Psychology of Love*. (pp. 68–99). New Haven, CT: Yale University Press.

Sinason, V. (1992) *Mental Handicap and the Human Condition: An Analytic Approach to Intellectual Disability. New Approaches from the Tavistock*. London: Free Association Books.

Sroufe, L.A. (2005) *The Development of the Person: The Minnesota study of risk and adaptation from birth to adulthood*. New York: The Guilford Press.

Tracy, J.L., Shaver, P.R., Albino, A.W. and Cooper, M.L. (2003) Attachment styles and adolescent sexuality. In P. Florsheim (ed.) *Adolescent Romance and Sexual Behaviour: Theory, research and practical implications* (pp. 137–159). Mahwah, NJ: Erlbaum.

Turk, V. and Brown, H. (1993) Sexual abuse and adults with learning difficulties: Results of a two-year incidence survey. *Mental Handicap*, 6: 193–216.

Van IJzendoorn, M.H. (1995) Adult attachment representations, parental responsiveness and infant attachment: A meta-analysis on the predictive validity of the Adult Attachment Interview. *Psychological Bulletin*, 117: 387–403.

Weiss J., MacMullin, J., Waechter, R. and Wekerle, C. (2011) Child maltreatment, adolescent attachment style, and dating violence: Considerations in youths with borderline-to-mild intellectual disability. *International Journal of Mental Health and Addiction*, 9: 555–576.

Weiss, R.S. (1982) Attachment in adult life. In C.M. Parkes and J. Stevenson-Hinde (eds) *The Place of Attachment in Human Behavior* (pp. 171–184). New York: Basic Books.

Willems, D.L., De Vries, J.N., Isarin, J. and Reinders, J.S. (2007) Parenting by persons with intellectual disability: An explorative study in The Netherlands. *Journal of Intellectual Disability Research*, 51: 537–544.

INDEX

Aamina (case example) 246–8
abandonment 134, 136, 188
abuse (ill-treatment; cruelty) 230
    autism spectrum disorder and 90
    in care/by caregivers 3, 104–5
    personality disorder and 226–7
    psychotherapy in 136
    sexual *see* sexual abuse
acting out 135
adolescents and young adults
    assessment 62
    autism spectrum disorder 89–90
    in residential care 156
    seeking support 165
    see also transition to adulthood
adult(s) (and later life)
    assessment 16, 62–5
        autism spectrum disorder
            and 82–3
        care staff functioning and
            attachment in 151–71
        with severe ID, key factors in
            interventions 145
        see also transition to adulthood
    emotional development and its
        implications for 174
Adult Attachment Interview
    (AAI) 16, 18, 38, 39, 40,
    62–4, 68, 154
    autism spectrum disorder
        82–3, 85
    criticisms 18
    excerpts from 151–2

Adult Attachment Projective Picture
    System (AAP) 68, 72, 203–7
    trauma and 197, 198, 203–7, 208,
        209, 215, 216
    case example 210, 212, 213, 214
Adult Attachment Q sort 63
Adult Attachment Questionnaire 63
Adult Attachment Scale 63
adult attachment styles, expanded
    model 248
Adult Attachment Styles (scale) 63, 64
affect (negative) and insecure
    attachment 229
Ainsworth, Mary 14, 60, 259
Ambulance (in Adult Attachment
    Projective Picture
    System) 203, 206, 213
anniversaries 176
antenatal screening 34–5
antisocial personality disorder
    (ASPD) 228, 237, 239
anxious-ambivalent/resistant
    insecure attachment 15, 16
    assessment of 60
    romantic relationships and 248
anxious-avoidant insecure
    attachment 15, 16
    assessment of 60, 63
    personality disorder and offending
        and 229, 232, 233, 236, 237
    romantic relationships and 248, 249
    sexuality and 253, 254
arousal cycle 176, 181

---

*Attachment in Intellectual and Developmental Disability: A Clinician's Guide to Practice and
Research*, First Edition. Edited by Helen K. Fletcher, Andrea Flood and Dougal Julian Hare.
© 2016 John Wiley & Sons, Ltd. Published 2016 by John Wiley & Sons, Ltd.

assessment (and measures) 59–78, 119, 232–4
  adults *see* adults
  autism spectrum disorder 84–6, 86–9
  case examples 73–5, 178, 189–90
  challenging behaviour 112–13
  children 60–2
  developed specifically for intellectual disability 66–70
  for psychotherapy 139–44
  strengths and limitations 70–2
  trauma and 199
Attachment Q-sort (AQS) 69
  autism spectrum disorder 84–5
attuned care 44, 173, 175, 176–7, 181
autism spectrum disorder (ASD) 79–103
  assessment of attachment 84–6
  case examples 49–52, 91–7
  clinical practice 86–97
  diagnosis of 79, 81, 82, 84
  impact on family 35–6
  early social development and 81–2
autonomous secure attachment *see* secure autonomous attachment
aversive methods (punishment) 106, 114, 118
avoidant insecure attachment *see* anxious-avoidant insecure attachment

Bed (in Adult Attachment Projective Picture System) 203, 210, 213
behaviour
  attachment, classification 14–16, 60–2
  challenging *see* challenging behaviour
  systems of 11–12
Bench (in Adult Attachment Projective Picture System) 203, 208

bereavement 125, 126
  case example 250, 252
best interests 107, 136, 181
Billy (case example) 223–4, 234–5
blank-screen approach 134–5
borderline personality disorder (BPD) 140, 227–8, 235, 239
boundaries (professional) 51, 177–80, 181, 183
Bowlby, John 9–14, 105, 153
  caregiving system and 251
  trauma and 105, 199–200
brain and neuroscience 21–2
Brief Symptom Inventory 139
bullying 201–2, 208–9, 215–16
  case example 213–15

Care Index for Infants 61
Care Index for Toddlers 61
caregivers (carers)
  abuse by 3, 104–5
  formal/professional/in general *see* professional caregivers
  informal
    parents *see* parents
    romantic relationships and 251–3
Cemetery (in Adult Attachment Projective Picture System) 203, 210, 213
challenging behaviour 104–29
  autism spectrum disorder 91
child (children)
  assessment 60–2
  development *see* development
  individual therapy with severe disability 132–3
  internal working models and 13
  of parents with ID 257–61
  see also adolescents; early childhood; infant; separation
Child Development Team (CDT) in case examples
  autism spectrum disorder 49–50, 52
  cerebral palsy 25

Christine (case example) 130, 131–2, 135, 136, 137, 138, 139, 140, 145–6
Circle of Security 23, 162, 163, 166
classification of attachment 14–16, 60–2
cognitive abilities in assessment 66
  case example 191
cognitive development, acknowledging person's level of 108–9
collaborative formulation 90, 95
commitment, ongoing 124–6
communication
  difficulties (and their management) 230
    in autism spectrum disorder 80, 83
  nurturing 183
community-based services 131
compassionate care 103, 105, 118, 123, 125
complaints, ongoing, families presenting with 45–52
conditioning models 111–12
confidence (therapist's) 135
confidentiality 135, 180, 184, 187
confirmation (to client) 157–8
consent 112–13, 181, 185–6, 208
  informed 185–6, 187, 207, 254
consistency (staff) 53, 175, 181
constriction 206
CONTACT (video-feedback intervention) 152, 157, 159, 160, 167
contact, physical 177
containment 53, 117–18, 187
  challenging behaviour 117–18
  pathological mourning 205
contract, therapeutic 183, 184–5
control, language of 112
Corner (in Adult Attachment Projective Picture System) 203, 204, 208, 210, 211, 214

countertransference 186
creative engagement 43, 53–4
criticisms of attachment theory 19
Crittenden's Dynamic Maturational Model of attachment 17, 61–2
cruelty *see* abuse
culture 18–19
current relationships 162, 250
  assessing 63, 68, 118

Dana (case example) 252–3
death (loss through) 199
  case example 252, 255
  see also bereavement; loss; mourning
defensive processing 199, 205
Departure (in Adult Attachment Projective Picture System) 203, 206
dependency
  overdependency 246
  realistic 111–12
derealization 206, 208, 213
despair (at separation) 10
detachment (at separation) 10
development
  adversity in 225, 230–2, 239
  emotional *see* emotional development
  social (early), and autism spectrum disorder 81–2
diagnosis
  autism spectrum disorder *see* autism spectrum disorder
  family-centred 54
  impact of 35–40
differentiation stage in early emotional development 143, 146
dismissing attachment 63
  adults and care staff and 155, 156, 157, 158, 159, 160, 164, 166
disorganized attachment 14, 15, 16, 61, 155

assessment 61
challenging behaviour and 109, 110
drawings in house, tree, person test 141–2
Dyadic Developmental Psychotherapy 23
Dynamic Maturational Model of attachment 17, 60–1
dynamics (attachment) 65, 130–50
  interviews about 66
  psychotherapy and 130–50

early childhood 152
  autism spectrum disorder and social development in 81–2
  emotional development *see* emotional development
  object relations 152
  trauma 90
ejection, resisting 116–17
emotion(s) 116–17, 233–5
  in assessment of challenging behaviour 113
  problems/disorders/distress 45, 224–5, 229, 233
    externalizing or internalizing 236
    personality disorder and 235–7
  regulation 229–30
  in therapy 187–8
  secure attachment and 173, 229, 233
  understanding 116–17
emotional development 142–4, 146–8, 180
  acknowledging person's level of 108–9
  becoming stuck/uncompleted/ arrested 144, 173–4, 174, 194
  case example 178–9
  early, observation 142–4
  later life implications 174
  Mahler's phases of 174
  stages/phases 142–4, 146–8

emotional safety and security 21, 113, 125, 146, 174–80
emotional support 172–91
empathy 123–4
ending of period of psychotherapy 188–9
engagement 162–4
  creative 43, 53–4
excessive attachment behaviours 160–1
externalizing of emotional problems 236
extroversion 236

families
  diagnosis and support centring on 54
  grieving models 40–2
  presenting with ongoing complaints 45–52
  see also parents
father *see* parents
feedback
  in psychotherapy 135
  video *see* video feedback
follow-up 122, 125, 182, 225
formulation
  attachment-focused 54
  case examples 92, 95, 178
  collaborative 90, 95
  shared with staff teams 180–2

generations, transmission of attachment across 18, 21, 153–4
'good enough care' 172, 173, 175–6, 181
Grace (case examples)
  first patient named so 49–52
  second patient named so 258–9
grief 40–2
  family models of grieving 40–2
  unresolved *see* unresolved losses
group level, functioning at 140
Gunel (case example) 254–6

history (personal - of
        attachment) 173, 180
    in assessment for
        psychotherapy 139
    continuing presentation of 110–11
    fragmentation 109
    staff 166
holding 117–18
house, tree, person test 141–2
human needs 104, 124, 125, 175,
        177, 194

ideas shared with staff teams 180–2
independence
    in autism spectrum disorder and
        transition to adulthood 89, 90
    program, case example 238, 239
individual (person)
    history *see* history
    permanence 160–1
    therapy 132–3, 138–9, 182–3
individuation stage in early emotional
        development 143, 173, 174
infant, assessment 61
infant–parent psychotherapy 23–4
Infant Strange Situation 61, 63, 68
informed consent 185–6, 187, 207, 254
insecure attachment 9, 14, 15, 16,
        60, 229
    anxious-ambivalent *see* anxious-
        ambivalent/resistant insecure
        attachment
    anxious-avoidant *see* anxious-
        avoidant insecure attachment
    emotional regulation and 229
insecurity 113
institutional/residential care
    abuse 104–5
    adolescents 156
intellectual capacity assessment 139–44
interactions (adult client–staff) 146,
        152, 156–9, 160
intergenerational transmission of
        attachment 18, 21, 153–4

internal working models 12–14
internalizing of emotional
        problems 236
International Association for the
        Scientific Study of ID Special
        Interest Research Group on
        Parents and Parenting with ID
        (IASSID SIRG) 258
interventions 22–7, 120–1
    attachment-focused 54
    autism spectrum disorder 91, 97
        case example 51
    challenging behaviour 106, 117,
        118, 120–1
        case example 107, 108, 126–7
    emotional support, case
        examples 178–9, 190–2
    severe disabilities *see* severe
        disabilities
    see also psychotherapy
interview (clinical), autism spectrum
        disorder 86–7
intimate relationships 244–65
    development 245–8
    romantic relationships 64, 65,
        248–57
introversion 236, 237
Isa (case example) 91–3

joint hypothesis in behavioural
        assessment 113–15, 120, 124
June (case example) 209–12

Leah (case example) 93–6
Lisa (case example) 73–5
loss(es) 19–20
    autism spectrum disorder
        and 90–1
    by death *see* death
    of 'healthy child' 33–58
    mourning for *see* mourning
    past 20, 40, 41
    proximal 20
    unresolved *see* unresolved losses

Mahler's phases of emotional development 174
Manchester Attachment Scale – Third Party (MAST) 69–70, 71, 72, 76
  case example 73, 74
Marital Q sort 63
Matt (case example) 189–92
meanings, understanding 186–7
measures of attachment *see* assessment
memories of attachment relationships, examining 63
Mental Capacity Act (2005) 6, 107, 181
mental health
  assessment (for psychotherapy) 139
  attachment influencing 11, 16, 164
  see also wellbeing
mental representation *see* representation
Mike (case example) 178–80
mindfulness 117, 182
  parents 21
mindless vs mindful state 21
mind-mindedness 21, 28, 191
mindset 165–6, 167
mother *see* parents
mourning 197–222
  failed 200, 207
  pathological/complicated 41, 197–222
    adults with ID 197–222
    case examples 209–15
  unresolved *see* unresolved losses

negative affect and insecure attachment 229
negative reinforcement 115
neuroscience 21–2
neuroticism 235
normalization 111
nurturing care 176–7, 181, 183

object relations 106, 142
  technique 140–1
observations
  autism spectrum disorder 87–9, 88
  early emotional development 142–4
offending 230–1, 232–3, 236, 239
one-person level, functioning at 140
oppositional behaviour 225, 231
overdependency 246

parents (incl. mother and other informal caregivers) 33–58
  in autism spectrum disorder 83, 85, 86, 89–90
  as cause 80
  becoming a parent 34–5
    people with ID 257–61
  caregiving abilities 42–4
  diagnosis and its impact on 33–40
  internal working models and 13
  mental representation 37, 154, 156
  neuroscientific developments 21
  psychotherapy involving infant and 23–4
  resolution or its absence *see* resolution; unresolved losses
  system of caregiving 12
  see also families; intergenerational transmission of attachment; separation
past losses 20, 40, 41
Patrick (case example) 249–50
Pauline (case example) 250–1
Peer Attachment Interview 63, 64
permanence, person 160–1
person *see* individual
personality disorder 225–8, 235–7, 239
  antisocial (ASPD) 228, 239
  borderline (BPD) 140, 227–8, 235, 239
  emotion and 235–7
physical contact 177
positive behaviour support 106, 119–22
positive reinforcement 115

post-traumatic stress disorder 235
practising stage in early emotional development 143, 147
pre-individuation phase 146, 174
premature birth 42, 43
prenatal screening 34–5
preoccupation with personal suffering 200, 209
preoccupied attachment 63, 64
  care staff and 158, 159, 160, 164, 165, 166
Preschool Assessment of Attachment 61–2
preterm (premature) birth 42, 43
professional caregivers (staff/team) 151–71
  adult attachment and functioning of 151–71
  autism spectrum disorder and working with 88, 90–1
  challenging behaviour and 115–27
  emotional security and development through support of 174–80
  ideas and formulation shared between 180–2
  introducing attachment concepts to, case example 115–16
  management 160–4
  risk and resilience 164–6
  separation by 202
  splitting in care team 53, 124
  sufficient amount of 138
  training and support 138, 180, 182, 191
  understanding their attachment strategies 17
  workshops 118
projective tests 139–44
protest (at separation) 10
proximal development, zone of 17
proximal losses 20
psychological health and wellbeing see mental health; wellbeing

psychotherapy 23–4, 130–50
  assessment for 139–44
  case example 26
  presenting issues and how to work with them 136–7
  working through 182–94
  see also interventions
punishment (aversive methods) 106, 114, 118

Q-sorts 16, 62, 63, 65, 68, 69
  autism spectrum disorder 84–5
questions to inform clinical observation of attachment strategies 80

rapprochement in early emotional development 143, 148, 179
Reaction to Diagnosis Interview (RDI) 37, 38, 39–40, 43
realistic dependency 111–12
reality orientation 108–9
referral 119–20, 125
  case examples 107–8
reflection 124–6, 184
refrigerator mother 80
reinforcement (of behaviour) 106
  negative 115
  positive 115
rejection 134, 136, 253, 256
Relationship Scales Questionnaire (RSQ) 232
Relationships Questionnaire (RQ) 63, 64, 232, 233, 236
reliability (staff/therapists) 137, 175, 181
representation (mental) of attachment 151–67
  Adult Attachment Projective and coding of 205, 208
  mental health and 164–5
  mindset and 166
  representational assessment 199
  support seeking and 165

residential care *see* institutional/
    residential care
resilience, professional 164–6
resolution, parental 37–8
    signs 38
reward 106
    interventions based on 91
risk, professional 164–6
romantic relationships 64, 65, 248–57
Rusty (case example) 231–2, 237–8

safety *see* security and safety
Sally and Tyrone (case example of couple) 260–1
School-aged Assessment of Attachment 62
screening, antenatal 34–5
secure autonomous attachment 13, 15
    adults and care staff functioning and 151, 152, 155, 157, 159, 165, 166
    in assessment 60, 63, 64, 65, 68, 69, 70
    autism spectrum disorder and 83, 84, 85
    disability and 39–40
    emotions and 173, 229, 233
    intimate relationships and 244, 245, 248, 249, 250, 251, 259, 260, 261
    personality disorder and offending and 226, 229, 232, 233, 236, 237, 239
Secure Base Safe Haven Observation (SBSHO) 68–9, 70, 71, 72, 76
secure unit 138, 213
security and safety 5, 138
    emotional 21, 113, 125, 146, 174–80
    five conditions for 113
    in therapy 184–5, 192–3
    see also Circle of Security
Security Scale, autism spectrum disorder 85

segregated systems 199, 206, 207, 208
    case example 210, 212
self, sense of 90, 140, 148, 173, 200
self-injury/self-harm 125, 136
    case examples 92, 234, 235
Self-report Assessment of Attachment Security (SRAAS) 66–8, 70, 71, 72, 73, 74
separation
    Bowlby on 10, 105
    by professionals or systems of care 202
    strange situation (procedure) *see* strange situation
services
    community-based 131
    emotional support and role of 172–91, 193–4
severe disabilities 108–9
    interventions
        individual therapy 132–3
        key factors 144–6
    limited independence 111
sex offenders 230
sexual abuse and assault 225, 230, 256
    case examples 209, 211, 213, 231
sexual behaviour, inappropriate 230, 231, 237, 256
sexuality 253–7
Shanice (case example) 256–7
social development (early) and autism spectrum disorder 81–2
sorrow, chronic 41
splitting in care team 53, 124
staff *see* professional caregivers
Stephanie (case example) 46–9
stereotyped behaviours 87, 162
    case examples 95, 107, 108
Steven (case example) 147
strange situation (procedure) 14, 15, 16, 18, 60, 84
    infant 61, 63, 68

styles of attachment 60
  adult, expanded model 248
  assessment *see* assessment
  emotions and 233, 236
  intimate relationships and 248–9
  personality disorder and 236
support
  of carers 124–6, 138
  emotional 172–91
  family-centred 54
  seeking 175
  in trauma and chronic unresolved mourning 202
    case examples 212, 214–15
  wellbeing benefiting from 162
Sylvie (case example) 25–7

termination of period of psychotherapy 188–9
Terry (case example) 213–15
theory (of attachment) 1–32
  care staff and 153–5
  challenging behaviour and 104–29
  criticisms of 19
  development 9–17
  disability psychotherapy and 172–3
  reactions to diagnosis and 36–40
  therapeutic (client–therapist/staff) relationship 156, 182–9
    assessment and the 70
    emotionally-nurturing 183–4
    ruptures and endings 188–9
three-person level, functioning at 140
Tom (case example) 107–8, 110–11, 115–16, 123, 126–7
Tommie (case example) 159
toolkit of assessments 72, 76
touch 117
training, staff 138, 180, 182, 191
transference 115, 186
transition to adulthood 165
  autism spectrum disorder and 89–90
Transition to Adulthood Attachment Interview 62

trauma (past) 90–1, 197–222
  autism spectrum disorder and 90–1
  Bowlby and 105, 199–200
  definition 198–201
  implications for research and practice 216–17
  mourning of *see* mourning
  psychotherapy 136–7
  trauma-informed care 131, 138–9
  see also abuse
trust in psychotherapy 133, 134, 135, 137, 138, 145, 146, 147, 148
two-person level, functioning at 140
Tyrone and Sally (case example of couple) 260–1

understanding
  language of 112
  of meanings 186–7
unresolved losses (grief and mourning), chronic
  adults with ID 200, 205, 206, 207
  case examples 209–15
  care staff and adult attachment 155, 157
  parents 37, 38, 39, 41, 42, 43, 202
  from past 20

video analysis research in autism spectrum disorder 81, 82
video feedback 23, 24, 156, 158, 159, 162
  CONTACT 152, 157, 159, 160, 167
video interaction guidance (VIG) 22–3
violence 230, 239
  personality disorder and 225–6

wellbeing, psychological 80–1, 113
  assessment 139
  support from staff contributing to 162
  see also abuse; mental health
Window (in Adult Attachment Projective Picture System) 203, 210

Winnicott, W.C. 144, 172
Winterbourne View Hospital 3, 104–5, 202
working through therapy 182–94
workshops, staff 118

young adults *see* adolescents and young adults

Zoltan (carer in case example) 252–3
zone of proximal development 17

Printed and bound by CPI Group (UK) Ltd, Croydon, CR0 4YY
28/09/2023